CIIE STORIES
进博故事

中国国际进口博览局
国家会展中心（上海）　编
中国新闻网

中国商务出版社
·北京·

图书在版编目（CIP）数据

进博故事 / 中国国际进口博览局，国家会展中心
（上海），中国新闻网编 . -- 北京：中国商务出版社，
2024.10. -- ISBN 978-7-5103-5426-7

Ⅰ . F752.61-282

中国国家版本馆 CIP 数据核字第 2024HV7816 号

进博故事

JIN-BO GUSHI

中国国际进口博览局

国家会展中心（上海） 编

中国新闻网

出版发行：中国商务出版社有限公司

地　　址：北京市东城区安定门外大街东后巷 28 号　　邮　编：100710

网　　址：http://www.cctpress.com

联系电话：010-64515150（发行部）　　　　010-64212247（总编室）
　　　　　010-64269744（商务事业部）　　　010-64248236（印制部）

责任编辑：张高平

责任校对：孙柳明　郭舒怡　周水琴

排　　版：北京天逸合文化有限公司

印　　刷：北京华联印刷有限公司

开　　本：787 毫米 × 1092 毫米　1/16

印　　张：24.5　　　　　　　　　字　数：352 千字

版　　次：2024 年 10 月第 1 版　　　印　次：2024 年 10 月第 1 次印刷

书　　号：ISBN 978-7-5103-5426-7

定　　价：189.00 元（全二册）

序　言

在全球伙伴共同见证进博会"越办越好"的进程中，一个个难忘的瞬间逐渐沉淀、累积，形成一篇篇引人入胜、深入人心的"进博故事"。

每一位亲历者分享的故事都展示了一个个经贸互惠、情感互信、文明互鉴的生动场景和真实细节，记录了全体"进博伙伴"的奋斗、成长与收获。

这些"进博故事"由全世界共同书写，是探寻创新之道、"天工人巧日争新"的故事，是携手共商共享共赢、"百花齐放春满园"的故事，是推进文明交流互鉴、"青山一道同云雨"的故事。

自首届以来，进博会如同巨大的引力场，已赢得众多"铁粉"。新一轮"进博故事"全球征集启动以来，线索蜂拥而至，已成为"进博引力"的生动注脚。

"进博故事"的讲述者有结缘进博的"头回客""回头客"和"全勤生"，有代表国家和国际组织参会的政界人士，也有参加虹桥国际经济论坛的专家学者。一年一度的携手相逢，365 天的精心筹备，8760 小时的殷切期待……参展参会的"进博伙伴"不仅收获了宝贵的订单和深厚的友谊，而且共同编织了一段段难忘的记忆。

虽然故事不尽相同，但相聚"四叶草"，共赴进博之约，已成为他们共同的选择。

进博之约是机遇之约。选择进博就是选择中国市场大机遇，融入世界大市场的怀抱。各国农产品搭乘"进博快车"走进千家万户，

知名药企参展后连年诞生"进博宝宝",百年老店借此打造全球合作链……主动扩大进口,让中国市场成为世界的市场、共享的市场、大家的市场。进博会为各国打开机遇之门,为世界经济注入"新动能"。

进博之约是发展之约。选择进博就是选择在休戚与共的地球村,共享普惠包容发展的成果。最不发达国家的土特产因进博成为爆款顶流,地球另一端的匠人在进博会现场签署供货协议,来自中国的订单增进遥远国度的民生福祉……作为全球共享的国际公共产品,进博会支持和帮助广大发展中国家共享中国发展红利,推动世界各国成为合作共赢的"众行者"。

进博之约是创新之约。选择进博就是选择创新引领的未来。跨国公司推动本土化创新"在中国,为全球",初创企业快速融入创新"生态圈",顶级专家在论坛碰撞智慧与创意……"四叶草"内外,创新科技和前沿理念汇聚激荡,全球企业共同探寻未来增长新引擎。作为中国构建新发展格局的窗口,进博会成为加快发展新质生产力、扎实推进高质量发展的重要平台,成为助力企业赢得未来的"能量场"。

进博之约是开放之约。选择进博就是选择以开放合作推动经济全球化不断向前。中国在进博会上宣布"干货满满"的扩大开放举措,虹桥论坛连续发布《世界开放报告》和最新世界开放指数,各国参展客商在"四叶草"开放合作的海洋中畅游……开放是世界繁荣发展的必由之路,也是当代中国的鲜明标识。作为推动高水平开放的平台,进博会高举开放旗帜、凝聚开放共识,成为促进贸易自由化和投资便利化的"助推器"。

这些与我们分享的"进博故事",记录了进博会背后的倾情奔赴与美好愿景,也记录了建设开放型世界经济、构建人类命运共同体的"进博足迹"。进博会将在推动经济全球化更加开放、包容、普惠、平衡、共赢的道路上谱写更多历史新篇章,而"进博故事"也将一直由你、由我、由更多的"进博伙伴"续写下去。

目录

机遇之门

创新之力

发展之美

开放之约

后　记

机遇之门

从法国农场到中国餐桌

民以食为天。远在亚欧大陆另一端的法国与中国一样，以美食享誉全球。如今，"舌尖上的法兰西"漂洋过海，"从法国农场到中国餐桌"走进现实，丰富着中国百姓的味蕾，满足着越来越多国人从"吃得饱"到"吃得好"的需求转变。

36 小时速达中国

"食在广州"，在以美食闻名的羊城，人们最懂得美味的食物源自新鲜的食材。来自万里之外法国的生蚝、龙虾、贻贝等海鲜经过最朴素的烹煮甚至直接生吃，便可让食客们在唇齿间还原大西洋的味道。

仅在两天前，这些海鲜刚刚打捞上岸，然后检验装箱、送往机场、直飞中国。在两国领导人共同推动建成的"从法国农场到中国餐桌"全链条快速协同机制的助力下，这些远道而来的新鲜水产品可以实现空中报关，落地便通过冷链配送直达商场超市、餐厅食肆。

滨海夏朗德省是法国重要的生蚝产区。该省生蚝养殖者雅克·科科洛斯（Jacques Kokolos）说，他们出产的生蚝最快不到 36 小时便可运抵中国。

对雅克·科科洛斯这样的水产从业者来说，中国是全球最大的水产品消费国之一，具有巨大的吸引力。随着生活水平的提高，人们对优质特色商品的需求更加旺盛，市场潜力巨大。滨海夏朗德省的生蚝出口商"朗贝尔生蚝"在接受法国电视台采访时说，他们对华生蚝出口量在2016年至2023年间增长了4倍多。

原汁原味的法国味道

位于天津市中心五大道的马克西姆餐厅是一家正宗的法式餐厅。在这里担任行政主厨的法国厨师阿兰·勒默尔（Alain Lemer）说，不少中国人对法国美食心怀向往，慕名前来品尝。

被许多普通客人所忽略的是，制作餐品使用的酱汁堪称美食的"灵魂"。伴随中法经贸关系的顺畅发展，制作酱汁的法国原产调料和食材不再难以获取，"客人们非常喜欢这种原汁原味的法国味道"。

在南开区一家超市，来自法国的食品品类丰富、品牌多样。市民刘洋说："我家小孩很喜欢吃法国品牌的奶酪，家长也

天津南开区一家超市出售多种来自法国等地的进口奶酪。【新华社记者王晖　摄】

第二届进博会法国国家馆展出的法国葡萄酒。【新华社记者张玉薇　摄】

3

对法国红酒情有独钟。现在进口渠道很多，根据需求能买到不同价位的法国红酒。"

法国肉制品同样正快速进入中国市场。法国猪业联盟驻华首席代表孟凡说，中国目前是法国在欧盟外最大的猪肉出口市场。法国畜牧及肉类协会外贸委员会主席马克桑斯·比加尔（Maxence Bigal）表示，法国肉制品企业正积极参与"从法国农场到中国餐桌"机制，将更多高品质的法国肉类产品引进中国市场。

互利共赢双向奔赴

近年来，中法农食产品贸易持续增长。据中国海关总署统计，法国是中国在欧盟第一大农产品进口地、第二大农产品贸易伙伴。截至 2023 年，法国水产品、乳制品、肉制品、种畜、种禽、水果等 200 余种农食产品获准对华出口，近 7000 家农食产品生产企业在华注册。

2023 年 4 月，在两国领导人的共同推动下，中法共同建立"从法国农场到中国餐桌"机制，为法国农食产品进入中国千家万户按下加速键。2023 年 11 月在上海举办的第六届中国国际进口博览会上，40 多家法国农食企业集体亮相，与中国采购商面对面洽谈。仅盒马一家就当场与 7 家法国企业签署协议，未来 3 年进口价值达 30 亿元的法国肉类、乳酪及红酒等产品。

除去农食产品贸易，中法双方还不断拓宽合作领域，强化农业科技合作、联合培养农业人才、开展农业农村政策交流，加强人员、机构和企业往来，促进农业领域合作取得更多丰硕成果。

2024 年是中法建交 60 周年暨中法文化旅游年，中国馆首次亮相历史悠久的法国国际农业博览会，法国也将受邀担任 2024 年中国国际服务贸易交易会和第七届中国国际进口博览会主宾国。中法两个农业大国携手合作，架起"双向奔赴"的桥梁。

文 / 彭梦瑶　杨骏　王晖

进博会助力"中美洲粮仓"加速对接中国市场

尼加拉瓜，素有"湖泊与火山之国"之称，位于中美洲中部，北靠洪都拉斯，南连哥斯达黎加，东临加勒比海，西濒太平洋。凭借得天独厚的地理位置和气候条件，尼加拉瓜盛产各类优质农产品，被誉为"中美洲粮仓"。自 2021 年 12 月中尼两国复交以来，借助进博会，尼加拉瓜的优质产品正在加速驶入中国市场"快车道"。

与一直期待的机会"相遇"

中尼两国复交后，"中国"一词越来越频繁地出现在尼加拉瓜民众的日常生活中。当地不少人意识到，如果本国的优质产品能够在中国市场打出名号，将为尼加拉瓜带来重要的经济发展契机。

复交不满一年，尼加拉瓜便参加了以线上方式举办的第五届进博会国家展。

2023 年，怀揣着开拓中国市场的愿景，尼加拉瓜派出高级别代表团赴华参加第六届进博会，向中国消费者展示咖啡、海鲜、牛肉和朗姆酒等当地优质产品。这也是该国首次线下参加进博会。

启程来华之前，尼加拉瓜代表团的部分官员就借媒体向外界释放出乐观信号。"我们对进博会抱有很高的期待。"尼加拉瓜总统

第六届进博会，尼加拉瓜首次线下参展。

投资、贸易和国际合作顾问劳雷亚诺·奥尔特加表示，"希望优质的尼加拉瓜商品能够获得中国市场认可，我们也希望了解中国市场对于我们商品的需求量。另外，我们想借此机会，吸引更多中国企业和企业家来尼加拉瓜投资，比如咖啡种植业、牛肉加工业等。"

尼加拉瓜财政和公共信贷部部长伊万·阿科斯塔·蒙塔尔万则讲出了尼商界人士的心声，他说："这是他们第一次接触如此巨大的市场，也是尼加拉瓜经济发展多年来一直期待的机会。"

首次来到"四叶草"的尼加拉瓜驻华大使迈克尔·坎贝尔也认为，进博会是尼商界期待已久的机会，同时还表达了对中国市场的信心。"我们有很多优质农产品，相信一定会打开中国市场销路。"他在接受媒体采访时说道。

借助"四叶草"敲开中国市场大门

"中国客商排起长队，就为了尝一口尼加拉瓜的优质牛肉。"第六届进博会闭幕一个多月后，尼加拉瓜发展、工业和贸易部部长贝穆德斯仍对当时的火热场面记忆犹新。

资料显示，尼加拉瓜牛肉产量位居中美洲各国之首。进博会期间，坎贝尔大使表示，牛肉是他心目中最骄傲的产品，希望更多中国家庭可以享受尼加拉瓜牛肉的美味。2024 年 4 月，坎贝尔大使与一家中国企业会谈时透露，目前尼加拉瓜牛存栏量达 600 万头，80% 以上出口欧美，计划未来 5 年存栏量翻倍，并把中国视为最有增长潜力的市场。

除了牛肉，来自加勒比海沿岸的尼加拉瓜大龙虾也在第六届进博会上成为"明星产品"。鲜甜肥嫩的龙虾肉同样引得观众排起长队，品尝这来自遥远国度的美味。看着人头攒动的队列，尼加拉瓜参展商热情地向大伙推介："我们今天提供的大龙虾源自加勒比海，请尝尝。还有这些蟹肉，也来自加勒比海，都非常受欢迎！"

通过进博会搭建的平台，尼加拉瓜商界近距离接触到了拥有 14 亿多人口的中国

第六届进博会国家展尼加拉瓜展台。【新华社供图】

大市场，并与多家中国公司建立了联系。尼加拉瓜的产品也因此敲开中国市场的大门。这让很多尼加拉瓜的商人感到无比振奋。

复交红利持续释放

近年来，通过积极参加进博会，尼加拉瓜的多种优质产品在中国市场逐渐打响知名度。这一成就离不开中尼复交以来持续释放的种种红利。

2021年12月，中尼两国恢复大使级外交关系。自此，两国关系呈现跨越式发展，各领域务实合作快速推进，为尼经济发展注入新动力。

次年7月，中尼两国签署《中华人民共和国政府和尼加拉瓜共和国政府关于自由贸易协定早期收获的安排》（下称《早期收获》），共同宣布启动中国—尼加拉瓜全面自由贸易协定谈判。值得一提的是，此后在进博会上大放异彩的尼加拉瓜牛肉，就在《早期收获》中约定的可向中国出口的农产品范围里。

2023年12月，中国和尼加拉瓜正式建立战略伙伴关系。在《中华人民共和国和尼加拉瓜共和国关于建立战略伙伴关系的联合声明》中提到，尼方愿积极利用中国

2021年12月31日，中国驻尼加拉瓜大使馆复馆仪式在尼加拉瓜首都马那瓜举行。
【新华社供图】

国际进口博览会等平台扩大对华出口。

2024 年 1 月 1 日，《中华人民共和国政府和尼加拉瓜共和国政府自由贸易协定》正式生效后，尼加拉瓜对华出口显著增长。海关总署最新数据显示，2024 年 1—8 月，中国自尼加拉瓜进口商品总值为 4750.8 万美元，同比增长 156.7%。

尼加拉瓜的对华出口正乘着东风快速增长，但新机遇与新挑战并存。坎贝尔大使认为，在当前的机会下，尼加拉瓜面临的挑战在于如何尽快提高现有产品的附加值，以及提供更多对中国市场有吸引力的商品和服务。面对这一挑战，他透露称，尼加拉瓜驻华大使馆计划参加在中国举办的进博会等投资和贸易促进活动。

眼下，第七届进博会大幕将启。从第五届线上参展，到第六届首次线下展示，再到第七届以主宾国身份参加进博会，尼加拉瓜一步一脚印，一年一台阶，一步步坚定地走向充满机遇的"四叶草"。

在第七届进博会国家展的舞台上，尼加拉瓜将在其展台设置文化展示、旅游亮点、出口产品和国家经济潜力等多个主题区域，全面展示该国综合形象、优势领域和独特魅力。

在中尼两国复交红利持续释放的背景下，届时，相信尼加拉瓜必将收获满满，观展者也必将大饱眼福。

（本文综合自：人民日报、新华社、CGTN、央视新闻客户端、环球时报、北京日报客户端、大湾区之声公众号、中华人民共和国外交部、中华人民共和国海关总署、湛江市冷链物流协会等。）

共乘开放东风，埃及"国宝"在"四叶草"大放异彩

有这么一个国家，既和中国同属四大文明古国，又是第一个同新中国建交的阿拉伯国家和非洲国家，还是中国在非洲地区重要的贸易伙伴，而且是首届进博会主宾国之一，并已连续6年参加进博会。

这个国家就是埃及。

传统产业搭上"进博快车"

"没想到埃及棉线质量这么好，接近国际一线品牌，价格又很实惠。"在第六届进博会埃及染色和加工公司展台前，几位来自浙江的编织品原料采购商驻足良久，他们看中了该公司生产的"布莱特"牌棉线。

埃及有着数不清的文物古迹，但被誉为"国宝"的，却是长绒棉，在世界上久负盛名，为国内纺织工业提供了上等原料。

在第六届进博会上，埃及染色和加工公司展台负责人努拉向客商介绍展品。【央视网视频截图】

纺织工业是埃及重要的传统支柱产业，也是埃及政府重点发展的产业之一。《2023 纺织业对外投资合作国别指南》显示，埃及现已发展形成三大纺织产业集群，首都所在的大开罗地区就是其中之一。此次前来参展的埃及染色和加工公司展台负责人努拉就来自开罗。短短几天下来，就有多家企业向她表达了线上和线下代理产品的意向。努拉表示："希望借助进博会的广阔平台，让我们的产品进入更多中国消费者的视野。"

香料产业也是埃及历史悠久的传统产业之一，早在数千年前的法老时期，埃及就有种植香料的传统。在古代，通过海上丝绸之路，大量香料从埃及等国运输到中国。如今，搭乘"进博快车"，埃及香料产业在遥远的东方迎来了新的发展机遇。

埃及 Retaj 出口商贸经理汉德来自埃及萨达特城，2023 年，她带着 30 多种埃及特产的植物香料首次参加了进博会。"我们来中国就是想为家乡的特产寻找商机，参加进博会后已经接到多个订单，有中国的，也有其他国家的。"谈及参展收获，汉德十分开心，"进博会真是个大舞台，不仅带来了订单，还收获了未来和希望。"

"网红外教"的进博之旅

来自埃及开罗的马哈茂德·苏莱曼（中文名"马晓宇"）是上海外国语大学东方语学院阿拉伯语系外籍教师，因多次被媒体报道，学生们称他为"网红外教"。第六届进博会上，这位网红外教化身"小叶子"志愿者参与视频直播，以埃及人的视角向世界讲述中国故事。

中国 2004 年加入联合国教科文组织《保护非物质文化遗产公约》，经过二十年的积极探索，形成了非遗保护的中国实践与中国经验。在一场直播活动中，马晓宇与搭档来到了进博会的文化长廊，

在第六届进博会上，网红外教马晓宇（左）参与直播活动。【中国日报网直播回放截图】

向观众介绍中国的非遗文化。穿梭在各地的文化展示馆内，他被中国丰富的非遗文化深深吸引，并对中国传统文化产生了浓厚兴趣。

　　除了传统文化，马晓宇还了解到全球高端制造领域的最新进展。在另一场名为"跑出智造加速度"的直播活动中，他与中国日报记者一起到技术装备展区探馆，"解码"新型工业化背景下的高端制造成果，体验难得一见的炫酷技术装备。

　　对于能以上外外教的身份参与进博会志愿者服务工作，马晓宇感到非常开心。"无论是从经贸合作还是中埃两国的文化交流来说，进博会都是一个很好的平台。所以我即使是一名教师，也非常想要参与并更深度地了解进博会。"他还表示，希望自己成为一座桥梁，积极地推动中埃经贸合作与文化交流。

文明古国共乘开放东风

　　中埃两大文明古国友好关系源远流长，企业间的合作潜力巨大。

棉线、香料、鲜橙、椰枣、锡瓦盐……参加进博会后，越来越多的埃及好物受到中国市场认可，提振了埃及商界对中国市场的信心。

进博会已连续 7 年被写入全国两会的政府工作报告。2024 年全国两会期间，埃及埃中商会秘书长迪亚·赫尔米接受采访时表示，"一带一路"和进博会都表明中国向各方张开双臂，实现合作共赢，有助于推动世界走向进步发展、共同繁荣的道路，中国的发展惠及世界。

2024 年 4 月，第七届进博会推介会在埃及首都开罗举行，埃及政府机构、企业及商协会代表共 150 余人参加。埃及展览和会议总局主席谢里夫·马瓦尔迪表示，埃及企业参加第六届进博会成效突出，进博会为埃及企业在全球范围内推广"埃及制造"提供了很好的机会。今年也有许多埃及企业准备前往上海参加第七届进博会。

在刚刚结束不久的中非合作论坛北京峰会上，进博会被写入《关于共筑新时代全天候中非命运共同体的北京宣言》。今年恰逢中埃建立全面战略伙伴关系 10 周年，让我们共同期待埃及机构和企业乘中国开放东风，亮相第七届进博会，把更多优质特色产品带到中国和全球市场。

当地时间 2024 年 4 月 23 日，第七届进博会推介会在埃及开罗举办。

（本文综合自：人民日报、新华社、光明日报、中国日报、中新社、中国青年报、湖南日报、江苏广电总台·融媒体新闻中心、观察者网、上海教育电视台、上海松江公众号、中国纺联国贸办、上外东方语学院公众号。）

推开"金色大门",携手建设中哈关系新的"黄金三十年"

哈萨克斯坦地处中亚腹地,是世界上最大的内陆国。中哈两国山水相连,经济结构互补性强,经贸合作有着得天独厚的优势。

自 1992 年正式建交以来,中哈两国关系走过了不平凡的发展历程,取得令世人瞩目的丰硕成果。而自 2018 年以来举办的中国国际进口博览会为中哈两国进一步加强经贸合作打开了一扇"金色大门",也为双方建设新的"黄金三十年"注入了强劲的动力。

为"出口加速计划"提供支撑

自 2018 年以来,哈萨克斯坦一直是进博会的积极参与者。自 2020 年起,哈萨克斯坦政府启动了一项"出口加速计划",进一步激发了哈企业参加进博会的热情。

据了解,"出口加速计划"旨在通过对哈企业出口机遇进行评估,帮助其开拓新的海外市场或扩大现有的出口规模。哈萨克斯坦贸易政策发展中心(以下简称"哈贸发中心")是该计划的主要实施方,对接中国市场和进博会是哈贸发中心工作的重要内容。

"哈萨克斯坦的出口商对进博会非常感兴趣。"哈贸发中心副主任阿谢尔·叶根别尔季耶娃（Egemberdieva Asel Yerikovna）表示，哈中两国已经建立起完备的物流路线，对彼此产品的需求也更加明确。参加进博会是向中国市场推广哈产品的有效渠道之一。

推开"金色大门"，收获的是实实在在的经贸成果。2023年，哈贸发中心组织了超过40家哈萨克斯坦机构和企业参加进博会，签下大批订单，收获颇丰。

推开"金色大门"，迈入的是更宽广的经贸通路。第六届进博会期间，哈萨克斯坦贸易和一体化部部长阿尔曼·沙卡利耶夫（Shakaliyev）在国家展团推介会上说："今天，哈萨克斯坦与中国签署了21份哈萨克斯坦农产品和食品出口议定书，这使得（哈萨克斯坦）向中国供应的农工综合体产品大幅增加。"

参展就有收获，参加进博会的效果让哈萨克斯坦中国研究中心主任古丽娜尔（Gurinal）赞不绝口："毫无疑问，进博会将是哈萨克斯坦实施出口加速计划的关键渠道，包括哈萨克斯坦在内的中亚国家都希望进博会能够继续在促进全球发展中发挥重要作用。"

2024年，哈萨克斯坦企业参加进博会

在第六届进博会上，哈萨克斯坦展台吸引众多客商前来洽谈。【新华社供图】

金骆驼集团有限公司总经理扎济拉·奥扎特克济在第六届进博会上向中国客商介绍展品。【新华社供图】

的信心更足。哈萨克斯坦贸易和一体化部部长阿尔曼·沙卡利耶夫透露，第七届进博会上哈萨克斯坦的参展规模将显著扩大，希望借助进博会展示更多商品种类。

为企业发展创造机遇

"为什么骆驼奶是咸香的？"在 2023 年进博会上，许多客商在第一次品尝哈萨克斯坦骆驼奶后问出了相似的问题。

在有"世界骆驼王国"之称的哈萨克斯坦，骆驼不只是一种交通工具。近年来，在当地乳制品企业的努力下，骆驼奶的深加工技术愈发成熟。金骆驼等品牌携骆驼奶连年亮相进博会，进一步扩大了哈乳制品的市场知名度。

面对客商们对骆驼奶的好奇心，金骆驼集团总经理扎济拉·奥扎特克济（Zazira Ozatkezi）用一口流利的中文耐心地解释道："骆驼在沙漠中吃的都是盐碱性食物，因此骆驼奶粉一般会有一点点咸味，还有醇厚的奶香味。"

连年奔赴"四叶草"，从未缺席进博会，让金骆驼被不少中国消费者熟知。目前，金骆驼产品已实现中国市场全覆盖，中国市场已占据金骆驼产品销路的半壁江山。

订单多了，企业发展也蒸蒸日上。如今，金骆驼集团拥有世界领先、全球规模最大的骆驼奶生产线，可日处理 100 吨新鲜骆驼乳。

回望过去数年参展历程，扎济拉·奥扎特克济感慨万分："2018 年参加首届进博会时，我们对参展效果有些担心。但之后连续几年参展，我们目睹了进博会一届比一届办得更好，我们觉得在中国市场大有可为，所以我们年年都愿意来参加进博会。"

在哈萨克斯坦，像金骆驼这样通过进博会拥抱中国市场的企业还有很多。不少当地企业负责人表示，希望进博会"朋友圈"不断壮大，为全球企业创造更多发展机遇。

为青年追梦搭建舞台

在第六届进博会哈萨克斯坦优选展台前，有一位特殊的参展商——哈萨克斯坦姑娘叶胜利。

说她特殊，是因为她曾多次以"小叶子"志愿者的身份参加进博会，如今却摇身一变成为参展商。

叶胜利称呼自己为追梦人，她和进博会的缘分始于 2020 年。彼时还在学校读书的她以"小叶子"志愿者的身份参加了第三届进博会，此后又连续两年成为进博会志愿者。感叹于这个平台能让这么多全球好物和贸易机会都汇聚一堂的同时，她也从中不断学习。3 年间，她服务的参展商从最初的一家增加到后来的二三十家。正是这段经历，让她找到了人生的努力方向。

"三届进博会志愿者的经历改变了我，让我从一个性格内向的小姑娘，变成外向开朗、对未来有明确规划的年轻人。"通过进博会搭建的大舞台，追梦人叶胜利找到了自己的梦想职业——从事哈中国际贸易，为两国经贸、文化交流贡献一份力量。第六届进博会上，叶胜利第一次以参展商的身份再赴"进博之约"。

哈萨克斯坦姑娘叶胜利（Botakoz Yelshibek）以志愿者身份首次参加第三届进博会。
【受访者供图】

　　闲暇时，叶胜利也像许多中国青年一样，喜欢在短视频平台分享自己的日常。她的账号中有一条用每届进博会的工作证剪辑而成的 vlog，获得了大量网友的点赞。

　　在叶胜利的影响下，她的妹妹爱民也报名参加进博会，成为一名"小叶子"。未来，也许还有更多哈萨克斯坦青年成为进博会志愿者，与中国"小叶子"一起逐梦"四叶草"，共同为建设中哈关系新的"黄金三十年"注入青春力量。

　　几年前，《共青团真理报》曾在报道中称，中国扩大外国商品进口的举措使更多国家在中国经济发展的进程中受益。哈萨克斯坦展商参加历届进博会的经历和收获，已成为这一报道的生动写照。

第七届进博会将再次向哈萨克斯坦人民敞开"金色大门",为中哈两国关系新的"黄金三十年"书写新的篇章。

(本文综合自:人民日报、新华社、央视网、央视新闻客户端、中新社、中国新闻网、黑龙江日报、解放日报、文汇报、国际商报、大庆日报公众号、哈萨克斯坦驻华大使馆公众号、驻哈萨克斯坦共和国大使馆经济商务处、普华永道官网。)

进博会让"铁杆朋友"越走越近

塞尔维亚地处巴尔干半岛中部，是中国在中东欧地区首个全面战略伙伴。长期以来，中塞两国缔造了深厚传统友谊和特殊友好感情。在面对一次次困难和挑战之时，中塞两国人民始终患难与共，彼此支持。

2016年6月，习近平主席首次对塞尔维亚进行国事访问。两国元首一致决定，将中塞关系提升为全面战略伙伴关系。

2023年10月，习近平主席会见来华出席第三届"一带一路"国际合作高峰论坛的塞尔维亚总统亚历山大·武契奇（Aleksandar Vucic）时说："塞尔维亚是中国的铁杆朋友，两国关系经受住国际风云变幻考验，堪称中国同欧洲国家友好关系的典范。"武契奇表示，对塞中铁杆友谊感到自豪。

2024年，习近平主席时隔8年再次访问塞尔维亚，对中塞关系提质升级具有重

第六届进博会塞尔维亚国家展展台。

要里程碑意义。两国领导人再次共话友谊、共商合作、共谋发展，规划两国关系发展新蓝图。

作为世界上首个以进口为主题的国家级展会，进博会自 2018 年首次举办以来，已成为全球共享的国际公共产品，全球好物在此"上架"，并迅速进入中国市场。前六届以来，塞尔维亚企业年年赴进博会参展，而且数量逐年攀升，越来越多来自塞尔维亚的优质产品从展品变为商品，逐步走进中国消费者的日常生活。

参会企业数量逐年攀升

在 2023 年第六届进博会上，作为主宾国参展的塞尔维亚第 4 次亮相国家展，并迅速因其独特的设计风格和独具特色的美食大放异彩。"面包与河流"的概念设计令现场观众印象深刻。在塞尔维亚，河流象征着富饶和团结，面包象征着喜悦和幸福。塞尔维亚人，选择了当地最具美好象征意义的元素来展示他们的热情与友好，这也吸引了许多观众排起长长的队伍，等待品尝塞尔维亚风味的红酒和面包。

正如 2021 年第四届进博会上塞尔维亚国家馆的主打标语"与中国分享我们最好的"所揭示的，自进博会举办以来，"铁杆朋友"塞尔维亚年年参展，不仅带来"最好的"展品，而且带来最坚定的支持。塞尔维亚总统武契奇在第三届进博会开幕式上以视频方式致辞，总理阿娜·布尔纳比奇（Ana Brnabic）两次现

塞尔维亚企业参加第六届进博会。【中国驻塞尔维亚大使馆供图】

场出席进博会开幕式并致辞，这充分体现出塞尔维亚政府对进博会的高度重视。

塞尔维亚企业也越来越多地出现在进博会的舞台上。自2018年至2023年，前来参加进博会的塞尔维亚企业数量由6家逐年递增至41家，展览面积也由最初的100平方米左右增至近700平方米，主要展品集中在食品和农产品等领域。塞尔维亚的葡萄酒、果汁、奶酪、麦片、蜂蜜、果酱、肉类等特色产品，开始常态化进入中国老百姓的购物车。

进博会让塞尔维亚企业感受到了实实在在的利好。泰尔齐奇的公司主要经营塞尔维亚的纯天然饮料和葡萄酒。他表示，参加进博会为他的公司带来了极大收益，公司与多家中国公司结成合作伙伴关系，出口产品销量得到大幅提升。在他看来，进博会为塞尔维亚的出口企业打开了机遇之窗，同时也促进了全球贸易交往。

一位酒商代理也感慨道，公司进军中国这些年，销量不断上升，随着进博会越办越火，中国开放的大门越开越大，相信塞尔维亚产品出口中国也会有越来越多的机会和优势。

中塞友谊之路越走越宽

进博会犹如桥梁，加速了中塞两国贸易往来和友谊升温。塞尔维亚总理布尔纳比奇在参加第六届进博会时表示，塞中合作日益密切，过去 10 年，塞尔维亚对中国的出口增长了 185 倍，这充分体现了中国的开放。

几乎可以肯定的是，中塞双边贸易额还将继续走高。2023 年 10 月，中国与塞尔维亚签署自贸协定，这是中国与中东欧国家签署的第一个自贸协定。协议约定，中塞双方将分别对 90% 的税目相互取消关税。其中，超过 60% 的税目在协定生效后立即取消关税，双方最终零关税税目的进口额比例都达到 95% 左右。"自贸协定生效后，关税将以 20% 的幅度逐年递减，这样在 5 年内我们就可以零关税向中国出口我们的葡萄酒了。"说起自贸协定，武契奇日前在接受中国中央广播电视总台采访时难掩兴奋。

塞尔维亚工商会中国代表处主任耶琳娜·格鲁伯·斯特凡诺维奇（Jelena Grubor Stefanovic）在结束了第六届进博会工作后，马上投入到第七届的准备之中。因为在她看来，塞中自贸协定签署后，许多塞尔维亚的优势产品出口中国将逐步实现零关税，这对塞尔维亚企业是利好消息。

据其了解，一些塞尔维亚企业在中国的业务进展迅速，正在吸引更多的塞尔维亚企业参加进博会，向中国消费者展示自己的产品，并仔细了解和研究中国消费者的需求。"进博会已成为重要的全球经济盛会，不仅为中国消费者提供了更多选择，也是各国企业进入广阔中国市场的绝佳平台。我们计划继续扩大展位面积，让更多塞尔维亚企业在进博会舞台上展览展示、获得商机。"耶琳娜·格鲁伯·斯特凡诺维奇说。

　　进博会是"中国开放的大门越开越大"的最好证明。"朋友是时间的果实",塞尔维亚的"进博故事",也将越讲越精彩。

　　（本文综合自：新华社、中国新闻网、中国网、21世纪经济报道、第一财经、澎湃新闻、文汇报、南方都市报、上观新闻、浦东发布。）

借进博东风，非洲特色农产品打开机遇之门

最不发达国家（Least Developed Countries，LDCs），是指经联合国认定的社会、经济发展水平以及人类发展指数最低的国家。根据联合国有关数据，截至2023年12月，全球共有45个最不发达国家，其中33个位于非洲。得益于多样的地理环境，许多非洲最不发达国家拥有各具特色的优质农产品。近年来，中国持续扩大非洲农产品进口，既促进了非洲最不发达国家农业现代化发展，又丰富了中国消费者的市场选择。

作为世界上首个以进口为主题的国家级展会，进博会已经成为中国构建新发展格局的窗口、推动高水平开放的平台、全球共享的国际公共产品。自2018年首次举办以来，无数全球好物在进博会收获商机。借助进博东风，来自非洲最不发达国家的特色农产品，也在"四叶草"打开了机遇之门。

"双向奔赴"

中国食品土畜进出口商会发布的《2023年中国与非洲地区国家农产品贸易概况》显示，2019—2023年，中国自非洲地区国家农产

进博会成为非洲最不发达国家共同的选择。

品进口额实现五连涨。在巨大的市场红利面前，诸多非洲最不发达国家不约而同地将进博会作为提高自身知名度、扩大对华农产品出口、进一步共享中国发展红利的选择。

不同的国家，共同的选择，背后是进博会与最不发达国家"双向奔赴"的生动故事。为了让更多国家分享中国发展红利，进博会从首届起便广泛邀请最不发达国家参展，并向每个最不发达国家提供2个免费标准摊位。自第五届起，进博会加大对最不发达国家参展的支持力度，将免费标准摊位的数量扩大至4个。免费标摊面积虽然不大，却承载着诸多非洲最不发达国家的展商寻求发展的美好希望。

除了免费标准摊位，进博会对最不发达国家的支持是多方位的。例如，挖掘各国有市场潜力的特色产品，积极引进参展；帮助展商对接采购商及合作伙伴，助力实现参展即有收获；创造媒体集中报道机会，扩大综合影响力……

进博会为帮助最不发达国家融入多边贸易体制所做的种种努力，让世界见证了中国建设开放型世界经济、构建人类命运共同体的决心与行动。

"繁花"争艳

在多重支持政策的加持下，历年进博会上总会出现众多非洲特色农产品。

自 2018 年以来，每年约有 30 个最不发达国家的企业来进博会寻求商机。其中，不少非洲最不发达国家曾在国际组织等机构的支持协助下参展。例如，马达加斯加、莫桑比克等国企业通过联合国

第六届进博会上的"非洲农产品专区"。【IC photo 供图】

国际贸易中心参展，中非共和国、尼日尔、安哥拉、索马里等国则借助欧美工商会等机构参展。

第六届进博会期间的一幕"火热场面"，让非洲最不发达国家的特色农产品进入更多人的视野。在第六届进博会上，中国食品土畜进出口商会汇集联合国国际贸易中心、比尔及梅琳达·盖茨基金会和阿里巴巴国际站等国内外资源，通过设立"非洲农产品专区"突出集中展示效果。专区汇集了来自尼日尔、苏丹、埃塞俄比亚、贝宁等9个非洲最不发达国家的20家农产品出口企业，受到广泛关注，形成了一派争奇斗艳的景象。

排队试吃的观众，洽谈咨询的采购商，围了一圈的媒体记者……"非洲农产品专区"的现场堪称"人山人海"。其中，芝麻、花生和大豆等非洲传统农产品是中国采购商关注的重点，来自埃塞俄比亚和卢旺达的咖啡豆等特色农产品更是咨询不断。

"非洲农产品专区"显著的影响力，收获了参展的非洲最不发达国家多方好评。来自苏丹的 Morshy 贸易公司表示，进博会为企业进入中国市场提供了绝佳机会，并将积极投入更多资源参加第七届进博会。尼日尔驻华使馆代表参观专区之后，对专区设计和企业参展效果十分满意，表示来年将组织更多出口企业参加第七届进博会，助力更多企业开拓中国市场，共享中国机遇。

"开放画卷"

多年来，非洲最不发达国家特色农产品在进博会频频展出，换来的是海量订单，带回的是民生福祉。赞比亚蜂蜜打响了知名度，带动更多当地居民加入养蜂队伍；几内亚比绍腰果开拓了中国市场，还惊喜地收到投资意向；埃塞俄比亚咖啡、卢旺达辣椒等特色农产品大受欢迎，诸多种植户因此获益……

第六届进博会上亮相的"非洲农产品专区"更是成果喜人。数据显示，展会期间，该专区接待超 300 家中方企业与非洲企业对接洽谈，意向采购金额超出预期，为非洲最不发达国家发展注入一针"强心剂"。

参加进博会不仅带来了实实在在的成果，同时也极大地提升了非洲国家产品的知名度。比如，2023 年进博会期间诞生的明星展品——"甜面包"贝宁菠萝。参展期间，贝宁展台观众络绎不绝，贝宁菠萝在互联网上的热度也迅速攀升，一跃成为"顶流"展品，并同步在贝宁电视台播放现场盛况。

众多非洲最不发达国家参加进博会的

在第六届进博会上，贝宁驻华大使西蒙·阿多韦兰德（Simon Pierre Adovelande）手捧两个贝宁菠萝向观众做介绍。【新华社供图】

故事向世界表明，作为全球共享的国际公共产品，进博会有力支持了最不发达国家的经济发展，彰显了构建人类命运共同体的中国胸怀。

（本文综合自：新华社、海外网、联合国官网、中国食品土畜进出口商会官网。）

从"共用一张桌子"到"拥有 60 平方米的展位"

在 2018 年首届进博会上的一个很不起眼的角落，阿克海洋生物（Aker BioMarine）在与其他中小企业共用的一张桌子上，展示着该公司的磷虾油原料产品。这家来自挪威的生物技术公司彼时不会想到，这方小小的展台日后将为公司发展带来大机遇。

小展台爆发大潜力

阿克海洋生物专注于海洋生物资源的可持续开发和利用，2015 年正式进入中国市场，通过与中国客户和商业伙伴合作以及参加各类行业展会，逐步在中国站稳脚跟，取得一定发展。

让阿克海洋生物意外的是，2018 年首次在进博会亮相，公司就一炮而红，不仅知名度得到提升，与本地企业的合作也频频加快，在中国的市场份额逐步扩大。

阿克海洋生物认识到，进博会不只是一场规模巨大的展览会，更是一个充满活力的平台。在这里，不仅仅可以展示产品和技术，更能够培养有意义的伙伴关系，促进思想和理念的交流与创新。此外，在进博会上获得大量曝光，对于中小企业提高品牌知名度、与中国潜在合作伙伴建立信任和联系非常有价值。

美食博主任芸丽在第六届进博会挪威海产馆进行现场直播。【挪威海产局供图】

　　首届进博会后，阿克海洋生物便一直是进博会的"全勤生"，每年都派出由市场、销售和技术专家组成的团队，用心设计展台，精心筹划准备，展示其创新产品和可持续发展理念。

　　在第五届进博会上，阿克海洋生物举办了一场主题为"海洋资源的可持续利用与健康未来"的专题讲座。到第六届进博会，阿克海洋生物已拥有面积达 60 平方米的独立展位，与近 30 家客户达成战略合作协议，并支持开展 7 场直播活动，打破了磷虾油产品以往的直播销售记录。

　　从"共用一张桌子"到"拥有 60 平方米的展位"，这段宝贵的进博会历程，让阿克海洋生物看到了中国市场的巨大潜力。

深谙进博"流量密码"

与阿克海洋生物"全勤生"的身份不同，挪威海产局在第五届进博会才首次亮相。

虽然是"新人"，但挪威海产局很快就"如鱼得水"，以"挪威，海产大国"为主题参展。在第六届进博会上，挪威海产局已深谙"流量密码"，邀请美食博主任芸丽在"挪威海产馆"进行现场直播。

这场直播制作的美食包括挪威北极甜虾芒果泰式沙拉、挪威三文鱼牛油果土豆轻食沙拉、具有沪上风味的葱烧挪威北极鳕鱼以及以云南小烧烤方式制作的无油脆皮挪威青花鱼。

美食博主对一条鱼的花式做法，将挪威海产品的美味口感展现得淋漓尽致，大众也了解到挪威海产走上中国餐桌的各种渠道。

挪威海产局相关人员表示："进博会不仅是一个展示挪威优质海产品的平台，更是一个增进国际交流、加深中挪海产贸易合作的重要平台。我们希望借助进博效应，进一步推动中挪在海产贸易领域的热度，加强挪威与中国在海产领域的合作与联系，以满足中国消费者对高品质海产的需求。"

2024 年第七届进博会，挪威海产局参加进博会的方式有所改进，将作为挪威国

第六届进博会挪威海产馆相关展品。【挪威海产局供图】

家馆的组成部分参展，以期更深入地了解中国市场。

凭借进博效应，挪威海产局迅速将"进博热度"化作"贸易热度"。

挪威海产局发布的最新数据显示，截至 2024 年 7 月，挪威对中国的海产品出口量约为 89856 吨，同比增长 14%，出口总额达 48.7 亿挪威克朗（约合 33 亿元人民币）。其中挪威三文鱼在中国的出口业绩格外亮眼，出口量达 26876 吨，出口额达 28.5 亿挪威克朗（约合 19 亿元人民币）。

挪威海产局总监毕思明（Sigmund Bjørgo）表示，2023 年，中国是世界上大西洋三文鱼消费增长最快的市场，共计消费 108128 吨大西洋三文鱼，同比增长 32597 吨，增幅为 43%，这使得中国大西洋三文鱼市场成为全球第八大市场。而且中国目前是亚洲地区最大的大西洋三文鱼消费市场，相较于排名第二的日本市场，高出逾 2 倍的消费量。

"进博推荐官"

对挪威海产品在中国市场的火爆情况，挪威首相斯特勒（Store）曾亲自体验。2024 年 9 月 10 日晚间，正在访华的斯特勒现身上海东虹桥中心，在简单参观后，便穿上蓝色围裙，现场"带货"自家海产品。他端着餐盘，一边邀请大家品尝挪威三文鱼和青花鱼，一边介绍道："快试试，很新鲜。"

斯特勒表示，希望将最新鲜的海产品出口到中国，并希望与中国相关部门合作，帮助中国消费者，消除所有让这些产品变得昂贵的障碍。

参加进博会让包括阿克海洋生物和挪威海产局在内的挪威机构收获满满，挪威官方也因此推动更多挪威企业和产品亮相进博会。

挪威创新署亚洲及中东地区司长奥立希（Ole Henaes）在第七届进博会挪威推介会上致辞。【挪威海产局供图】

第六届进博会挪威海产馆展位。【挪威海产局供图】

　　当地时间 2024 年 5 月 13 日，第七届进博会挪威推介会在奥斯陆举办，这是进博会推介活动首次走进挪威，获得当地欢迎。

　　会上发布的数据显示，在第六届进博会上，挪威有近 30 家企业参展，参展企业数量和总面积均创历史新高。

　　阿克海洋生物公司代表王黎明在推介会上化身"进博推荐官"，强烈推荐挪威企业赴进博会参展参会。

　　挪威创新署亚洲及中东地区司长奥立希表示，有越来越多的挪威企业开展对华贸易投资，两国企业在清洁能源、海产品等诸多领域持续开展合作。进博会是展示最新产品和技术、促进合作和交流的很好平台。挪威创新署致力于将挪威的优质产品推向包括中国在内的国际市场，将继续组织企业参展，帮助挪威企业开拓中国市场。

文 / 缪璐

中国市场给秘鲁羊驼制品手工艺人带来更多发展机遇

6月下旬，位于南美洲的秘鲁南部高原城市阿雷基帕刚刚入冬，空气中弥漫着一丝清冷。但在当地手工艺人奥斯瓦尔多·马马尼家中，一家人忙着画图、缝制、为羊驼毛玩偶梳毛，劳作的气氛格外热烈。

奥斯瓦尔多·马马尼开心地向记者展示一只用羊驼毛制作的大熊猫玩偶，介绍说："2023年11月，我和妻子带着这个特别的设计去了中国的进博会。"

手工艺人奥斯瓦尔多·马马尼（Oswaldo Mamani）在秘鲁阿雷基帕展示用羊驼毛制作的熊猫玩偶。【新华社供图】

"带着我们的作品去中国参加进博会，是我们的梦想。"奥斯瓦尔多·马马尼激动地说，作为秘鲁传统手工艺人，"我们非常感谢中国和中国消费者欣赏、认可我们的作品。"

已年满50岁的奥斯瓦尔多·马马尼从青少年时期就开始制作、售卖羊驼毛装饰品。

羊驼皮毛和手工制作羊驼玩偶所使用的工具。【新华社供图】

2016 年，中国顾客马玉霞来到奥斯瓦尔多·马马尼的小店选购了两只羊驼玩偶，自此他的羊驼玩偶走进了中国市场。

"起初，他们向我们购买 1000 只羊驼玩偶，我叫上了家里的兄弟姐妹一起制作完成这笔订单。"奥斯瓦尔多·马马尼说。随后，双方开始了长期合作。

"中国市场有潜力，消费力强，近年需求增长快，现在每两个月交付一次订单，每次在 8000 至 1 万件。"奥斯瓦尔多·马马尼说。

在产品的质量和丰富性方面，奥斯瓦尔多·马马尼一家也下足功夫。"我们是传统的秘鲁手工艺人，在每天的制作过程中也不断

羊驼皮毛和羊驼玩偶。【新华社供图】

完善细节，力求完美，"他说，"面对更加多样化的市场需求，我们也制作鸭子、海豚等更多品类，玩偶尺寸也更加丰富。"

谈及新作品大熊猫玩偶，奥斯瓦尔多·马马尼介绍说："我们知道熊猫是中国的一个标志，在中国备受喜爱，就有了用羊驼毛制作熊猫玩偶的想法，在进博会上我们也注意到吉祥物是一只大熊猫。"

在繁忙的工作中，奥斯瓦尔多·马马尼一家也享受到"羊驼经济"为他们带来的实在好处，原本只有一层的手工作坊已扩建至三层。"我们热爱制作手工艺品，现在不仅赚的钱更多了，生活也更好了。"奥斯瓦尔多·马马尼说。

秘鲁国旗中央绘有一只金黄色的羊驼。秘鲁是世界上羊驼数量最多的国家，也是最大的羊驼毛纺织品生产国。秘鲁安第斯山区不少家庭以养殖羊驼及制作羊驼毛纺织品为生。

在奥斯瓦尔多·马马尼看来，"中国为我们的产品打开了市场"。近年来，中国市场不断开放、扩大，欢迎他们手工制作的多样化产品，对秘鲁当地手工业增长作出贡献。

亚历杭德拉·贝德雷加尔（Alejandra Bedregal）是奥斯瓦尔多·马马尼与中方合作品牌的秘鲁合伙人之一，主要负责品控和发货。"得

手工艺人制作羊驼玩偶。【新华社供图】

益于中国市场的快速恢复，我们的销售额增长强劲，"她说，"自我们同奥斯瓦尔多·马马尼一家合作以来，许多手工艺家庭来找我们寻求合作。"

亚历杭德拉·贝德雷加尔认为，中国和秘鲁政府为产品发展提供了支持，"特别是进博会让我们大开眼界，对中国市场有了更深入的了解，督促我们要一直创新和改进"，自贸协定也发挥了重要作用。

由于中国市场需求巨大，亚历杭德拉·贝德雷加尔希望"能同当地更多手工艺人达成合作，生产销售更多产品，同时不断改进细节、创新品类"。奥斯瓦尔多·马马尼也表示，希望"能开设面积更大的工作坊，聚集更多家人一同生产、一同受益"。

"2024年进博会我一定要再去中国看看。"亚历杭德拉·贝德雷加尔说。

文 / 席玥 朱雨博 李木子

发 展 之 美

"甜面包" 遇见 "金钥匙"

贝宁是联合国公布的最不发达国家之一。从太空俯瞰，其版图形状像一把钥匙，从几内亚湾直通西非腹地。钥匙常被视为机遇的象征。当地人在进行招商引资时，也会把自己形容为"打开非洲大门的钥匙"。

贝宁南部盛产一种被称为"甜面包"的菠萝。2023 年 9 月，中国与贝宁签署鲜食菠萝输华植物检疫要求议定书，贝宁菠萝正式获得中国检疫准入。为加快菠萝输华步伐，贝宁人来到"四叶草"，找到了快速进入中国市场的"金钥匙"。

助力贝宁菠萝实现"最快输华"

菠萝是贝宁主要出口农产品之一，在当地种植面积达 6000 余公顷，年产量约 40 万吨。不同于常见的圆形和椭圆形菠萝，贝宁菠萝呈棒槌形，表皮常为绿色，口感独特，素有非洲"甜面包"的美称，是贝宁特有品种。"这样甜度的菠萝在我们国家，也只有南部的阿拉达高地上能够种得出，因为那里有理想的气候和优质的土壤。"贝宁驻华大使助理爱力舍（Alisher）介绍道。

近年来，进博会已经成为世界各国优质水果进入中国市场的"金钥匙"。通过进博会，比利时朱樱红啤梨、秘鲁沙漠蓝莓、厄瓜多尔麒麟果等水果相继与中国消费者"结缘"。从决定参加第六届进博会起，这把"金钥匙"便为"甜面包"贝宁菠萝打开了快速进入中国市场的大门。

在进博会的推动下，从 2023 年 9 月获得检疫准入，到 11 月首批鲜果入境，"甜面包"贝宁菠萝仅用时两个月就实现了"最快输华"。贝宁驻华大使西蒙·阿多韦兰德（Simon Pierre Adovelande）对此十分感慨："中国政府部门让每个过程都非常顺利。"

与此同时，进博会还为贝宁等最不发达国家提供了免费标准摊位等多重支持政策，进一步帮助贝宁菠萝等特色农产品进入中国市场。

第六届进博会开幕前夕，西蒙·阿多韦兰德亲自前往上海浦东国际机场海关检疫现场，迎接首批贝宁菠萝入境。在他眼中，参加第六届进博会是自己职业生涯的重要一刻，对整个贝宁也具有重要意义。这意味着经过中贝两国的共同努力，一个庞大的市场向"甜面包"贝宁菠萝敞开了大门。

共建"一带一路"结出果实

"民以食为天"，在数千年饮食文化的熏陶下，中国消费者对食物有着极高的兴趣和关注度。深厚的饮食文化背后，是中国巨大的农产品消费市场。在文化和市场的双重驱动下，历届进博会上展出的优质水果，总能成为各方关注的焦点。"甜面包"贝宁菠萝正是其中之一。

"入口甜，鲜嫩多汁。""很细腻，而且带有一种香味。""形状像是不倒翁似的，很可爱。"……"甜面包"贝宁菠萝在第六届进博会首次亮相便吸引了众多采购商排队品尝。贝宁参展商菲尔曼

（Firman）介绍说："当你切开它的时候，里面的果肉白皙香甜，这也是'甜面包'这个名字的由来。"

输华速度快，热度和订单来得也快。置身"四叶草"，才能更直观地感受到进博会这把"金钥匙"的强大影响力。贝宁菠萝开启中国首秀后，很快就引爆了中文互联网。一夜之间，"甜面包"贝宁菠萝成为成千上万网友热议的对象。与极高关注度同时到来的，还有海量订单。另一位贝宁参展商贝蒂耶·盖迪贝（Bettier Gedibe）兴奋地说道："我早就听说过进博会，很高兴2024年作为参展商过来，并与中国企业签下大单。希望更多中国消费者喜欢'甜面包'贝宁菠萝！"

"甜面包"贝宁菠萝在第六届进博会取得的骄人成果，成为中贝双方经贸往来的新亮点。在阿多韦兰德看来，此次贝宁菠萝借第六届进博会首次亮相中国，是中贝双方共建"一带一路"结出的果实。同时，他对中贝双方经贸往来有了更多的期盼："'一带一路'倡议使中国市场向世界开放，希望贝宁的腰果、棉花等特色农产品也可以在未来进入中国。"

观众在第六届进博会食品及农产品展区的贝宁菠萝展台品尝"甜面包"菠萝。【新华社供图】

为中贝两国人民带来福祉

在第六届进博会期间，观众来到贝宁展台不仅可以品尝美味的"甜面包"菠萝，还可以通过屏幕上播放的影片了解产地的情况。如此一幕，持续了整个展期，让人体会到"小菠萝"身上承载的民生"大福祉"。

随着贝宁菠萝借助进博会这把"金钥匙"实现快速输华，国内民众不用出国就可以品尝到来自贝宁的独有美味。而远在万里之外的贝宁人民，也有了一条致富增收的新路子。"贝宁农民与中国消费者都会从中受益。"阿多韦兰德说道。

"我们每天早上7点就来到菠萝地，目的是清除杂草、整理田地和种植菠萝。"听闻"甜面包"贝宁菠萝在中国打开了销路，正在田间劳作的当地种植户布莱兹·博巴特（Lez Bobart）表达了自身的喜悦，"我们对于自己种植的菠萝可以进入中国市场感到很自豪，这将增加我们的出口，同时我们的收入也会发生变化。"

贝宁菠萝在第六届进博会惊艳首秀，还为其带来了潜在的投资机遇。"除了订购贝宁菠萝外，我们还计划在贝宁当地投资建厂，输出种植技术和先进管理经验。"一家上海公司的非洲业务总负责人表示，

生长中的"甜面包"菠萝。【新华社供图】

进博会让贝宁菠萝走进中国消费者视野，公司目前正积极与贝宁政府洽谈合作。他说，希望借此推动贝宁本土产业规范化、规模化发展。

中贝两国传统友谊历经51周年，如今依然充满活力。2023年9月，中贝关系提升为战略伙伴关系。站在新的起点上，中贝经贸合作将进一步深化。2024年4月，第七届进博会全球推介走进贝宁。属于"贝宁菠萝"的进博故事，仍将续写新章。

（本文综合自：人民日报、新华社、光明日报、央视网、中国日报网、中国新闻网、环球时报、北京日报、浙江日报潮新闻、第一财经、中国小康网、国际商报、《中国经贸》杂志官网、北京日报客户端。）

进博会为媒，寻味"千丘之国"

　　位于非洲中东部赤道南侧的卢旺达是一个内陆国家，因地形多山丘，素有"千丘之国"之称，也是联合国公布的 45 个最不发达国家之一。近年来，卢旺达经济增长势头强劲，和中国的经贸往来日渐频繁，其中就包括积极参加进博会。自 2018 年首届进博会以来，

第二届进博会卢旺达国家展展台。

卢旺达已经连续6年参展，带来的咖啡、茶叶、辣椒、蜂蜜等特色产品为"四叶草"注入了酸甜苦辣等不同风味。

卢旺达人连年参展的动力，源自实实在在的收获。作为世界上首个以进口为主题的国家级展会，进博会带着"向世界开放市场"的承诺，让中国大市场一步步成为卢旺达的"大机遇"。

辣椒"爆卖"

卢旺达盛产辣椒，其中哈瓦那辣椒的辣度更是位居世界前列。但正因太辣，加上本地消费能力较弱，卢旺达辣椒时常面临着"有质无市"的尴尬处境。

进博会为卢旺达辣椒打开了新的销路。首届进博会后，卢旺达发展委员会与中国某新零售商超签署了合作备忘录，旨在推动卢旺达本地产品进入中国，卢旺达辣椒由此迎来了转机。被称为"卢旺达老干妈"的辣椒酱迅速在中国市场走红，引发了一股购买热潮，甚至成为春节期间的热门年货之一，频繁出现在中国消费者的餐桌上。在第三届进博会上，卢旺达辣椒酱还进行了包装升级，以全新面貌吸引了更多关注。

此外，辣椒油和干辣椒也广受欢迎。从首届进博会上价值两百万美元的辣椒油订单，到第四届17吨的干辣椒订单，卢旺达辣椒一次次点燃了采购商们的热情。

订单纷至沓来，辣椒热潮同样席卷卢旺达全境。一批在互联网时代成长起来的年轻人，返乡种上了辣

卢旺达辣椒酱为中国市场量身打造的全新包装。【新华社供图】

椒。此前，他们像候鸟一样散落在不同工地，日均收入不足 10 元人民币。而在众多卢旺达辣椒种植户中有一位特别的人，他是毕业于中国科学院的博士赫尔曼（Herman）。他曾算过一笔账，按一个当地农民种 1 公顷辣椒来算，种植、收获周期 8 个月，平均日收入可以达到 50~60 元，这是他们以前打工收入的 5~6 倍。

实际上，每一份订单不仅是单纯的产品买卖，背后还有长长的产业链供应链，可以带动相关国家产业发展、民生改善。这也是进博会的一大魅力所在。

2021 年 3 月，中卢两国政府签署了《关于卢旺达干辣椒输华检验检疫要求议定书》。8 月，首批来自卢旺达的辣椒运抵湖南，卢旺达成为首个向中国出口干辣椒的非洲国家。根据协定，2026 年前，卢旺达供应商将向中国出口 5 万吨干辣椒。

一秒售出 3000 包

"喝起来感觉有点甜。""令人联想到蓝莓、红苹果和柑橘的酸甜味道。"……卢旺达的火山质土壤赋予了当地咖啡豆独特的果香和花香，入口甘醇、余韵绵长。因其优质的品质，卢旺达咖啡"突出重围"，成为多届进博会的"明星展品"之一。

其中，卢旺达"大猩猩"牌咖啡与进博会有着特殊的缘分。2018 年，这款咖啡通过首届进博会与中国消费者见面。这些年，生产该咖啡的卢旺达农民咖啡公司不断发展壮大，咖啡烘焙工厂拉动了当地就业，也提高了咖啡种植者的收入。

"进博会是一个促进贸易和机会共享的开放交流平台，为卢旺

进博会展出的卢旺达"大猩猩"牌咖啡产品。【《中国与非洲》杂志供图】

达产品，尤其是咖啡豆，提供了机会。"卢旺达大猩猩咖啡公司首席执行官戴维·恩加兰贝（David Ngarambe）表示，参加进博会以来，公司在中国市场的销售额不断增长，并发展了多家商业合作伙伴，逐渐融入国际市场。

卢旺达驻华大使詹姆斯·基莫尼奥（James Kimonyo）也表示，进博会拉近了卢旺达农民和中国消费者之间的距离，当地咖啡豆种植户现在每售出一包咖啡就可以多赚 4 美元。

得益于进博会强大的溢出效应，卢旺达咖啡在中国市场的知名度迅速提升。第四届进博会期间，一些卢旺达品牌顺应中国的电商直播趋势，与头部电商主播达成合作，让更多中国消费者领略到卢旺达咖啡的独特魅力。"有一次，我们在短短一秒钟内售出 3000 包咖啡，而我们甚至没有准备那么多库存。"卢旺达驻华使馆商务参赞沙米尔（Samuel Abikunda）笑着回忆道："这是一个巨大的惊喜。"次年，在第五届进博会上，沙米尔亲自上阵，到直播间做起了"咖啡推荐官"，还带来了一杯专为进博会设计、融入中国元素的咖啡。

卢旺达咖啡俘获了消费者的心，巨大的商业机遇也吸引着越来越多展商奔赴进博会的舞台。

"这几天见了不少人，我们带的样品都不够用，因为很多人路过这里就觉得好香，都想尝一尝。"来自卢旺达的安迪·盖塔拉（Andrew Gatera）满脸兴奋。他熟练地切换中英文，向驻足在展台前的观众介绍自己的咖啡品牌，拿下了不少订单。

第六届进博会是安迪首次参展，但早在第五届时，他作为普通观众便在此深刻感受到了中国巨大的消费能力和市场潜力。此外，进博会还通过提供部分免费展位等实实在在的支持，推动当地各类产品进入中国市场，让世界经济发展成果更加均衡普惠包容。"希

望能借助进博会的平台推广我们的产品，同时吸引更多中国消费者到卢旺达去一探究竟。"安迪充满期待地说道。

高山茶"泡出"致富经

卢旺达地处高海拔地区，得天独厚的自然环境孕育出香气高远、轻苦回甘且滋味浓厚的高山茶，这种颇受消费者青睐的茶叶已成为当地人民致富的法宝。中国驻卢旺达大使王雪坤表示，在茶叶等产品的推动下，2023 年卢旺达对中国的出口增长了 87% 以上，达到创纪录的 1.31 亿美元。

茶叶是卢旺达重要的出口创汇来源之一，也是历届进博会上的"常客"。卢旺达高山茶公司就是在第二届进博会上完成了首秀。参展前，公司的工厂经理哈米姆·卡巴加穆贝（Hameem Kabagamube）就对进博会充满期待，希望通过此次展会接到来自中国的订单，进而打开中国市场的大门。

哈米姆·卡巴加穆贝的期待没有落空。在展会现场，卢旺达高山茶公司与中国某进出口贸易商达成合作意向，公司旗下全系列七款高端茶饮被正式引进中国，并在电商平台销售。这也是卢旺达高山茶首次进入中国。这些茶叶主要产自卢旺达南方省，而随着 2022 年卢旺达胡耶 66 公里公路的建成，当地的交通运输条件得到了极大改善。作为中卢两国共建"一带一路"合作项目之一，这条平整的双向沥青公路沿着连绵起伏的山丘蜿蜒盘旋，使得新鲜茶叶能够迅速运送至沿线城镇，经加工后出口至其他国家。"以前交通条件太差，茶叶运输是个大问题。现在我们可以及时把新鲜的好茶叶运出去，销路越来越好。这是一条改善生活的幸福路！"一名茶商感慨道。

卢旺达高山茶全系列七款产品。【DUNIVERSE 进口馆供图】

　　火爆的辣椒、飘香的咖啡、回甘的茶叶，来自卢旺达的美味通过进博会走进中国千家万户，让中卢两国民众走得更近。随着卢旺达政府积极推动夏威夷果、牛油果等优质产品进入中国市场，不久的将来，进博会上将解锁更多卢旺达的优质产品，让我们一起期待！

　　（部分内容综合自：人民日报、新华社、人民网、央视新闻、北京日报、经济导报、今日中国、参考消息、上观新闻、澎湃新闻、看看新闻、中国与非洲、中非经贸合作研究院、中非贸易研究中心、北京周报网、杭州网、相关企业官网等。）

埃塞俄比亚咖啡插上"进博翅膀"飞抵中国千万家

　　一筐筐拥有独特香气和口感的埃塞俄比亚（以下简称"埃塞"）咖啡豆，经过加工处理，配以精美的外包装设计，漂洋过海转运至国内，在电商平台上迅速捕获了中国消费者的心。一句"今天在进博会看到，明天就能网购到手"，完美诠释了进博会展品变商品的

往届进博会埃塞俄比亚国家馆。

魅力。埃塞俄比亚驻华大使塔费拉·德贝·伊马姆（Tefera Derbew Yimam）也曾欣喜地表示："我在中国的咖啡连锁店就能喝到埃塞咖啡，我们太高兴了。"

作为世界知名精品咖啡产区，近年来，埃塞咖啡在中国市场销量以每年 27% 的速度快速增长。中国海关数据显示，仅 2023 年 1—11 月，中国就从埃塞俄比亚进口了 2 万吨咖啡生豆。依托中国市场及电商平台的数字化赋能，埃塞咖啡插上"进博翅膀"迅速飞抵中国消费者的家中。

"展品一键变商品"

进博会和跨境电商作为海外品牌进入中国的有效路径，为埃塞企业带来了许多机遇。

埃塞咖啡品牌 Gera 早在第三届进博会就收获满满。品牌旗下耶加雪菲及西达摩咖啡现场签约入驻知名跨境电商平台，实现展品一键秒变商品，让消费者能够第一时间在网上买到"进博同款"优质咖啡。

彼时，Gera 品牌电商项目负责人凯文·朱（Kevin Zhu）感慨道，参加进博会让品牌加深了对中国市场的了解，第三届团队更是首次携带咖啡熟豆产品参展，并同步上线跨境电商销售。"这与埃塞之前农产品出口商的身份相比，是一个巨大的转换，多亏了进博会以及中国庞大的进口消费者们。"

在第五届进博会上，以橙黄色为主色调包装的埃塞高山咖啡吸睛十足，在某电商直播间亮相后，仅一

第五届进博会食品及农产品展区的埃塞俄比亚咖啡。【新华社供图】

晚便售出了1.7万盒。而第六届进博会期间，得益于强大的溢出效应，埃塞咖啡线上销量同比增长300%。

过去，在埃塞咖啡生豆出口贸易中，咖啡种植加工环节的收益仅占产业链收益的不到10%，绝大多数利润都在流通销售环节。借助进博会实现跨境电商销售，有效降低了贸易成本，让埃塞本土咖啡农获益的同时，也让中国消费者以更优惠的价格品尝到原产地精品咖啡豆。

据大使塔费拉·德贝·伊马姆称，现在中国成了埃塞咖啡的主要进口国之一，埃塞咖啡在历年进博会上广受好评，许多企业都希望在进博会上推介产品。"从使馆方面，我们努力为埃塞企业参展提供便利。"他看到埃塞产品越来越受中国消费者喜爱，非常高兴。

埃塞好物进博推

咖啡贸易只是中国与埃塞俄比亚贸易的一角，芝麻、绿豆等埃塞农产品也频频出现在中国的超市、商店和零售市场。

7年来，进博会让众多埃塞好物被寻到、被看见，也为它们背后的企业铺垫起入华"快车道"。他们带着家乡最优特产共赴进博之约，为全球经济注入活力。

第六届进博会上，埃塞芝麻贸易商杜卡工程贸易有限公司（Duka Engineering & Trading Plc）与山东的瑞福油脂股份有限公司达成初步合作意向，签订了6000吨的芝麻采购意向订单。据悉，瑞福油脂将用这批采购的高品质芝麻生产其老字号香油产品。

"之前我们公司和瑞福油脂股份有限公司通过中介进行交流，而进博会让我们实现了面对面签订合同。"Duka Engineering &

在第六届进博会上，芝麻、绿豆等埃塞俄比亚农产品吸引专业观众前去洽谈。

Trading Plc 公司的库拉格·德加（Kulag Degas）说。在这里，来自世界各地的企业有机会探索和建立新的合作关系，成功案例也在各方互动中不断涌现。

"进博会推动了全球贸易的自由化、便利化。节约了我们的时间和花费，却让我们得到更大收益。"埃塞商人德杰·梅斯克尔（Dejay Meskell）感触颇深，通过进博会，不仅结识了很多中国客商，还与多国商家建立了联系。阿联酋、墨西哥等国商家都对他的农产品很感兴趣。他表示，未来肯定还会前来参展。

进博会让埃塞与中国双边贸易关系日益密切。大使塔费拉·德贝·伊马姆说："未来一两年，我希望能在中国市场看到埃塞牛油果。我们会逐渐出口越来越多产品到中国，不仅是初级产品，还有纺织品和皮革制品等制成品。"

拥抱中国大市场

自 2018 年首届进博会以来，一场场签约、一笔笔订单，践行着进博会"一展惠全球"的承诺。

身为埃塞俄比亚咖啡出口商协会总经理吉萨特·沃库（Geisart Overkoo）对大大小小的本土咖啡出口企业十分熟悉，而进博会则帮助吉萨特拓宽了视野，看到了埃塞咖啡的未来目标市场。

"只要想做生意就不可能错过中国"，他表示，进博会为全球出口商进入广阔的中国市场提供了重要而独特的机会。"中国对于埃塞咖啡出口来说潜能巨大，不容忽视，要将开拓中国市场放在首位。"

在第六届进博会上，展台工作人员介绍埃塞俄比亚展品。

埃塞俄比亚商会和行业协会主席西赛·阿斯马尔（Cisay Asmar）也曾在第五届进博会上表示，进博会为埃塞农产品出口中国市场提供了巨大的机会，成为会见潜在客户并建立业务伙伴关系的有效平台。

企业热情高涨，政策利好频出。2023年10月，中埃两国双边关系升级为全天候战略伙伴关系。中方在联合声明中表示愿继续鼓励并支持包括农食产品在内的埃塞俄比亚产品对华出口，欢迎埃塞方用好非洲农产品输华准入"绿色通道"。

始于咖啡，远不止咖啡。"要把最好最新的产品带到进博会。""进博会带给我们的不只是订单，还有希望。"……中国市场为埃塞产品出口提供源源不断的动力，期待第七届进博会上，埃塞的特色展品继续"挥舞翅膀"，为企业带来广阔商机。

（部分内容综合自：人民日报、新华社、央视财经、海外网、光明网、人民政协网、国际金融报、国际商报、走进埃塞公众号、海报新闻、天下泉城客户端、阿里巴巴商品创新孵化中心、埃塞俄比亚 FANA 广播公司等。）

坦桑尼亚特色产品搭上"进博快车"

坦桑尼亚位于非洲东部，以热带气候为主，农业占国家经济主导地位。近年来，中坦双边贸易额增长显著，坦桑尼亚从与中国的合作中受益匪浅。自首届进博会以来，坦桑尼亚已经连续 6 年参展。通过进博会这个广阔的平台，坦桑尼亚参展商带着咖啡、腰果、麒

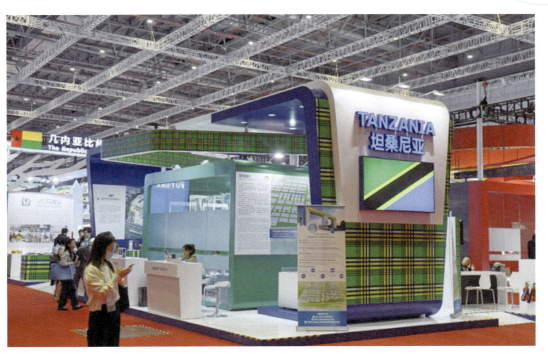

第六届进博会坦桑尼亚国家展展台。

麟菜等特色展品走出非洲大陆，走进中国市场，走向世界舞台。

2024 年是中国与坦桑尼亚建交 60 周年。60 年来，中坦关系一直走在中非合作前列，已成为中非关系和南南合作的典范。2023 年，中坦双边贸易额达 87.8 亿美元，同比增长 8.9%。中国已连续 8 年成为坦最大贸易伙伴。为促进双边贸易发展，中方给予坦 98% 税目输华产品零关税待遇，批准坦牛油果、水产品、腰果等优质特色农产品输华。进博会无疑是推动中坦贸易发展的绝佳平台，是促进中坦经贸往来的重要窗口。

"黑色黄金"

咖啡是坦桑尼亚传统出口作物之一，被誉为"黑色黄金"，主要种植在乞力马扎罗山、阿鲁沙和姆贝亚等南部高地地区。特别是乞力马扎罗地区，其肥沃的火山灰赐予了这里的咖啡浓厚的质感和柔和的酸度，独具特色。坦桑尼亚 90% 以上的咖啡均用于出口，2022—2023 财年出口总量达 8.15 万吨，出口额达 2.3 亿美元。第六届进博会前夕，坦桑尼亚咖啡生产企业非洲茶和咖啡搅拌器有限公司（1963）［Afri Tea & Coffee Blenders （1963） Ltd］负责人阿比杜哈基姆·毛拉（Abdulhakim Mulla）先生表示，他曾多次来到中国，该公司目前使用的设备也全部从中国进口，但一直没有能够同中国企业建立贸易合作关系。事实上，农产品进口的手续要比普通产品更加复杂，而进博会在展品通关方面提供了诸多便利政策，使其咖啡首次进入中国变得容易。在第六届进博会上，该企业成功找到了咖啡代理商。不过，订单不是最终目的，Afri Tea & Coffee Blenders 看中的是进博会的大平台。他们想以进博会作为打开中国市场的契机，找到稳定合作伙伴，进而构建稳定的产业链和供应链。

参展商非洲茶和咖啡搅拌器有限公司（1963）负责人阿比杜哈基姆·毛拉先生（前排左一）向驻坦桑尼亚大使陈明健（前排左三）介绍该公司生产的咖啡。【解放日报供图】

2024 年 5 月，坦桑尼亚投资顾问沙约应邀参加了上海国际咖啡文化节，他感叹道，中国咖啡产业规模在过去几年大幅增长，2023 年产值已达到 367 亿美元。如果坦桑尼亚利用本国经济特区和出口加工区以及东非重要的国际港口达累斯萨拉姆港将咖啡输入中国市场，那将大幅增加收入并实现真正的互利共赢。

"网红展品"

坦桑尼亚是非洲乃至世界最大的腰果生产国之一，其腰果主要种植区域集中在姆特瓦拉、林迪、滨海、鲁伍马和坦噶等省。其中，姆特瓦拉省和林迪省占全国腰果产量的 87% 以上。目前，坦桑尼亚

的腰果年产量约 80 万吨，是出口最多的经济作物，市场规模已达到 6.9 亿美元，但其年加工能力仅为 10 万吨，因此 90% 的坦桑尼亚腰果以带壳的原料形式出口。

中国是坦桑尼亚腰果主要出口目的地之一。2021 年，来自中国湖南的一家国际贸易公司参与坦桑尼亚政府组织的腰果拍卖活动并顺利中标，拿下坦桑尼亚对华开放腰果出口后的第一单，成为具备坦桑尼亚腰果直采权的中国企业。400 吨高品质腰果也因此可直接出口至中国。

2023 年，第六届进博会坦桑尼亚意向成交取得可喜成果。其中，腰果在所有坦桑尼亚展品中销量最大，也成为进博会上最受欢迎的坦桑尼亚特色产品。

"绿色黄金"

麒麟菜是产自坦桑尼亚桑给巴尔岛的特色海藻，既可以直接作为凉菜食用，也可以用作工业原料，被当地誉为"绿色黄金"。到 2022 年底，桑给巴尔岛每年生产超过 12000 吨麒麟菜。

第六届进博会前夕，在坦桑尼亚举办的进博会专场推介会令坦桑尼亚企业信心倍增。在中国驻坦桑尼亚使馆经商处的协

坦桑尼亚腰果。【潇湘眼供图】

助下，像纳苏尔·达基（Nasur Daki）一样的坦桑尼亚企业家首次带着用麒麟菜制作的香皂、茶叶以及精油来到进博会。纳苏尔·达基说，桑给巴尔岛约有 2.3 万名麒麟菜种植者，其中90%是女性。在桑给巴尔岛，男性捕鱼，女性种海藻，是常见的家庭分工方式。未来麒麟菜如果能在中国打开销路，将会助力当地女性就业发展，有力提升其经济收入和生活水平。

麒麟是中国古代神话中的一种瑞兽，寄托了人们的美好希冀，蕴藏着与人为善、宽以待人的理念。在构建中非命运共同体理念指导下，中坦共建"一带一路"倡议助力深化两国合作。坦桑尼亚通过扩大农产品对华出口来增加国家收入，中国企业在坦实施了铁路、桥梁、港口、水务工程等一系列项目，给坦桑尼亚带来飞跃性变化。作为世界上首个以进口为主题的国家级博览会，进博会引来八方宾客，助力以中国式现代化新成就为世界发展提供新机遇。越来越多原本不为中国消费者所熟知的坦桑特色产品，通过进博会进入中国市场，成为中坦两国发展互利共赢经贸合作关系的生动写照。

坦桑尼亚麒麟菜制作的凉拌菜、香皂、茶叶以及精油。
【新华社供图】

2024 年中非合作论坛峰会于 9 月在北京举办，中坦领导人共商中非友好合作大计，共绘中非发展美好蓝图，共筑高水平中非命运共同体，必将为中非合作插上翅膀。在第七届进博会上，中坦企业将继续在这一推动高水平开放的平台上共享发展机遇，展现中坦务实合作成果，实现"一带一路"倡议，让中坦贸易合作取得新进展，互利共赢再上新台阶。

（本文综合自：新华社、解放日报、潇湘眼等，驻坦桑尼亚使馆经商处供稿。）

中老农产品合作在进博会"开花结果"

志合者，不以山海为远。近年来，中国秉持亲诚惠容理念，同老挝等周边国家开展友好合作，共同发展振兴。自 2021 年 12 月开通运营以来，中老铁路助力中国和老挝在贸易往来、产业对接、人才交流等领域实现互联互通。在亲诚惠容理念的引领下，以进博会为媒，两国人民进一步发挥中老铁路的优势和作用，一道携手共赴美好未来。

野生古茶树焕发新生

在老挝南部占巴塞省巴松县的"36 公里村"，一片片古茶树园傍山而建，制茶工厂和包装基地坐落其中。到了收获季节，茶园产出的古树茶便会在这里打包，通过中老铁路出口到中国市场。

这些为当地带来巨大经济效益的古茶树，早年却并不是民众眼中致富增收的"香饽饽"。

"我们这里有好山好水好茶，但因缺少销售渠道等原因，茶叶产业长期发展不起来。"巴松县县长披蓬回忆道，以前当地人不知道种植茶树也能带来经济效益，许多几百年甚至上千年树龄的古茶树一度面临被砍伐的风险。幸运的是，与进博会结缘后，老挝茶企打开了中国这一全球最大茶叶消费市场的销路，为巴松县的古茶树带来新生机。

第六届进博会上老挝展商带来的古树茶。【新华社供图】

2018年，当地茶企36庄园携老挝古树茶参加了首届进博会。极具热带特色的茶叶和天然醇厚的茶汤，令古树茶成为进博会的"明星展品"，订单也纷至沓来。次年起，36庄园等老挝茶企便开始向中国市场出口古树茶。

随后几年，除了36庄园，金占芭、少占、寮国古韵、SAN WAN LAO等老挝茶企也多次携古树茶参加进博会，丰富了中国消费者的茶叶品类选择。持续提升的知名度，让古树茶成为老挝国家农产品新名片。

2021年12月，中老铁路开通后，茶叶的运输成本显著降低。中国消费者可以用更优惠的价格品尝到老挝古树茶，老挝古树茶的市场竞争力也得以进一步提升。

"铁路通车后，老挝古树茶运往中国可以节省三分之二的时间。我们期待充分利用这些有利条件，借助进博会平台及中国市场，将老挝古树茶推向全球，以茶产业造福更多老挝民众。"老挝工贸部贸易促进司司长赛宋鹏·诺拉辛说道。

千余种植户迎来发展机遇

老挝是一个以农业为主的国家，农业发展关系着千家万户的收入。位于老挝北部的琅南塔省气候条件优越，种植辣椒能实现全年采收，当地有不少农户掌握着一定的辣椒种植经验。第六届进博会后，辣椒为当地千余农户带去了新的发展机遇。

开幕第三天，琅南塔省农林厅与贵州安广国际供应链有限公司（下称"安广国际"）签署农业国际经济技术合作协议，包括优质辣椒种植、采购供应链合作项目。

安广国际工作人员透露，该项目涉及的辣椒种植品种包括毕节皱椒、遵义子弹头、铜仁二荆条、林卡辣椒等。项目落地后，将带动琅南塔省 2000 余农户加入种植合作，并依托中老铁路、保税站场和冷链物流，惠及双边人民，促进地方经济发展。老挝琅南塔省农业与林业厅厅长平焦·塔拉新（Pingio Tarasin）表示，该项目将为当地百姓解决就业、增加收入。

可喜的是，2024 年以来，这一在第六届进博会上达成的合作项目正逐渐"开花结果"。

截至 2024 年 5 月，安广国际已在琅南塔省成功选培出 4 个优质辣椒品种，目前正在申报优质农产品原产地证书。此外，以琅南塔省示范基地带动的优质辣椒种植区也在申请进入输华农产品清单。届时，

琅南塔省辣椒小样种植试验田。【天眼新闻供图】

预计每个季度可收成优质鲜椒 4500 余吨、干椒 1000 余吨。2024 年全年预计收成 15000 余吨，可实现对华出口额 7000 余万元人民币。

从双方在"四叶草"达成合作，到项目在老挝"开花结果"，再到未来辣椒依托中老铁路输华，满足中国百姓味蕾，中老两国合作成果将持续造福两国人民。

老挝"小叶子"收获温暖经历

国之交在于民相亲，民相亲在于心相通。无论是中老铁路还是进博会，联通的从来都不仅仅是市场、技术、理念，还有温暖的民心。第六届进博会期间，一位来自老挝的"小叶子"志愿者对此有深切的体会。

作为老挝第一条现代化铁路，中老铁路的可持续发展离不开专业人才的输送。去年 10 月，老挝青年邓涛和几位同学搭乘中老铁路澜沧号列车来到中国，成为上海应用技术大学轨道交通学院招收的第三批老挝留学生。毕业后，他们将成为老挝首批现代化铁路的工程师。

1 个月后，第六届进博会开幕。邓涛以"小叶子"体验官的身份零距离见证了这一全球共享的国际经贸盛会。

开幕当天一大早，邓涛就和他的 4 人小队一起来到"四叶草"外待命。作为体验官，他们的任务是制作短视频来宣传进博会。邓涛需要在展馆内外穿梭，敏锐地捕捉鲜活的素材。

步入展区，邓涛被眼前的经贸盛景深深震撼。在逛展过程中，他还留意到一些国家的特色展品或许也契合老挝市场的需求。得知这一点后，队友们决定将此作为视频的重点。视频出炉后，邓涛计划把它带回自己的祖国，和亲朋好友们分享进博会的盛况。也许在不久的将来，他们之中会有人带来继古树茶、辣椒之后的老挝名优产品。

开幕第三天下午，邓涛来到志愿者中心，陪同小队里的中国同学过集体生日，并用镜头记录下这一刻。

"每当我找不到存在的意义，每当我迷失在黑夜里，夜空中最亮的星，请指引我靠近你……"看着大家挥舞手臂一起合唱《夜空中最亮的星》，邓涛不知被什么触动了心弦，流下了眼泪。进博会不仅促进了中老两国经贸往来，也在两国青年心中埋下了友谊的种子。或许在多年后，邓涛还会记得这一瞬间的温暖，记得进博会。

纵观历届进博会，中国和最不发达国家"双向奔赴"的故事数不胜数。2024 年 11 月，第七届进博会将在上海举办，开放的中国将继续与老挝等最不发达国家谱写共同发展新篇章。

老挝留学生邓涛化身"小叶子"体验官。【央视网视频截图】

（本文综合自：人民日报、新华社、央视网、中国新闻网、农民日报客户端、文汇报、《人民铁道》报、青年报、贵阳日报、中国江苏网、多彩贵州网、天眼新闻、贵州省人民对外友好协会、上海应用技术大学公众号。）

带花香的大米，你吃过吗

东埔寨位于中南半岛，因丰富的文旅资源和多样的农产品闻名世界。自 2018 年首届进博会以来，东埔寨已连续 6 年参展。在亲诚惠容理念的引领下，在进博会的推动下，中东两国经贸往来持续深化，双方经贸合作成果正转化为实实在在的红利，惠及两国人民。

东埔寨香米走上中国餐桌

提起东埔寨，许多人首先想到的是吴哥窟、洞里萨湖等著名的文化遗产和自然景观。但除此之外，洞里萨湖地区还是东埔寨的"鱼米之乡"，盛产稻米、甜薯等多种农产品。

作为世界主要大米出口国之一，多年来，许多东埔寨出口商积极拓展海外市场。参加进博会让他们看到了更多新机遇——既能提升产品知名度，又能促进产品深入中国市场，开拓更广阔的发展空间。

在第六届进博会上，许多客商被东埔寨大米的品质所吸引，尤其是散发浓郁独特茉莉花香的香米，吸引不少观众驻足围观。展期，东埔寨展馆内总能听到："茉莉香米卖多少钱一袋？"

"我相信东埔寨大米在中国会越来越受欢迎。"东埔寨稻米协会主席松萨兰（Sonsaran）表示，参加进博会后，东埔寨大米对华

第六届进博会上的柬埔寨大米产品。

第六届进博会上的柬埔寨腰果。

【云南日报供图】

出口显著增加，"希望通过进博会，把纯天然无污染的柬埔寨大米带给更多的中国百姓。"柬埔寨稻米联盟秘书长伦延（Lenjen）也深表赞同，他认为进博会对柬埔寨大米向中国出口起到很大促进作用。

柬埔寨稻米联盟 2024 年 1 月发布的统计数据显示，2023 年全年柬埔寨累计出口大米超 65 万吨，其中向中国出口大米 21.28 万吨。中国已成为柬埔寨大米的最大出口目的国。

得益于进博会强大的溢出带动效应，除了大米外，龙眼、紫衣腰果等其他柬埔寨特色农产品也逐渐赢得了中国消费者的青睐。在进博会上，许多贸易商纷纷涌向柬埔寨展馆，积极洽谈采购，寻找商机。

新鲜水果直通中国大市场

芒果，被誉为"热带果王"，深受中国消费者的喜爱。柬埔寨地处热带地区，是东南亚主要的芒果产区之一。阳光充足、雨水丰沛，这样得天独厚的地理环境，使得柬埔寨产区的芒果口感细腻、香气浓郁。

2021 年 5 月，跨越一千多公里，一艘满载柬埔寨"高乐蜜"芒果的冷柜集装箱货轮靠抵钦州港大榄坪南作业区 3 号泊位。这是柬埔寨新鲜芒果首次出口中国，也是继香蕉之后，柬埔寨第二种直接出口到中国的生鲜水果。

此前，中柬双方已经签署并交换了柬埔寨芒果输华植物检疫议定书，为柬埔寨芒果顺利进入中国市场铺平了道路。

顺利输华仅是一个起点，柬埔寨芒果要想真正打开中国市场的大门，进博会无疑是一把关键的"金钥匙"。仅仅六个月后，这些金黄饱满、果香四溢的"高乐蜜"芒果便在第四届进博会上完成了首秀，吸引了众多观众驻足品鉴。采购商们争相咨询产品包装、品质、成熟度等信息，并留下联系方式，期待下一步的合作机会。

进博会为柬埔寨优质产品进入中国市场提供了广阔的舞台，也为提升其在中国市场的知名度提供了绝佳的机会。柬中关系发展学会会长谢莫尼勒（Semonil）表示，出口到中国的柬埔寨新鲜芒果，将通过进博会被中国市场乃至全球所了解。

随着《中华人民共和国政府和柬埔寨王国政府自由贸易协定》和《区域全面经济伙伴关系协定》（RCEP）的生效实施，中柬双边贸易规模不断扩大，双边经贸关系持续深化，柬农产品输华按下"加速键"，助力更多柬优质商品出口中国。

中柬文化交流持续升温

近年来，随着中柬经贸合作不断加深，两国在文化领域的交流也日渐频繁。

吴哥窟的仙女"阿帕莎喇"雕像、莲花、木雕……在首次亮相第五届进博会的柬埔寨国家航空有限公司（简称"柬国航"）的展

台上，陈列了一系列具有柬埔寨特色的装饰品，给观众带来了一次独特的文化体验。

"中国游客喜欢到柬埔寨旅游，探访吴哥窟。我们希望借助进博会这一舞台，架起两国人民交往的'空中之桥'，助力文化交融、旅游往来。"柬国航上海代表处总经理尹征说道。

2024 年适逢"中柬人文交流年"，这不仅是加强中柬人文往来的重要契机，也开启了两国友谊新篇章。自 2024 年年初以来，中柬两国

在第五届进博会上，柬埔寨国家航空展台展示具有柬埔寨特色的装饰品。【柬埔寨国家航空供图】

已成功举办了多项人文交流活动，包括新春招待会、柬埔寨国立马德望大学孔子学院举办的国际中文日系列活动等，吸引了众多中柬文化爱好者的积极参与。

尽管柬埔寨是最不发达国家，但其丰富的旅游资源仍吸引了众多中国游客。据柬埔寨旅游部统计，2024 年一季度，柬埔寨吸引中国游客 19 万人次，同比增长 43%。2024 年前 5 个月，柬埔寨著名景点吴哥窟的门票收入同比增长 38.2%。

在此背景下，柬埔寨对参加进博会的热情更加高涨。近日，柬埔寨商务部发文称，柬埔寨将于 2024 年 11 月如期赴约上海参加进博会。

柬埔寨商业部发布文件呼吁该国企业积极参加第七届进博会。【柬埔寨高棉时报网供图】

柬埔寨商业部国务秘书兼发言人佩恩·苏威切特（Penn Sovicheat）表示，进博会展现了中国坚定不移促进全球贸易和多边主义以及向世界开放中国市场的决心。相信随着两国在"四叶草"碰撞出更多火花，中柬双方将在经贸合作、文化旅游等领域迎来更加广阔的共赢天地。

（本文综合自：人民日报、新华社、经济日报、中国新闻网、人民论坛网、中国旅游报、看看新闻、东方国际、云南日报、相关企业官微、高棉时报等。）

华商企业与进博会"彼此成就"

　　既是"外来客",又是"东道主",这是华商企业(海外华侨华人创办的企业)参加进博会时的独特感受。他们以各种方式支持和参与这场全球盛会,进博会也为华商企业成长打开了机遇之门。进博会越办越好的背后,华商企业与进博会"彼此成就"。

感情深厚的"东道主"

　　"每年参加进博会既是明智的商业考虑,背后也

第三届进博会金光集团 APP 展台。【企业供图】

往届进博会正大集团展台。【企业供图】

有着一种强烈的情感共鸣。"金光集团 APP（中国）副总裁翟京丽表示，7 年来，金光集团 APP 一直如期奔赴"进博之约"。"我们把进博会看作每年最值得期待的盛会，我们既是'外来客'，也是'东道主'。"

进博会的举办为包括金光集团 APP 在内的华商企业提供了展示自我、对接国际资源的平台。

拥有逾百年历史的老牌华商企业正大集团，1921 年成立于泰国，1979 年进入中国，是改革开放后第一家进入中国大陆的外资企业，已在中国设立 600 多家企业。

历届进博会都有正大集团的身影。"进博会为正大集团搭建了重要的交流合作平台。"正大集团资深副董事长、正大投资股份有限公司总经理兼 CEO 谢毅分析说，一方面，进博会深化了正大集

第四届进博会上好佳展台。【企业供图】

团"买全球，卖全球"的贸易战略；另一方面，进博会吸引了全球采购商和合作伙伴，有助于正大集团开拓新市场渠道和寻找新合作伙伴。

益海嘉里金龙鱼粮油食品股份有限公司总裁穆彦魁同样对进博会感情深厚。他说："这是一个由'中国搭台、世界共享'的平台，我们见证着进博会越办越好，进博会也拓宽了我们的业务发展。"

菲律宾晨光有限公司是已为中国消费者所熟知的"上好佳"品牌的创立者，从1946年在菲律宾马尼拉起步的小型家庭手工作坊，到1966年扩转为有限公司，再到1993年在中国投资设厂，"上好佳"的品牌知名度越打越响。上好佳（中国）有限公司董事长施学理是在菲律宾出生和长大的第三代华人，在他的主导下，菲律宾唐人街、

"菲华三宝"等元素被"搬"到了进博会的展台上。在他看来，参加进博会坚定了上好佳扎根中国的信心。

融入中国的"快速路"

从"全球展会"到"世界平台"，进博会圈粉全球华商企业。华商企业深度参与进博会，也拉近了住在国与中国的距离。以参展进博会为契机，华商企业加速融入中国市场，共享中国机遇。

金光集团由印度尼西亚知名华人黄奕聪于1938年创立，旗下的浆纸业集团APP早在1992年便进入中国，如今APP的产品和业务遍及全球。

"进博会不仅帮助印尼企业更好地融入中国市场，也是通向中国市场不可或缺的'快速路'。"翟京丽表示，进博会是展示产品和技术的舞台，更是了解中国投资政策、寻找合作机会的重要窗口。过去6年间，APP在进博会上收获的意向订单总额超过7亿美元，这充分展现了进博会国际采购功能的强大动力。

"中国有一句话叫'水涨船高'。"在谢毅看来，进博会溢出效应不断释放，正大集团在中国取得了非常好的发展业绩，

往届进博会丰益国际展台。
【企业供图】

农牧食品、商业零售、制药、地产、金融等业务有了长足发展，投资区域遍及所有省份。

除了助力自家企业把握进博机遇，华商企业也积极为住在国企业开拓中国市场牵线搭桥。在第五届进博会上，施学理抽出更多时间为菲律宾食品"代言"。

菲律宾被称为"太平洋的果盘"，香蕉、芒果、木瓜等丰富的热带水果畅销全球。施学理表示："中国巨大的市场和潜力对菲律宾企业极具吸引力。资源共享、市场联通，中国市场就是世界的市场、共享的市场和大家的市场，中国所倡导的全面深化改革和扩大开放将为菲律宾企业的发展创造无限商机。"

连接世界的"架桥者"

7年来，华商企业与进博会共同书写开放合作、共享未来的新篇章，依托进博会溢出效应，华商企业快速走向全球各地，为构建开放型世界经济架起一座座桥梁。

让施学理念念不忘的是，上好佳在首届进博会上偶遇了乌兹别克斯坦副总理带队的政府代表团。接触后，上好佳在乌兹别克斯坦置地建厂，正式投产该项目。他直言："这样的机遇可遇不可求，而这正是进博会带给我们的惊喜。"

从一个生产休闲食品的企业成长为多元化的跨国食品集团，如今上好佳正在积极拓展更多的海外市场，在更多国家组建产品线，把更多新产品和新服务提供给市场和消费者。"作为华商，我和父辈一样，始终对中国抱有充分的信心，期待从上海出发，收获更多的惊喜。"施学理说。

不仅组织26个业务板块参加第六届进博会，还发挥华商企业优势，帮助中国各地特色优质产品销往全球，形成了正大集团的"双重奏"。

谢毅表示，正大集团"买全球，卖全球"，十分希望能够协助更多中国企业开拓东南亚市场。"我们愿意发挥资金、技术、文化融通等优势，搭建更多交流合作平台，为中国与世界各国多领域合作搭建桥梁和纽带。"

在翟京丽看来，持续参加进博会也是倒逼企业提升自身发展进步、拓宽商业版图和自身影响力的重要推动力。"一花独放不是春，万紫千红春满园。"翟京丽说，"未来，我们可以帮助更多中国企业走出去，开拓更大的市场与商机。"

虽然华商企业的进博体验各不相同，但参加一年一度的进博会已是他们的共同约定，华商企业与进博会共同成长、彼此成就的故事未完待续。

文／范宇斌

创新之力

"四叶草"里成长的"进博宝宝"

2024 年 2 月 29 日是第 17 个国际罕见病日。如今,世界上被人们所知的罕见病已超过 7000 种,仍不断有新的病种被发现,保守估计我国的罕见病患者在 2000 万人以上。

自 2018 年首次举办以来,进博会为企业多个罕见病在内的医疗创新方案和成果亮相提供了展示平台,推动全球医疗企业在华创新、投资,已成为企业加速新品引入和落地的"驱动器"和"孵化器",为中国医生和病患群体带来更多全新的用药选择。

对于这类通过进博会实现展品变商品、在中国落地投入使用的创新药品和器械,展商们亲切地称呼它们为"进博宝宝"。"四叶草"孵化过许多这样的"进博宝宝",也见证着"进博宝宝"的苗壮成长。

"进博宝宝"诞生落地

7 年来,一大批创新药品、医疗器械在"四叶草"登台亮相,并借力进博会首度落地中国,实现从"零"到"一"的华丽转变。

"与通常的审批过程相比,节省了一半时间。"西门子医疗大中华区总裁王皓对进博会溢出效应感受颇深。在第四届进博会展出后,西门子医疗全球首款光子计数 CT 仅用时两年,就实现从首秀到上市的蜕变。王皓表示:"借助进博会,世界顶尖医疗药械得到

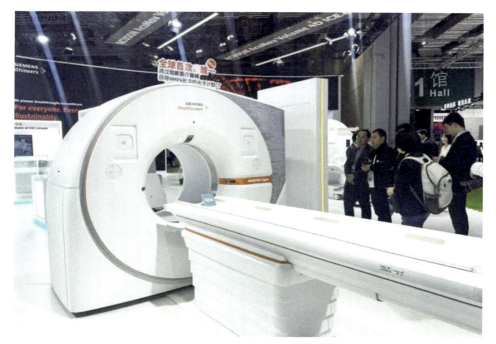

第六届进博会西门子医疗展台上的光子计数 CT。【新华社供图】

药监、医保等多个层面的关注。政府主动推动，使得创新药械以最快的速度，服务医疗机构和广大患者。"

在第五届进博会首秀的吉利德如愿拥有了自己的"进博宝宝"——安必速®，这是一款治疗侵袭性真菌病的药物。其全球副总裁、中国区总经理金方千感慨道："进博会为推进创新药物上市的整体进程提供了重要的助力。"展会后仅三个月后，该展品就获得中国国家药监局上市批准，为患者提供了新的治疗选择。2023 年 6 月，吉利德宣布安必速®正式在华上市。

未来，随着进博会溢出效应的不断显现，诞生于"四叶草"的"进博宝宝"们将加速迈向更广阔的中国市场，为广大中国患者谋求更大福祉。

新适应证接连获批

适应证是指药物、手术等方法适合运用的范围、标准。从进入博鳌先行先试到新适应证正式获批，武田制药旗下消化领域创新产品瑞唯抒®的在华发展历程，成为"进博宝宝"与进博会共同成长的缩影。

用于治疗罕见病短肠综合征（SBS）的"孤儿药"瑞唯抒®于2022年亮相第五届进博会。会上，武田制药与海南博鳌乐城国际医疗旅游先行区进行现场签约，不到6个月，该药就进入博鳌医疗机构先行先试。2024年2月23日，瑞唯抒®正式获得中国国家药品监督管理局批准，得以造福更多短肠综合征患者。历时15个月，从进博首秀到正式获批，武田"拓维中国"战略刷新加速度。

对另一位"进博宝宝"赛诺菲旗下明星产品达必妥®来说，进博会加速药品新适应证获批的作用进一步凸显。

达必妥®在第六届进博会展出。【21世纪经济报道供图】

"达必妥®是进博会强大溢出效应的亲历者，实现了一款产品多年进博之旅多个适应证在华获批上市。我们将开拓进博新机遇，为饱受慢性呼吸系统疾病困扰的患者带来新的希望。"在第六届进博会上，赛诺菲特药中国区总经理谢丽娟介绍，达必妥聚焦中国慢性呼吸疾病领域巨大未满足需求，展示其 2 型哮喘新适应证，可用于 12 岁及以上青少年和成人哮喘患者的维持治疗。闭幕一周后，赛诺菲宣布该适应证正式获批，"进博宝宝"达必妥®的"技能包"再度迭代升级。

本土化进程不断加速

进博会持续凝聚开放共识，释放合作红利，不仅成为"进博宝宝"诞生的摇篮，也持续推动着展商加大在华投资、加速本土化战略实施。

自参加进博会以来，常驻客波士顿科学接连迎来了 6 个"进博宝宝"。由此，波士顿科学切实感受到中国市场蕴藏的巨大机遇，也窥见了本土化布局的契机。

2022 年 9 月，首台 Polaris 血管内超声系统从上海捷普工厂下线，标志着波士顿科学首个中国生产、供应本土的产品正式落地。该产品早在 2019 年首次参加进博会时，就吸引了上海药监部门的关注，

波士顿科学 Polaris 血管内超声系统。
【波士顿科学供图】

并于 2022 年 7 月正式获颁本土注册证，得以迅速实现本土生产并同步供应全球。借此机会，波士顿科学也实现了从"在中国为中国"到"在中国为全球"的华丽蜕变。

罗氏制药也在连年参展中尝到了甜头。受益于中国速度，公司旗下淋巴瘤创新药物格菲妥单抗于第六届进博会期间在华获批上市，成为"进博宝宝"。2023 年 9 月，罗氏中国加速器大楼在上海正式落成，旨在为初创企业有针对性地提供包括资金渠道、合作机会、研发经验、先进的实验设备等资源，助力本土创新"幼苗"成长。

从加速引进创新药、在华落地上市，到加码孵化本土创新，罗氏紧握进博会这把"金钥匙"，看到了中国市场更大的价值与红利。

共筑"健康中国"美好未来

近年来，随着《"健康中国 2030"规划纲要》的出台，中国医药市场前景更加明朗，为全球药企在华发展开辟新机遇。乘着进博会东风，一些"进博宝宝"不仅实现了在华获批上市，还纳入了医保目录。

在第六届进博会上，生物医药公司葛兰素史克（GSK）携旗下"进博宝宝"倍力腾已连续五年参展。5 年来，得益于进博会溢出效应的持续释放，倍力腾的成人及儿童系统性红斑狼疮适应证已先后被纳入医保目录。

GSK 副总裁、中国特药及呼吸业务负责人余锦毅表示，GSK 一直在关注中国百余万狼疮患者的未尽之需。目前，"进博宝宝"倍力腾正在积极推进成人狼疮肾炎适应证进入医保目录，希望惠及更多患者。

武田制药旗下"进博宝宝"富马酸伏诺拉生片的反流性食管炎适应证，也于 2020 年纳入医保目录。"未来，我们会继续加速更多重磅产品落地中国，并积极参与中国医疗创新生态圈的建设，赋

第二届进博会期间展出的倍力腾。【澎湃新闻供图】

能中国医药高质量发展，共筑健康中国 2030。"武田制药全球高级副总裁、武田中国总裁单国洪表示。

（本文综合自：新华社、中国新闻网、中国网、21世纪经济报道、第一财经、澎湃新闻、文汇报、南方都市报、上观新闻、浦东发布。）

搭乘进博快车，"行李箱"不断扩容

　　在每届进博会上，医疗器械及医药保健展区总是"新"意满满，总能汇集大量极具科技含量的首发、首秀、首展展品，成为人气最热的展区之一。

　　2023 年，全球领先的生物制药公司吉利德科学第二次参加进博

第六届进博会吉利德科学展台。【企业供图】

会。从"头回客"到"回头客",吉利德的"行李箱"容量大增:展台面积扩大 5 倍,创新产品业务展示区域扩大 2 倍,并专门开设研发管线展览区,集中介绍吉利德全球的研发管线布局以及在中国开展的临床研究与新产品上市计划。

2024 年,吉利德科学第三次与进博会牵手,"行李箱"再度扩容,在 500 平方米的展台上将再次展示其不断扩大的产品组合与创新成果,全面展现其医学创新实力以及与各方伙伴紧密协作、惠及中国患者的优异实践。展品不仅覆盖吉利德中国聚焦的病毒学、肿瘤学与真菌学等领域,而且包含多款首次展示的在研药物。吉利德全球副总裁兼中国区总经理金方千也表达了对三赴"进博之约"的美好期待。

"进博宝宝"频频现

吉利德总部位于美国加利福尼亚州福斯特市,在全球超过 35 个国家和地区运营。2017 年,吉利德在中国开启商业运营。7 年来,已有 11 个吉利德全球领先的药物在中国获批,其中 8 个药物已被列入国家医保目录。

中国是吉利德全球三大重要战略市场之一。吉利德已两次参加进博会,见证了进博会带来的溢出效应,亲历了展出药物的快速上市。

在进博会医疗器械及医药保健展区,展商们习惯于把通过进博会实现"展品变商品"、在中国落地使用的创新药物和器械亲切地称为"进博宝宝"。

每年的进博会后,都会有一批"进博宝宝"诞生。吉利德在 2022 年首次参加进博会后,便如愿拥有了自己的"进博宝宝",包

观众在吉利德科学展台观展。【企业供图】

括抗真菌和肿瘤领域的两款新药。其中，抗真菌领域药物安必速®在展会后仅三个月就获得了中国国家药品监督管理局上市批准，见证了创新药物加速可及的"中国速度"。

在 2023 年第六届进博会上，吉利德计划在中国上市的"明星产品"长效 HIV 新药 Lenacapavir 首次亮相就吸引了众多关注。

金方千认为，进博会为推进创新药物上市的整体进程提供了重要助力，已然成为促进药物创新发展的"加速器"。

扩大医疗合作"生态圈"

两度参展，进博会在潜移默化中成为推动吉利德在华发展的"加速器"。借助这一开放的大平台，吉利德持续加强与各方的合作交流。

吉利德科学在进博会上展出的药品。【企业供图】

在第五届进博会上，吉利德与中国预防性病艾滋病基金会启动了一项为期3年的丙肝病例随访管理合作项目，支持国家消除丙肝公共卫生危害行动。

在第六届进博会上，吉利德与中国性病艾滋病防治协会签署HIV快速启动项目合作协议，倡导HIV感染者及早获得规范治疗，并与北京市希思科临床肿瘤学研究基金会合作建立"希思科—吉利德肿瘤研究基金"，推动肿瘤领域科研转化。

这些项目是吉利德通过进博会与中国医疗生态圈深化合作共赢关系的生动缩影。金方千说，期待借助进博会平台，进一步扩大在医疗生态系统的"朋友圈"。

加大在华研发投入

作为外资企业分享中国发展机遇的重要平台，进博会成为全球头部医药企业连接中国市场的重要渠道。吉利德通过参加进博会，切身感受到"展品变商品"的平台效应，深刻体会到中国与全球各国共享发展机遇的决心，进一步坚定扎根中国市场、深耕本土医药创新的信心。

吉利德科学的"进博宝宝"。【企业供图】

如今，中国市场作为"世界的市场、共享的市场、大家的市场"已经成为一种国际共识。2022年以来，吉利德中国大力投入本土研发，启动多个临床研究项目，包括与全球同步的三期临床研发，覆盖了癌症、病毒学领域的多个疾病，旨在推动更多创新疗法在中国国内"同步"上市，造福更多有需要的患者。

吉利德致力于突破不可能。金方

吉利德科学全球副总裁兼中国区总经理金方千（中间）在进博会展区与嘉宾交流。
【企业供图】

千表示，未来，吉利德将持续以患者为中心，与各方探索创新合作、加强多渠道建设，不断提升已上市药物的可及性，持续推动本土研发能力的建设，让更多创新药物早日惠及中国患者。

文 / 范宇斌

载入企业"大事记"的标志性事件

"中国市场是开放的，也是富有魅力的。"进博会正持续向世界发出这一强烈信号。刚刚出任东京海上日动火灾保险（中国）有限公司总经理的结城一郎已经感受到了这个信号传递出的重大价值。在他看来，带领企业参加第七届进博会，是他今年上任后的"优先事项"。

"通过参与进博会，我们可以学习各行业的最新举措，了解最尖端的技术动向，并与自身业务结合构筑新的商务模型。"结城一郎认为，以共创实现共赢，进博会是"启发思考的绝佳平台"。

在华深耕

东京海上创建于 1879 年，是日本历史上第一家财产保险公司。作为世界 500 强企业，东京海上在中国开展业务已满 30 年。

许多跨国公司将进博会视为了解和进入中国市场的"新航道"，而对于在华深耕多年的"老牌"外企而言，进博会有着更为深厚的意涵。

"进博会为我们打开了把握合作契机与通往市场的大门，助力我们在实现经济价值的同时，提升社会价值。"结城一郎表示。

1992 年，上海成为中国内地第一个在保险领域对外开放的试点

东京海上日动火灾保险（中国）有限公司董事兼总经理结城一郎。【康玉湛 摄】

城市，多家外资险企先后落"沪"。1994 年，东京海上在沪开设分公司，这是中国第一家外资财险公司的营业机构。

落"沪"30 年，东京海上既是中国保险行业发展的"见证者""受惠者"，也是"参与者"和"推动者"。

"优先事项"

梳理 30 年的发展轨迹，东京海上将"连续 3 年参与进博会"作为标志性事件，载入企业在华发展"大事记"。"老牌"外企参与的展会数不胜数，缘何参与进博会是"优先事项"？

"进博会为东京海上提供了一个展示自身实力和成果的平台。"在结城一郎看来，进博会也是企业领略全球发展趋势，调整自身在华发展战略的"风向标"。

"中国拥有庞大的市场规模、快速的经济增长以及不断优化的

营商环境。"曾在广州、深圳和上海工作过的结城一郎对中国市场有着自己的观察和了解。在他看来，随着中国居民财富增长和风险保障意识提升，中国的保险市场需求呈现出多元化、个性化的趋势，加之政策环境不断完善。"这都为外资保险公司提供了广阔的发展空间。"结城一郎说。

多年在华工作经历让结城一郎感受到中国市场的快速变化，以及持续发生的技术创新。"在这样的环境下，企业更加需要通过参与解决社会议题，来适应中国市场的成长。"结城一郎说。

节能低碳成为企业运营的重要方向，康养产业和适老化创新成为新的商业增量空间，大批企业正在开展产业升级……进博会上的"前沿风"，正是外企把握中国市场脉搏的绝佳机会。

2021 年，以"提供安心、安全，贡献可持续发展的未来"为主题，东京海上首次亮相进博会。2022 年，东京海上日动（中国）将"可持续发展战略"纳入到公司经营战略中，并结合中国国家战略与市场趋势，确定了绿色转型、健康养老、防灾减灾、产业升级 4个优先领域。

跨界合作

"在当下，我们面临的社会议题变得越来越复杂，例如气候变化、人口老龄化等等问题。"结城一郎感受到，这些社会问题绝非一家企业可以单独应对，需要企业间更广泛的合作，共商对策。

结城一郎表示，通过持续参加进博会，东京海上日动（中国）遇到了新的合作伙伴。"用中文来说，我们的'朋友圈'在不断扩大。"他说。

在进博会的大舞台上，"共创"不仅发生在企业之间，不同领域行业间也正接连擦出跨界合作的新火花。

在第五届进博会上，分属保险、电器制造、自动化解决方案三个不同产业领域的东京海上日动（中国）、松下电气设备（中国）有限公司、欧姆龙（中国）有限公司，签约成立"健康促进产业联盟"。三家在华日企在"进博舞台"上达成跨界合作，充分发挥各自产品服务优势，协同构建大健康服务生态圈。

作为跨界共创的深入延续，在第六届进博会"中日健康促进与创新技术发展论坛"上，东京海上日动（中国）与中国康复技术转化及发展促进会携手，展开政产学研跨界对话，共同为智慧健康产业多领域融合发展探索新道路。

"通过参与进博会，我们不仅能够与国内外同行进行深入交流和学习，还能发现更多的合作机会和潜力市场，实现公司

在第五届进博会上，"健康促进产业联盟"签约成立。【企业供图】

2024 年是东京海上在华开展业务 30 周年。【企业供图】

经济价值与社会价值的同步提升。"结城一郎表示，进博会带来的启示是：企业携手共创，就可以实现稳步前进。

第七届进博会恰逢"东京海上在中国展业 30 年"。结城一郎表示，参与第七届进博会是东京海上在中国发展的里程碑，也是共创共赢的新起点。

"请大家务必来我们的展台看看。"结城一郎向各界人士发出邀请。

文 / 李姝徵

常驻客的"顶流"项目

欧莱雅与进博会结缘来自 2018 年的一封信。

这一封信阐述了中国正筹办进博会，希望邀请外商共享中国发展机遇的计划。

欧莱雅中国时任董事长兼 CEO 安巩看完信后的第一反应是"这个想法太棒了"。欧莱雅很快就成为首批进博会"粉丝"，一马当先入驻展会。

作为进博会的常驻客和连任五届的参展商联盟理事会轮值主席，欧莱雅集团 2024 年连续第七年参展，并再次担任参展商联盟理事会与日化消费品专业委员会会长单位的"双料主席"。

展品、商品、爆品

坚定选择进博会，是因为欧莱雅对中国的未来发展充满信心。欧莱雅每一年都为参展量身定制主题，把全球"pick"最新潮和最让中国消费者心动的新品牌、新产品、新科技、新理念带到进博会。

如今，进博会已成为欧莱雅在全球范围内的"顶流"项目，是欧莱雅全球新品首发、科技首秀的首选平台。

7 年来，欧莱雅在进博会首发了近 20 个国际新品牌和数十个美妆黑科技，很多新品在进博会平台上从"展品变商品，又从商品变爆品"。

欧莱雅深度融入进博会，并持续加码。2024 年，欧莱雅将设立第七届进博会日化消费品行业单个最大展位，在 672 平方米的舞台上，打造一个充满"艺"境的主展台，为观众献上一场融合科技、文化与艺术的美之盛宴。

届时，不仅有全球新品、爆款美妆科技及可持续消费跨界合作项目的首发首秀，欧莱雅更将解码护肤、彩妆、美发、香水四大品类背后的科学"艺"境。

进博会不仅是全球新品、科技首秀的舞台，也是跨越不同文化、促进国际交流合作的盛会。2024 年恰逢中法两国建交 60 周年，法国将作为主宾国亮相进博会，不但向世界展现中法两国源远流长的友谊，而且充分展示中法务实合作的丰硕成果。

作为中法友谊的见证者和参与者，欧莱雅将入驻法国馆，以实际行动献礼中法友谊"一家子 / 一甲子"，让法式优雅与中国风韵交相辉映，共同谱写中法合作美美与共的乐章。

共享、共创、共赢

进博会上的合作故事一直在延续。2019 年，欧莱雅在第二届进博会上遇到了东方美谷，共同开创了"BIG BANG 美妆科技创新计划"，与具有前沿科技的初创企业一起共创共赢，推进美妆科技开放式创新。

2023 年 4 月，法国总统马克龙访华期间，在两国部长的见证下，"BIG BANG 美妆科技创新计划"中的法国赛道正式升级为中法战略项目。一年后，东方美谷与 2023 BIG BANG 中国—法国赛道获奖企业 CTIBIOTECH 签署战略合作备忘录，帮助 CTIBIOTECH 进军中国市场。这次合作的达成进一步彰显出进博会的溢出效应。

在第六届进博会上，欧莱雅北亚美妆科技共创孵化展揭幕。【企业供图】

　　进博会欢迎行业"领头羊"带来自家的黑科技，也大力支持初创企业带上自己的看家本领，登上这个世界级的大舞台。

　　进博会支持"开放、合作、创新、共赢"与欧莱雅的 BIG BANG 项目不谋而合。2023 年，欧莱雅的 BIG BANG 项目成功从中国拓展至日本和韩国。借此契机，欧莱雅邀请了日本、韩国、法国的创新企业共同亮相进博会，探索中国市场的无限机遇。

　　这些海外初创企业表示，进博会给他们留下了深刻印象。在这里，他们不仅感受到中国市场的活力与创新氛围，结识了志同道合的伙伴和潜在合作方，也收到来自中国各地各级政府送上的政策"服务包"。它们都渴望有机会与支持开放创新的中国有更多次的"亲密接触"，像欧莱雅一样，从进博会的"头回客"变为"回头客"，再变为"常驻客"！

　　进博会的溢出效应让欧莱雅感受到了中国市场的活力和潜力，

欧莱雅 BIG BANG 美妆科技创造营北亚赛区获胜企业颁奖典礼。【企业供图】

也更加坚定了欧莱雅深耕中国市场的决心。2024 年，欧莱雅加大对中国市场的投入，位于江苏苏州的智慧运营中心于 2024 年 4 月正式启动，希望进一步满足中国消费者越来越个性化的消费升级需求。

作为进博会的老朋友，欧莱雅将继续支持进博会。在第七届进博会招展启动仪式上，欧莱雅早早预定了第八届进博会的"入场券"。

文 / 范宇斌

从 46% 到 71%，看见可持续未来

自诞生起就与竞速赛事结缘的米其林，在进博会上"抢了个先"。2023 年 9 月下旬，米其林的一款创新产品——可持续材料使用占比

第六届进博会米其林展台。【企业供图】

高达 63% 的轮胎，经上海海关快速审核后"秒放"通关，成为第六届进博会的首票进境展品。这款"绿色"轮胎在进博会上进行"亚洲首秀"后，很快就成为"明星"展品。

需求引领创新

2021 年 46%、2022 年 53%、2023 年 63%……随着可持续材料占比在一届又一届进博会上持续提升，米其林的"进博故事"也在不断"上新"。在第七届进博会上，米其林将继续展现其对可持续

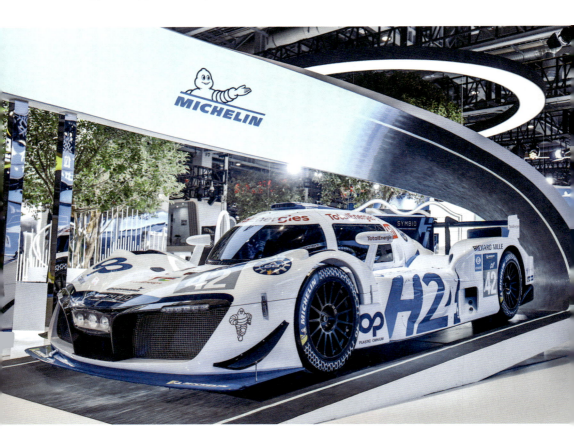

米其林在第四届进博会搭载 46% 可持续材料比轮胎的 Mission H24 氢能源赛车。
【企业供图】

材料的追逐和将突破性技术付诸实践的能力，再次展示"亚洲首秀"产品——可持续材料占比 71% 的新款轮胎。

可持续发展关乎人类社会的长期繁荣，已成为全球共识和行动指南。米其林提出，到 2050 年，其轮胎产品将 100% 使用生物基、可再生及可回收的可持续材料生产。

自 1895 年米其林成功研制出汽车充气轮胎以来，轮胎始终是汽车产业链中至关重要的一环。近年来，电动化及智能化成为汽车市场新兴增长点，全球配套轮胎销量逐步恢复，中国市场增幅显著。2023 年，中国乘用车配套轮胎销量达 1.32 亿条，位居全球主要地区之首。

随着全球汽车生产对轮胎的要求不断提升，轮胎向高端化、绿色化迈进是大势所趋。米其林在中国看到了汽车产业对高质量发展的巨大需求。

中国 2009 年成为全球第一大新车市场，目前已是当之无愧的汽车生产和消费大国。中国汽车工业协会公布数据显示，中国汽车产销量连续 15 年蝉联全球第一，2023 年全年产销分别实现了 3016.1 万辆和 3009.4 万辆。2024 年前 8 个月，中国汽车产销分别完成 1867.4 万辆和 1876.6 万辆。

中国超大规模市场需求的持续释放，让包括米其林在内的企业加速迈上创新赛道，或调整战略，或升级产品，满足市场新需求，实现自身发展。

米其林中国区总裁兼首席执行官叶菲介绍，目前在高端新能源汽车市场上，米其林品牌轮胎搭载率超过 30%。

"我们希望在中国探索绿色发展的新前景。借助进博会的平台效应，企业既能够更好地展示尖端创新成果，也能够建立更为多元

的连结。尽管米其林在中高端新能源汽车市场市占率较高，但仍需要灵活地根据市场和客户的需求进行生产调整，才能跟得上当前中国汽车产业快速发展的步伐。"叶菲表示，每年举办的进博会正是企业快速获取需求和反馈的重要时机。

竞争激发创新

米其林总部位于法国克莱蒙费朗，致力于提高人类及货物的可持续移动性。1989年，米其林在北京成立首个中国内地的代表处，将先进科技和高质量产品带到中国。2001年，米其林（中国）投资有限公司在上海成立，在中国目前已拥有近7000名员工和3家工厂。

百余年来，米其林秉持"竞，以求进"的理念，从未停止过追逐与创新的脚步。在进博会这一行业领军企业同台竞技的"超级秀场"，大众、丰田、现代等12家世界500强车企，米其林、Prometeon等3家头部汽车轮胎企业携新产品"争奇斗艳"。米其林倡导"一切皆可持续"的理念，在这些展品中独树一帜，引领创新前沿。

在第六届进博会上，米其林将展台布置成一个逾500平方米的"米其林赛道乐

米其林在第六届进博会展出的63%可持续材料比轮胎。
【企业供图】

园"，展现其在可持续发展过程中的多元成果。在叶菲看来，赛事运动更像是真实世界的技术实验室，在创新可持续解决方案方面发挥着至关重要的作用。

2024 年，米其林第 4 次参加进博会，将以"米其林奇遇号"为主题，展示从道路到天空乃至太空的创新科技，让观众看到一个"创新不止于道路"的米其林。同时，米其林将在第七届进博会上"亚洲首发"可以适应月球上极端恶劣条件的"月球探测车免充气轮胎"。叶菲表示，在中国，米其林希望用因地制宜的创新，引领行业变革，重塑人们的生活。

依托进博会，包括米其林在内，众多企业的新产品、新技术、新服务在"四叶草"首发首秀，并进入中国大市场，带动中国产业升级和消费升级，助力高质量发展，也为世界提供更多新机遇。

合作促进创新

在进博会上，参展商与业务伙伴合作洽谈、握手签约的场景频现，一份份互惠互利的协议成为"合作共赢"理念的生动注脚。

"合作"同样是米其林参加进博会的关键词。通过进博会平台，米其林与消费者、合作伙伴走得更近，有机会获得产业链上、生态圈中更多周边企业的合作意向，进而为创新储备更多资源。

叶菲表示："参加进博会，让我们拥有更多与产业链上下游企业加强合作交流的机会，能够和其他企业共同探索可持续发展的经验和技术，携手推动行业向更绿色、更可持续的方向迈进。"

在往届进博会上，米其林达成了一系列合作，包括采购订单、轮胎业务、赛事业务等合作，收获了对中国市场和消费者的更多了解。

第三届进博会米其林展台。【企业供图】

　　进博会是推动对话、促进合作的平台。深谙"交流才能带来合作"的米其林在第六届进博会上举办 7 场不同主题的对话交流，邀请不同领域的专业人士参与讨论。在叶菲看来，这种和全球同行、政府人士、专家学者及行业领袖等直接对话的机会非常难得。

　　一展汇世界，一展惠全球。展望未来，进博会将携手米其林等"进博老友"以及更多新的合作伙伴，以创新驱动发展，为人们带来更加美好的生活体验，持续助力可持续发展。

文 / 范宇斌

在进博会实现"三级跳"

一根根黑色的线条在银白色地面纵横延伸，贯穿其中的是美国勒布朗·詹姆斯创新中心和上海新江湾城一处街道的经纬度坐标……

在第六届进博会这个颇具设计感的舞台上，耐克宣布将在上海设立耐克中国运动研究实验室。这成为进博会推动"展商变投资商"、

耐克中国运动研究实验室高科技研究装备亮相第六届进博会。【企业供图】

推动更大力度吸引和利用外资的又一个生动案例。

对这家体育用品百年老店来说，这一全新的运动研究实验室意义非凡，堪称其"创新大脑"。该实验室成立后，将成为耐克在亚洲设立的首个运动研究中心。

为何选择在进博会上宣布这一重要决策？耐克大中华区政府及公共事务副总裁马征说："在全球化背景下，进博会是一个推动各国经济开放、促进世界对话和交流的绝佳平台，也是耐克参与中国经济发展、共创美好未来的契机。我们有强烈的意愿参与其中。在每年的进博会上，耐克不仅会展示全球创新成果，也会宣布在中国的重要投资项目。这已经成为我们的惯例。"

在中国，为全球

在第六届进博会上，耐克展出了"创新大脑"的一部分"神经元"，引得参观者纷纷驻足"打卡"。足部扫描仪，可以记录脚型数据，进而做出更加合脚的鞋楦；压力映射及测力板，进行步幅识别步幅，并根据个人走路、弹跳等着力点不同，判断在鞋底的哪个位置需要缓震，以减少压力……

曾现身进博会的前中国男篮运动员认为，运动研究实验室是耐克展台"最吸引人的地方"，在实验室的帮助下，运动员们可以获得更适合自己的运动装备。

据马征介绍，中国"创新大脑"的启用，将帮助耐克更好地了解中国运动员和消费者，为设计和制造更加贴合本地市场需求的创新产品提供助益。"从某种意义讲，这将会引领耐克的全球创新。"马征认为。

几年前，耐克大中华区团队发现，中国女性需要的是一双兼具行走轻松舒适和独特风格的运动鞋，并将这一洞察成功转化为创新

耐克中国运动研究实验室发布现场。【企业供图】

产品。这款名为 NikeMotiva 的产品一经推出，就得到了全球消费者的认可，并在进博会上亮相。

马征说："这是我们基于中国消费者需求反哺全球创新的典型案例。"从"在中国，为中国"到"在中国，为全球"，进博会成为耐克这一改变的"催化剂"。

"三级跳"，步步高

耐克可谓全球 500 强企业中抢抓中国机遇的"早鸟"。早在中

耐克进入中国市场 40 年展亮相第四届进博会。【企业供图】

国改革开放初期的 1980 年，它就与天津和上海的鞋厂签订生产协议。1981 年，耐克在上海设立中国总部。

2021 年，第四届进博会恰逢耐克进入中国市场的"不惑之年"。在进博会展台上，耐克展出了进入中国的 40 个经典瞬间，并将在华发展历程中的重要产品作为展品，展示其与中国体育共同成长的生动故事。

经过 40 多年的发展，中国在耐克全球市场中的地位实现了"三级跳"：从全球重要的制造和出口基地，一跃而成除美国之外的全球第二大单一市场，再跃成为原有定位基础上全球重要的前沿创新中心。

进博会则在耐克"三级跳"进程中发挥了重要的助跑作用。马征认为："进博会不仅是为期 6 天的展会，更是贯穿企业全年发展计划和发展目标的活动。不管从投资的角度，还是从技术和品牌发展的角度，参与其中的企业都获得了很好的溢出效应。"

与进博，共"升级"

2020 年，第三届进博会首设体育用品及赛事专区，耐克即成为首批参展商。"四叶草"更是频频成为耐克宣布重要投资项目的舞台。

"中国正逐渐成为全球创新的中心，对耐克来说也不例外。我们把在中国获得的宝贵经验知识和创新精神通过进博会分享给全球。"马征说。

耐克已连续 4 届参展，成为"进博老友"，且每年在进博会上都有代表性项目落地。

耐克首套废旧运动鞋自动化拆分工艺流程在进博会展示。【企业供图】

　　在第四届进博会上，耐克宣布在深圳建设耐克中国技术中心，加快数字化转型步伐，让耐克牢牢地把握住线上机遇。在第五届进博会上，耐克宣布在其中国物流中心建立"全自动无人立体仓"，可以实现高度智能自动化和熄灯运营，极大地提升供应链的效率和韧性。

　　除了项目，进博会也为耐克产学研联动提供了平台。在第六届进博会上，耐克宣布与清华大学在可持续发展领域达成深度合作，双方携手开展"碳中和产学研深度融合专项计划"合作；耐克还与同济大学生态文明与循环经济研究所合作开发首套废旧运动鞋自动化拆分工艺流程，通过回收旧鞋，建造环保运动场。

　　在马征眼中，进博会近几年在不断升级，参展商的获得感越来越强。在第七届进博会上，耐克将与进博共"升级"。据马征透露，耐克将以"跑步"为"秘密武器"，进一步展示未来的发展空间及对中国市场的长期承诺。

文／缪璐

"全勤生"与中国发展同频共振

融合空调和新风功能于一身的"六恒气候站"、电池资产管理和延长寿命的云分析服务"BetteRRRy"、应用 5kW 纯氢燃料电池的冷热电三联供项目……作为进博会"全勤生",松下每年都带来不少首发首秀的"黑科技"。

在进博会的大舞台上,松下的新产品、新技术收获了极大的曝光机会。松下控股株式会社全球副总裁、集团中国东北亚总代表本间哲朗表示,松下将进博会定义为"全球性战略性展会",每年都会带来很多创新产品和技术成果,并发布集团在华战略。

展示最新产品　加快成果落地

从 2019 年第二届进博会开始,参加进博会成为本间哲朗从未缺席的固定日程。每一次,他都会来到松下的展台,现场与观众互动,演示其产品和服务。

往届松下进博会展台。【企业供图】

"对于外国企业来讲，进博会是我们向中国展示最新产品及最新解决方案很好的舞台。"本间哲朗表示，通过进博会将最新研发的高科技产品和概念展现给中国消费者，可以加快成果落地，获取市场反馈。

参加进博会，松下收获的不止是业务曝光度。7年来，松下不断拓展朋友圈，在展会现场与众多合作伙伴签订多份合作备忘录，仅第六届进博会签订的合作协议就多达 15 份。

作为一家历史悠久的日本企业，松下在中国市场上有着广泛的认知度。自 1978 年与中国结缘，松下从最初的显像管、家电业务，发展到现今的健康智能住空间、新能源汽车零部件、智能制造三大重点事业，这些板块全部与中国经济社会紧密相连。

2019 年，松下集团成立了将事业和地域统括职能合二为一的地区事业公司——中国东北亚公司。这一年，松下在进博会上首次提出打造"健康养老 No.1"品牌事业战略，推动在中国建设首个养老社区——雅达·松下社区。

当时，松下希望在中国推进的康养事业还只是一个概念。随着进博会的持续举办，凭借在日本 20 多年的养老经验，松下展示的适老化产品和方案得到了政府、企业、消费者的欢迎。2022 年，雅达·松下社区正式竣工。如今，这样的家电与住宅融合项目在中国达到了 35 处。

往届松下进博会展台。【企业供图】

洞察市场变化　紧跟中国步伐

本间哲朗表示，中国是制造大国，也是消费大国、工程大国、创新大国。中国拥有巨大的国内市场需求、完备的产业链供应链，对新技术接纳能力强，经济发展潜力很大，为外资企业在华发展提供了广阔机遇。对松下而言，中国是推动其整体业绩上升的重要市场。

在他看来，从全球范围看，中国市场无疑独具特色。"对于外企来说，中国市场的吸引力不仅在于庞大的规模，更在于消费者对于新概念和新技术的乐于接受。"

对于跟松下一样的外资企业来说，进博会是了解中国市场最新动态和变化的绝佳平台。"通过进博会，我们提升了快速适应新技

往届松下进博会展台。【郭志华　摄】

术和市场变化的能力，使得松下能够紧跟中国市场的步伐，与中国的发展同频。"本间哲朗说。

从首届进博会的百年企业全系列家电、到后来的"健康、养老""清洁""生活和环境"，直至第七届的"Smart Life，Smart Society"……不难发现，松下在进博会的展示主题一直紧随中国的市场变化和消费趋势。

本间哲朗说，进博会汇聚了来自世界各国优秀企业的优秀产品和技术，是让世界了解中国、让中国了解世界的重要平台和窗口。"通过进博会，让我们深切感受到中国开放的大门越开越大，感受到中国市场在全球发挥着越来越重要的作用。"

百闻不如一见　以开放创未来

在第六届进博会上，松下集团 CEO 楠见雄规首次来到进博会的新品发布平台。他评价说："中国速度就是全球速度，中国成本就是全球成本。"他要求松下以"中国速度""中国成本"来推进全球业务。

"中国开放的大门将越来越大，对在华开展事业 40 多年的松下而言，是很大的鼓舞。"本间哲朗透露，在过去的一年间，松下几乎所

往届进博会松下展示的新产品。【企业供图】

有事业部门的高管都曾访问过中国，了解市场趋势，寻求合作机会。松下也将在第七届进博会上继续展示新品，并公布新的投资计划，继续与中国经济共创未来。

"百闻不如一见，我也希望有越来越多的外企高管来到中国，亲眼目睹这个日新月异、不断创新的市场，加深对中国市场的理解。"本间哲朗说。

文 / 范宇斌

交通银行：
为高水平对外开放贡献金融力量

　　左滑、右滑、握拳……在一个空气全息屏前，参观者只要轻轻滑动手指，就可以详细了解金融推动高质量发展的全球服务案例。在进博会上，交通银行通过这样的布展，让无形的金融产品和服务变得更"有感"。

　　进博会是全球首个以进口为主题的国家级展会，在这个舞台上，

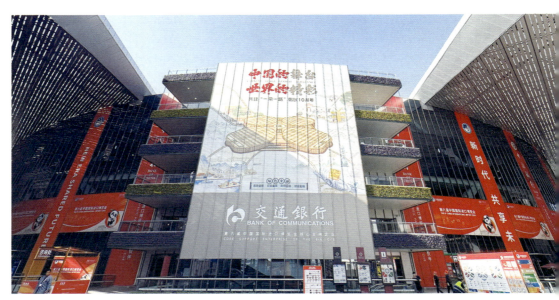

交通银行亮相第六届进博会。【企业供图】

国际采购、投资促进的需求不断增加。交通银行坚持把服务实体经济作为根本宗旨，着力发挥金融"血脉"作用，聚焦跨境金融服务，创新综合化金融服务方案，搭建对外开放"金融桥"。

数字转型，为跨境贸易赋能

发布"数字贸服"跨境金融服务方案、推出"丝路电商"跨境电商综合金融服务平台、揭晓对公渠道及数字新生态服务方案……在第六届进博会上，交通银行"大招"频出，向世界展现其数字化金融服务创新成果。

借助 AI 算法、大数据分析等金融科技手段，交通银行不断推动产品优化，着力提升普惠小微外贸客群金融支持力度，做大做强跨境电商等外贸新业态金融服务。

眼下，数字化已成为金融机构转型的大趋势。交通银行积极融入数字化发展浪潮，发挥金融科技优势，为进博会提供高效优质的一站式金融服务，持续助力释放进博会溢出效应。

第七届进博会前夕，交通银行为进博会核心支持企业和指定保险服务商成功办理多边央行数字货币桥跨境人民币结算业务。该笔业务为航贸场景项下的首笔再保险费支付业务，交通银行通过数字货币桥的"点对点"新型技术实现快速清算，减少传统跨境支付中存在的延迟和手续费高的问题。

交通银行还加大对市场、客户需求的研究力度，稳健开展新型离岸国际贸易金融服务，融入粮食、能源、矿产等大宗商品跨境交易场景，不断提升场景化金融服务能力和科创企业知识产权项下跨境贸易支付便利化水平。

在第六届进博会的创新孵化专区，交通银行展示了企业网银、企业手机银行新版本、开放银行、小程序等一系列"数字化新交行"建设成果。其中，交行开放银行聚焦各类进出口企业或平台机构需求，提供针对性涉外汇款服务，并围绕外贸新业态场景，打造全流程、线上化、场景化的跨境收汇服务方案。

据悉，交通银行发挥资本项目数字化试点产品优势，以更大力度吸引和利用外资为突破口，2024年上半年业务金额同比增幅超过130%。

绿色金融，为低碳转型加力

交通银行展台上的数字人民币废弃瓶回收箱，吸引着参观者纷纷驻足。投入废弃水瓶，即可获得交行的数字人民币红包。交通银行希望通过这种互动，吸引大众关注绿色发展。

除了在展台布置上下功夫，交通银行还广泛参与虹桥国际经济论坛及进博会配套活动，围绕"发展绿色投资贸易 共建全球生态文明""新时代外贸高质量发展与贸易便利化"等主题分享交行观点、贡献

交通银行亮相第六届进博会。
【企业供图】

交行智慧，携手共建开放生态圈。

为将服务上海国际航运中心建设与绿色低碳发展相融合，交通银行主办第六届虹桥国际经济论坛航运金融会员论坛，以"聚力高能级航运 服务新发展格局"为主题，邀请政府机构和业内专家学者等齐聚一堂，共同探讨航运金融低碳化、数字化等前沿发展趋势，打造航运产融协作"中国方案"。

论坛上，交通银行子公司交银金租牵头启动"中国航运租赁创新联盟"，推动航运高能级产业链聚集，开辟航运业新发展格局。

交银科创，为创新更添动能

在助推科创企业发展道路上，交通银行"股债贷租托"多管齐下，为推进高水平科技自立自强注入金融动能。

在其主办的第六届虹桥国际经济论坛"聚力新科技 交融创未来"科技金融会员论坛上，交通银行邀请政银企各界代表共聚一堂，深入探讨科技与金融的融合与未来。其间，交通银行首次发布"交银科创"品牌，为科技型企业打造全生命周期服务方案，助力产业集群发展壮大。

上海，是我国科技创新的重要策源地。在这片沃土上，交通银行发挥主场优势和全球经营网络，为本土科创园区搭建互通交流平台，提升科技创新"软环境"。通过进博会平台，交通银行首次推出"交融环宇启帆科创"交银科创全球创新枢纽服务方案，集中展示了交通银行为提升本土科创软环境作出的努力。

作为一家综合性金融控股集团，集团子公司也积极为优质科创企业全球业务的开展提供"硬支撑"。第六届进博会期间，交银投

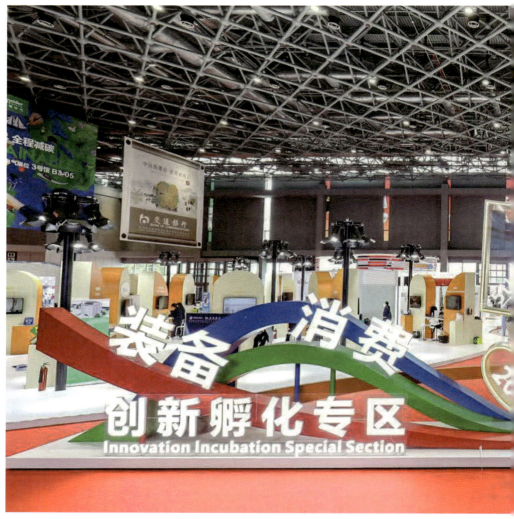

交通银行亮相第五届进博会。【企业供图】

资、交银国信、交银人寿与相关企业共同发起专注上海区域科创企业投资的母基金，并联合多家知名硬科技投资机构，设立基础软件、集成电路、先进制造、光电芯片与商业航天等四支行业主题子基金。交银金租积极为科技型企业提供专业化、定制化金融服务方案，创

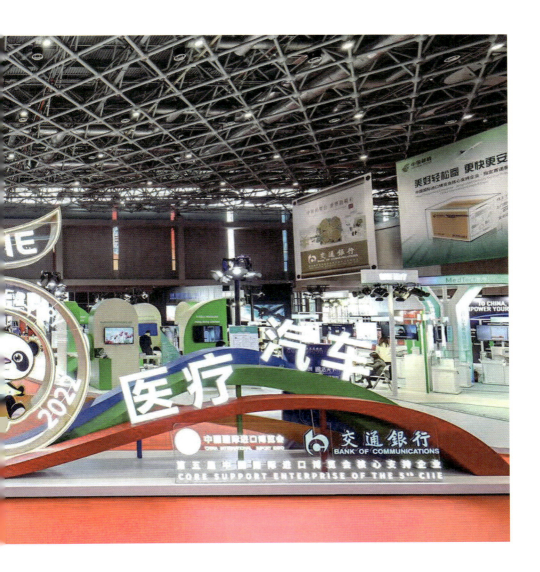

新推出科创"快易租""信易租"系列产品体系，帮助更多科技型中小企业获得高效的金融租赁服务，并通过自贸区 SPV 模式机制突破，协同产业伙伴推进产融结合，加快设备引进。

交行"货轮",从"四叶草"出发驶向"一带一路"

一艘名为"交通银行"的货轮满载集装箱驶向远方,这艘货轮的上方写着"跨境金融服务,境内外、离在岸、本外币一体化"。这是交通银行进博会主题海报上描绘的场景。

交通银行支持共建"一带一路"重大标志性工程和"小而美"民生项目,加大对绿色、数字、科技等共建"一带一路"合作新领域的支持力度。

数据显示,交通银行运用保函产品为共建"一带一路"项目提供增信支持,2024 年上半年开往"一带一路"共建国家的保函金额同比增长 92%。交通银行还持续丰富"一带一路"共建国家可兑换币种,近年来先后推出阿联酋迪拉姆、匈牙利福林、波兰兹罗提等 9 个"一带一路"小币种即远期结售汇和外汇买卖产品,代客可兑换货币达 27 种,为企业降低汇兑成本,促进双边贸易和投资。

在服务进博会展商的过程中,交通银行与企业间彼此信赖,不断拓宽业务合作深度。例如,进博会一展商子公司需紧急办理"贸易外汇收支企业名录"登记以满足首笔进口付汇需求,由于其法定代表人为境外个人,按照当时政策,名录登记需派人亲赴外汇局柜面办理,费时费力。交通银行深入排摸客户需求,推荐最优业务办理方案,最终精准把握时间节点满足其货物贸易收支需求。

2024 年,交通银行将第七度参与进博,也是第三次作为"核心支持企业"支持进博。交通银行将凝聚全行之力、统筹全行资源,一如既往为进博会提供高效优质的一站式金融服务，助力放大进博会溢出效应，持续为中国经济发展注入活力，为全球经济发展提供助力。

文 / 缪璐

开放之约

"七年不痒"，进博会魅力依然

　　第七届中国国际进口博览会将于 2024 年 11 月 5 日至 10 日在上海举行。开幕倒计时 100 天之际，时任中国国际进口博览局副局长孙成海公布了一份成绩单：截至目前，超过 50 个国家和国际组织确认参加国家综合展，企业商业展签约展览面积超过 36 万平方米，

交易团和专业观众组织工作进度快于 2023 年同期，预计有更多专业观众参与第七届进博会。

"七年不痒"，进博会何以魅力不减？

让进博好物从"四叶草"走向大市场

"纽仕兰作为依托进博赋能成长起来的进口品牌，既是进博开放的见证者，更是受益者。"新西兰纽仕兰乳业亚太区 CEO 盛文灏说。

七届进博会，纽仕兰从未缺席，且年年都有首发新品亮相。2024 年，纽仕兰将首发一款"全链路低碳牛奶"，从牧场端的无圈养，到运输端的氢燃料，再到工厂端的可再生地热能使用，展示企业对绿色新质生产力的探索发展。盛文灏说："全球经济增速进入慢车道，跨国企业都在探寻增长新引擎，重塑全球供应链。中国持续培育发展新质生产力，为跨国企业创新转型提供了广阔空间，我们相信，'下一个中国还是中国'。"

进博会的溢出效应有多大？上海市商务委主任朱民介绍，上海紧紧围绕"展品变商品、展商变投资商"的功能定位，持续放大进博会溢出带动效应。进博好物从"四叶草"场馆走向国内大市场，体现在三个"明显"上：

——"丝路电商"带动效应明显。上海"丝路电商"合作先行区建设全面铺开，已经举办上海网上年货节、丝路云品电商节等促消费活动，促进进博展品变为电商商品。

——常年展示交易平台效应明显。虹桥品汇 2023 年交易额 170 亿元，累计开设苏州、绍兴等 23 个分中心。绿地全球商品贸易港开设国家馆 63 个，累计开设 13 个分港，推动 5000 余款进博同款商品进入国内市场。南京东路的进博集市城市会客厅已有 20 多个国别和地区的进博产品集中展销，成为全球游客了解进博新品、体验国别商品的打卡场所。

——首发首展效应明显。六届进博会以来，上海累计引进了首店 5840 家，其中，亚洲级别以上首店超过 80 家。

让参会获得感转为营商环境满意度

不仅是"买全球、卖全球"，进博会向世界展示了中国扩大高水平开放的决心，搭建了中外企业携手共进的平台。

连续 6 年参加进博会的乐高公司，其乐园主题度假区项目一期建设已初具规模；第四届进博会参展商士卓曼，其高端种植体产业化项目一期已经启动，预计 2025 年达产；七届进博会"全勤生"乐斯福，通过进博会与上海清美集团牵手，深入合作打造适合国外消费者口感的中式面点，助力清美开拓国际市场。

乐高悟空小侠大篷车活动。
【受访单位供图】

从 6 天参会体验的获得感，升级为 365 天营商环境的满意度，上海持续优化营商环境吸引外商投资。全面对接国际高标准经贸规则，上海深入推进高水平全方位制度型开放，实施促进外商投资全球伙伴计划，擦亮"投资上海"系列活动品牌，召开市、区两级多层次的政企沟通圆桌会议，举办外资企业政策速递活动，促进与进博展商的"双向奔赴"。2024 年上半年，上海新设外资企业 3007 家，同比增长 18.3%。全市新认定跨国公司地区总部 29 家、外资研发中心 14 家，分别累计认定 985 家、575 家。

欧莱雅北亚公共事务联动部高级经理章恺兰介绍，欧莱雅是进博会的"全勤生"。进博会已成为欧莱雅集团在全球范围内的"顶流"项目，是全球新品首发、科技首秀的首选平台。6 年来，欧莱雅在进博会首发了近 20 个国际新品牌和数十个美妆黑科技，很多新品在进博平台从"展品变商品，又从商品变爆品"。

货真价实的进博溢出效应，让欧莱雅充分感受到了中国市场的巨大活力和潜力，也坚定了进一步投资中国的决心。在第二届进博会上，欧莱雅与东方美谷共同开创了"BIG BANG 美妆科技创新计划"；2022 年，在上海落地了总部之外的第一家投资公司美次方；2024 年 4 月，位于苏州的智慧运营中心正式启动。

让全球企业找到新项目新伙伴新机遇

从 73 家到 150 家再到 300 家，2021 年第四届进博会首设创新孵化专区以来，越来越多的科技型创新初创小微企业搭上了中国创新的快车。

孙成海副局长介绍，截至目前，第七届进博会创新孵化专区参展规模已超过 2023 年整体水平，并将首次聚焦数字经济、绿色低碳、

生命科学、制造技术四大赛道进行策展，继续举办评奖活动，打造以项目、政策、投资、金融、宣传于一体的创新孵化生态圈，为全球初创小微企业开拓中国市场提供科技资源与合作机遇。

在华韩国创新中心（KIC中国）2024年首次以推荐机构的身份参加第七届进博会，将携手6家人工智能、生物医药、新材料等领域的韩国科技型初创企业进入创新孵化专区办展。"进博会是全球最具影响力的展会之一。希望通过这一平台，对接中国的投资方和合作方，提升韩国初创高新技术产业的竞争力。"在华韩国创新中心代表金钟文表示对首次进博之旅充满期待和信心，"中国拥有全球最完善的产业供应链，与中国产业对接合作提高技术水平很有必要，希望借助进博会推进两国科技领域的合作。"

西班牙国家创新中心2024年将携20家西班牙初创企业参展进博会创新孵化专区，涉及领域包括数字经济、航天航空、制造技术等。该中心相关负责人表示："2024年参展的西班牙初创企业不仅有高科技含量，更重要的是对中国的市场有着充分的信心和热情，有强烈意愿加入中国市场。我们希望通过进博会平台，找到中国的合作伙伴，找到发展的新机遇。相信此次参展，将为未来更深层次的合作打下良好的基础。"

"进博会平台本身一直在跟随中国市场的新需求不断升级。"同样是进博会的"全勤生"，全球领先的科技创新企业3M在前六届进博会中，分别亮相消

首届青浦"四叶草之夜音乐节"奏响开放包容新乐章。【主办方供图】

费电子及家电展区、科技生活展区、医疗器械及医药保健展区、技术装备展区、能源低碳及环保技术专区。在第七届进博会上，3M将入驻首次设立于技术装备展区的新材料专区，围绕低碳、可持续主题，带来一系列全球领先的气候科技与解决方案。3M全球资深副总裁兼中国区总裁丁泓禹说："进博会的集聚效应，让企业得以一站式把握中国市场的前沿脉搏。6年多来，3M以新产品满足新需求，以新动向激发新灵感，推动更多源于本土、产自本土、面向世界的产品走出去。"

文／人民日报　田泓

（本文首次刊发时间为 2024 年 7 月 30 日）

开放强音汇新质

作为世界上首个以进口为主题的国家级博览会，7年来，中国国际进口博览会的"朋友圈"越来越大，新面孔、新科技、新观点汇聚激荡。以进博会为纽带，更多外资企业依然看好中国、坚定投资中国。

时任中国国际进口博览局副局长孙成海介绍，第七届进博会将于2024年11月5日至10日在上海举办。截至目前，签约展览面积已超过36万平方米，已有超过150家企业连续7年签约，书写合作共赢新篇章。

第七届进博会除了老朋友如约而至，更有新朋友奔赴而来。

来自新西兰的品牌萃斯2024年将第一次参加进博会，作为一个2024年6月才正式进入中国市场的品牌，其口服美容产品正好赶上了"6·18"购物节，第一个月的销量就突破了1000万元人民币，这也让品牌方直呼"表现远超预期"。

运动生活方式品牌lululemon也于近日宣布将首次参展进博会，lululemon全球首席执行官卡尔文·麦克唐纳（Calvin McDonald）说："进博会有着举世瞩目的影响力，我们很荣幸能与四海宾朋共赴这场'东方之约'。"

据介绍，目前有超过50个国家和国际组织确认参加2024年的

第七届进博会食品及农产品、医疗器械及医药保健展区展前供需对接会现场。
【新华社记者方喆 摄】

进博会国家综合展，其中，挪威、贝宁、布隆迪等国家以及联合国儿童基金会等国际组织将首次参展。企业商业展中，三菱商事等世界 500 强企业将首次参展，新材料专区的立邦、英威达和交通出行领域的安波福、阿尔斯通等行业龙头企业首次签约，成为进博会"朋友圈"不断扩容的见证。

在第七届进博会的展前供需会上，参展商与采购商亲密对接，"新质生产力"成为现场的高频热词。

"当前跨国企业都在寻找增长新引擎，中国以创新为驱动、以全要素生产率提升为核心标志的新质生产力，正在全球经济版图里形成新的吸引力。"纽仕兰亚太区首席执行官盛文灏说，2024 年纽仕兰将以"进博新质"为关键词，紧抓"绿色 + 数字"两条主线，推动成果在中国落地。

在展区设置上，第七届进博会深度挖掘科技前沿领域的展览展示潜力，为加快发展新质生产力贡献"进博力量"。其中，最引人关注的便是首次设立的新材料专区。目前，确定在新材料专区首秀

一名外国参展企业工作人员（左）向采购商介绍企业产品。【陈浩明　摄】

的，有来自美国、日本、德国、新加坡、巴西、意大利等多个国家的世界500强和龙头企业，还有一些细分行业的"隐形冠军"企业。

"中国始终是我们全球业务增长和投资的战略重心，首次亮相进博会选择新材料专区，是因为和我们的业务发展方向非常契合。"英威达亚太区尼龙上游业务副总裁李凯（Kyle Redinger）说。

作为进博会重要部分的第七届虹桥国际经济论坛，将以"坚持高水平开放，共促普惠包容的经济全球化"为主题，举办主论坛以及相关分论坛，同时将继续发布《世界开放报告2024》和最新世界开放指数，为推动世界共同开放贡献智慧。

以开放姿态，集纳全球智慧。创新孵化专区旨在为全球的科技型初创小微企业提供展示和交流的机会，自第四届进博会上首次设立以来，已有500多个海外的创新成果亮相进博会的平台。

第一年专区参展企业有 73 家，第二年增至 150 家，第三年再增至 300 家……截至目前，2024 年创新孵化专区参展企业数量已超过上届，预计将达到 350 家的新高。第七届进博会创新孵化专区宣介路演暨进博会签约仪式上的这组数据令人印象深刻。

"2024 年将共计有 20 家西班牙初创企业亮相进博会创新孵化专区，涉及领域包括数字经济、航天航空、制造技术等。"西班牙创新中心对外事务副总裁安赫尔·普列托（Angel Prieto）说："此次参展的西班牙初创企业不仅有高科技含量，更重要的是他们有强烈意愿加入中国市场。目前，我们还在与中国各地政府、产业园区进行积极对接，以推动更多项目落地中国。"

"进博会的举办，显示中国以普惠和包容的姿态，同更多国家合作释放发展动能。"中国人民大学重阳金融研究院执行院长王文说。

文 / 新华社　周蕊　王默玲

（本文首次刊发时间为 2024 年 7 月 26 日）

进博会推动中国与世界互惠共赢

从 2018 年起，每至金秋时节，东海之滨，黄浦江畔，中国国际进口博览会总是如约而至。四海宾朋同赴"东方之约"，共襄合作盛举。

"中国国际进口博览会不仅要年年办下去，而且要办出水平、办出成效、越办越好。"习近平主席在首届进博会开幕式上的庄严承诺言犹在耳。

循此前行，进博会已经成功举办六届。"进博故事"持续上演，进博效应不断释放，一幅中国与世界深度交融、共赢发展的美丽画卷徐徐铺展。展品变商品，商品进万家。中国用实实在在的行动把开放的大门越开越大，为各国共享中国发展红利、为各国企业深耕中国市场打开机遇之门，书写出共享机遇、共同发展的新华章。

以开放姿态拥抱世界

2017 年 5 月 14 日，北京，习近平主席在"一带一路"国际合作高峰论坛上宣布：中国将从 2018 年起举办中国国际进口博览会。翌年仲春，海南博鳌，习近平主席再次向世界郑重推介进博会："这不是一般性的会展，而是我们主动开放市场的重大政策宣示和行动。欢迎各国朋友来华参加。"

此后，从上合组织青岛峰会到中阿合作论坛部长级会议，从金砖国家工商论坛到中非合作论坛峰会，中国多次向世界发出"进博邀约"。

国际社会对此充满期待：世界上首个以进口为主题的国家级展会，将给世界经济带来怎样的活力？

2018 年 11 月 5 日，首届进博会开幕，一场在人类历史上留下光辉印记的"东方之约"点亮世界。来自 16 个国家的元首首脑，11 个国家的王室代表、副元首首脑及 13 个国际组织的负责人齐聚上海，部级以上外方嘉宾超过 400 位。3600 多家企业参展，超过 40 万名境内外采购商到会洽谈采购，展览总面积达 30 万平方米，按一年计，累计意向成交额达 578.3 亿美元。

回首首届进博会，阿斯利康全球执行副总裁、国际业务主席及中国总裁王磊颇为感慨："没想到这个展会的规格如此之高、中国政府的支持力度如此之大，也没想到全世界的参与力度如此之大。进博会展现的平台效应，是其他展会无法比拟的，绝对是一个创举。"

此后，无论世界风云如何变幻，进博会总是如约而至。关注度越来越高，参展商越来越多，成交额持续攀升。

第六届进博会按一年计意向成交金额 784.1 亿美元，比上届增长 6.7%，72 个国家和国际组织亮相国家展，128 个国家和地区的 3486 家企业参加企业展，集中展示了 442 项代表性首发新产品、新技术、新服务。参展的世界 500 强、行业龙头企业以及创新型中小企业，数量均为历届之最，全球十五大整车品牌、十大工业电气企业、十大医疗器械企业、三大矿业巨头、四大粮商等悉数参展。

进博会越办越好，溢出效应持续放大。国内外政要、知名企业负责人、各领域专家在进博会汇聚一堂，谈创新、话开放、促合作，脑力激荡，互相启发。非洲媒体《投资非洲》评论称，进博会为各

国提供了展示商品的国际平台，也是各国讨论外贸、世界经济、全球治理等重大问题的平台。

各国企业纷纷将进博会作为其全球新品首发地、前沿技术首选地、创新服务首推地，积极加入进博大家庭，从新朋友变成老朋友，从"头回客"变成"回头客"。越来越多的进博故事被书写，中国市场是"世界的市场、共享的市场、大家的市场"成为国际社会共识。

施耐德电气执行副总裁、中国及东亚区总裁尹正表示，进博会充分展现了中国高水平对外开放的成果，为全球企业深耕中国、合作共赢提供了重要机遇，参加进博会已经成为施耐德电气最为重视的"中国之约"。施耐德电气连续 6 次参展，展台规模逐年扩大，参展产品和解决方案越来越绿色先进，覆盖行业持续增加，"朋友圈"不断扩大。

进博效应释放广阔机遇

展会是人类文明成果的汇聚地，也刻画着东道国兴盛繁荣的轨迹。1851 年，英国成功举办第一届万国工业博览会，彰显了英国世界工厂的主导地位。1933 年，美国芝加哥世博会吹响了工业科技的号角，福特汽车装配线让人们看到一种崭新的生产生活方式。如今，进博会以开创历史的方式，为处于阴霾中的世界经济照亮了前路，注入了信心。

中国大市场的无限潜力，被国际社会普遍视为中国经济行稳致远的重要支撑，也是各国企业继续投资中国的重要聚焦点。着眼于中国经济高质量发展的内在需求，顺应国际社会合作共赢的普遍期待，中国把自身发展置于人类发展的坐标系中，通过进博会等开放举措，主动向世界开放市场，让各国搭乘中国发展的快车、便车。

从历久弥新的百年老店，到搏击潮头的初创公司；从实力雄厚的世界 500 强，到产品精小的中小企业；从连续参加进博会的老朋友，到首次参会的新面孔……参展商们竞相在进博会上展示企业竞争力，探寻合作新可能，表达出对中国大市场的坚定信心和对进博会溢出效应的无限期待。

东帝汶的咖啡、瑞士的巧克力、新西兰的牛奶……越来越多的国外优质商品通过进博会进入中国市场，让消费者不出国门就能"买全球"，充分享受经济全球化带来的红利，也为中国消费市场提质升级创造了更大空间。

一场场签约、一次次合作，也进一步激活了中国企业的创新精神，增加了发展机遇。国内外企业"手拉手"，共同把市场蛋糕做大，为世界经济复苏和发展带来澎湃动力。

医疗科技企业美敦力连续 6 年参加进博会。美敦力全球董事长兼首席执行官杰夫·马萨（Jeff Massa）表示，进博会是跨国医疗企业共享中国市场机遇、展示全球前沿医疗科技的重要平台。正是得益于进博会强大的市场影响力，美敦力的产品和服务才能更快地惠及中国患者。

德国卡赫集团霍克品牌董事会主席托比亚斯·瓦尔（Tobias Val）表示，搭乘"进博快车"，卡赫多款清洁产品率先完成市场占位，开启进入中国市场的机遇之门。参加进博会取得显著成果，让卡赫坚定了继续深耕中国市场的信心，不断加码在华投资，实现了从"展商到投资商"的身份转换。

在进博会，不仅发达经济体参展阵容庞大、引人注目，发展中国家同样书写着自己的精彩故事。

首届进博会期间，孟加拉国达达公司展出该国贫困妇女编织的黄麻手工艺品，受到采购团的欢迎。在中国合作方的帮助下，该公司产品进入上海百货卖场，还开设了网店，试水线上销售。

来自马里的展商库拉得知进博会主办方邀请马里企业家参展，不仅不设门槛，还提供免费摊位，于是她毫不犹豫地报名参展。她惊喜地发现马里展品在进博会广受欢迎，短短几天，展台的装饰品和小手工艺品就收获了可观的成交额。

坚定推进经济全球化

近年来，世界经济复苏乏力，经济全球化遭遇逆风，保护主义、单边主义甚嚣尘上。同时，新一轮科技和产业革命正孕育兴起，国际分工体系加速演变，全球价值链深度重塑，这些都赋予经济全球化新的内涵，孕育新的发展动能。

国际社会充分认识到，经济全球化是社会生产力发展的客观要求和科技进步的必然结果，闭门筑墙、逶过他人不是解决问题的正确方法。让世界经济的大海退回到一个个孤立的小湖泊、小河流，不符合历史潮流。各国利益日益交融、命运更加休戚与共是大势所趋，不断创造更加美好的生活是各国人民的共同期待，让经济全球化更好地造福全球人民是各国政府的共同责任。

举办进博会的初心和追求，折射着中国对世界发展大势的清晰思考和科学判断。正因如此，中国坚定引领经济全球化朝着更加开放、包容、普惠、平衡、共赢的方向发展。

跨国公司是经济全球化的推动者，也是受益者。当逆全球化思潮和贸易保护主义抬头，全球经贸形势不确定性显著增多时，跨国公司生产经营遭遇重重挑战。中国通过举办进博会，向世界宣示：中国真诚向各国开放市场，真诚邀请各国参展商加深与中国市场的相互了解、互相交流、相互促进、相互成就。

有国际专家认为，中国举办进博会，是支持经济全球化继续发展的一项有力举措，是"握住了通向明天的钥匙"。

国际货币基金组织总裁格奥尔基耶娃（Georgieva）表示，过去数十年，全世界从经济全球化中受益匪浅。经济全球化是所有人迈向更加繁荣未来的动力，这就是进博会如此重要的原因，也是国际社会需要进博会这一平台的原因。

一花独放不是春，百花齐放春满园。与举办进博会同步，中国推动更高水平对外开放的一系列重大举措相继落地，更低关税水平、更短负面清单、更便利市场准入、更透明市场规则……各国企业进入中国市场的制度环境不断优化，共享中国机遇的渠道变得更加便捷。

国际社会清楚地看到，中国举办进博会不是权宜之计，而是面向世界、面向未来、携手各国共同发展的务实行动和长远考量。一个改革不停顿、开放不止步的中国，一个致力于推动经济全球化发展、建设开放型经济的中国，正以更加开放包容的姿态拥抱世界，携手各国共同发展、共建人类命运共同体。

第七届进博会尚未开幕，不少参展商已经提前预订第八届进博会门票。2024 年 7 月 3 日，2025 年第八届进博会招展启动仪式举行，26 家企业现场签约，成为第八届进博会首批参展商，签约展览面积1.5 万平方米。各国企业用行动清晰地表达了这样的共识：经济全球化是人心所向，其潮流不可阻挡，中国则是推动时代潮流滚滚向前的中坚力量。

进博搭桥，全球合作。进博会这一国际贸易史上的创举，正推动新时代的中国与世界共享美好未来！

文 / 经济日报　袁勇

（本文首次刊发时间为 2024 年 7 月 12 日）

第七届进博会有望为众多企业搭建稳固的成长平台

　　报名参加本届进博会的企业纷纷表示，中国市场需求强劲，商业环境日益改善，将为希望进一步拓展业务的企业提供重要增长机会。

　　第七届中国国际进口博览会（进博会）将于 2024 年 11 月 5 日至 10 日在上海举行，本周六（7 月 27 日）将进入 100 天倒计时。

　　在 7 月 24 日举行的新闻发布会上，举办方时任中国国际进口博览局副局长孙成海表示，随着一批新参展商的加入，本届进博会参展面积已超过 36 万平方米。

　　2024 年，日本贸易公司三菱商事、美国材料供应商英威达、法国运输公司阿尔斯通、爱尔兰汽车技术供应商安波福，以及新西兰美容营养饮品品牌萃斯健康都将首次亮相进博会。

2024 年 7 月 24 日，在上海举行的第七届进博会对接活动现场。【陈梦泽　摄】

孙成海副局长表示，2024 年将首次设立专门区域，展示在新材料、自动驾驶技术、低空经济和汽车储能等领域企业取得的进展。

萃斯健康首席营销官王查理（Charlie Wang）表示："近年来，我们注意到中国健康产品市场空间广阔。女性消费者对于饮品的需求不断增长。我们的产品于 5 月底登陆天猫国际（阿里巴巴集团旗下跨境电子商务网站），第一个月销售额就突破 500 万元人民币（687132 美元），位居同类产品之首。我们希望通过进博会，让更多消费者了解这个品牌。"

总部位于上海的折扣零售商好特卖 2024 年也将首次作为买家参加进博会。该公司联合创始人张尼克（Nick Zhang）表示，进博会是一个重要的平台，能帮助中国企业和消费者了解"世界其他地区的发展"。

他说："我们店里销售的很多产品都刚刚进入中国市场，就出乎意料地得到了中国消费者的认可。我们期待与进博会的参展商合作，接触更多创新产品，并希望每届都能回来参加"。

法国美妆巨头欧莱雅参加了过去全部六届进博会。通过这个平台，欧莱雅已在中国市场推出了 20 多个新品牌，占该公司迄今为止在中国推出的 31 个品牌的绝大部分。2024 年，他们将在进博会期间首次推出一款新型空气干燥机，该空气干燥机通过应用红外线技术，效率更高。

更重要的是，欧莱雅在进博会上宣布增加投资，进一步扩大了在中国的市场布局。

2022 年 5 月，欧莱雅正式宣布在中国市场设立首家投资公司：上海美次方投资有限公司。四个月后，美次方作出首次投资，收购了中国香水品牌闻献和生物科技公司深圳杉海的少数股权。2024 年

2月，欧莱雅又宣布对中国本土高端香水香氛品牌观夏进行少数股权投资。

欧莱雅北亚及中国公共事务总裁兰珍珍表示："这一切都源于中国巨大的市场需求和增长潜力。"

据孙成海副局长介绍，超过150家公司将连续第七年参加进博会。新西兰乳业巨头恒天然就是其中之一。

恒天然上海创新中心于2020年投入运营。恒天然大中华区副总裁戴俊琦指出，恒天然在中国的第六个应用中心落户湖北武汉，已于2024年5月破土动工，9月投入运营。

上海市商务委员会主任朱民表示，进博会参展企业在中国的业务范围都在不断扩大。丹麦积木玩具公司乐高已参加过去六届进博会，其在上海的乐高乐园主题公园一期已初具规模。瑞士牙科植牙公司士卓曼集团参加过第四届进博会，其位于上海市中心的植牙项目一期将于2025年投入运营。

文 / 中国日报　施婧　王鑫

（本文首次刊发时间为 2024 年 7 月 26 日）

五洲客来，相约进博

第七届进博会大幕将启。五洲客来，相约进博。而正在加快"五个中心"建设步伐的上海，将经历进博会的又一次淬炼，把"不一般"的精彩华章呈现给世人。

展品变商品，"首发经济"更出彩

已经成功举办的六届进博会，与上海国际消费中心城市建设双向奔赴。

虹桥进口商品展示交易中心（虹桥品汇）作为进博会"6天+365天"常年展示交易主平台，2023年交易额达170亿元，累计开设苏州、绍兴等23个分中心。另一家进博会"6天+365天"常年展示交易平台——绿地全球商品贸易港开设国家馆63个，在国内累计开设13个分港，推动5000余款进博同款商品进入国内市场。

进博会的成功举办，更为上海"首发经济"添上重重一笔。六届进博会以来，上海累计引进首店5840家，其中，亚洲级别以上首店超80家。2024年6月，亮相第六届进博会的全球首款光子计数CT在上海瑞金医院正式投入运行，更低辐射，更高分辨率的性能，能让更多患者受益。

在第七届进博会迎来开幕倒计时100天之际，雅培宣布将再次

塞尔维亚美酒节新品首发仪式在进博会常年交易服务平台绿地全球商品贸易港举行。

参展，并将继续带来一系列新品。在历届进博会上，它们共展示了数百款生命科技创新产品。其中，在第五届进博会上首秀的 AVEIR VR 单腔植入式无导线心脏起搏器，已在中国正式获批上市，并于近期完成首批手术，为心动过缓患者带来全新治疗选择；自进博会首秀之后，用于二尖瓣反流微创治疗的 MitraClip 经导管二尖瓣夹及可操控导引导管，也已成功落地中国，用微创技术填补国内治疗空白。

连日来，第七届进博会参展企业争相"剧透"百日后将闪亮登场的首发新品：奥索将带来多款假肢仿生产品，其中新品"暴风飞毛腿大地运动脚板"为全球首发，适用于高活动级别的用户；纽仕兰将携 4.0 A2 全链路低碳牛奶开展全球首发。所谓全链路，是指企

奥索公司的进博展品帮助更多残障人士重建生活。【田泓 摄】

业在已经完成牧场端、工厂端的低碳实践后，在运输端，2024年又投入使用了新西兰首个新能源奶罐运输车队，更洁净的氢能源将帮助乳业运输趋近"零排放"；恒天然预计将带来近20款创新产品，其中包括助力健康老龄化营养支持的新品。

第六届进博会开幕前夕，《关于在上海市创建"丝路电商"合作先行区的方案》获国务院批复同意。自那以来，上海已经成功举办上海网上年货节、丝路云品电商节等促消费活动，促进进博展品变为电商商品。上海还推动线上线下联动，打造"丝路电商"国家馆。

2024年4月，巴基斯坦国家馆在外高桥开馆，成为第六届进博会巴基斯坦参展商品进入中国市场的首选平台。2024年以来，上海

共新增 3 个"丝路电商"国家馆，总数达到 26 个。据悉，连日来，这些"丝路电商"国家馆的工作人员都在加紧备货，待百日后盛会开幕之际，启动场外多场直播，线上线下联动，为第七届进博会"打 Call"。

展商变投资商，外资高地更牢固

除了"最新最潮"的商品，全球企业争相通过进博会平台，展现持续在华投资的诚意。六届进博会的成功举办，也进一步夯实上海外商投资高地的牢固地位。

2023 年，即便在全球经济复苏乏力的大环境下，上海新设外资企业仍达到 6017 家，同比增长 38.3%。2024 年上半年，上海新设外资企业 3007 家，同比增长 18.3%。全市新认定跨国公司地区总部 29 家、外资研发中心 14 家，分别累计认定 985 家、575 家。

作为进博会的"全勤生"，3M 将又一次站在进博会的舞台，并入驻第七届进博会技术装备展区首次设立的新材料展区。3M 全球资深副总裁兼中国总裁丁泓禹介绍，六届进博会以来，3M 多款创新成果从"展品到商品"。不仅如此，他们在 2022 年第五届进博会期间，宣布对 3M 上海金山工厂的增资扩产进行立项，"在全球董事会的大力支持下，不到一年，该项目便进入实质性启动，预计到 2024 年年底正式投产"。据悉，该项目的增资规模达到 4 亿~5 亿元，是近 10 年里规模比较大的一次增资。"另外，3M 在新能源、消费电子、可持续发展等领域，还会对位于上海的 3M 中国研发中心进行持续投入。"

在第六届进博会上，3M 多款创新产品吸引观众。【中新社记者汤彦俊 摄】

另据介绍，3M 全球已宣布，为履行对环境的承诺，未来 20 年里，在全球的可持续发展领域拟投入 10 亿美元。"在中国可持续发展领域的投入势必会占相当大的权重。"丁泓禹说。

"参展商变投资商"，汉高与进博会也一直在同频共振。"进博会平台让汉高见证并参与了中国产业和经济的发展，更加坚定了要始终致力于通过本土可持续创新服务、通过持续投资来支持当地产业和人才发展的企业战略。"汉高大中华区总裁安娜介绍，2024年年初，汉高消费品亚洲研发中心在上海落成启用，该中心投资约 1 亿元，将作为汉高消费品牌在亚洲最大的研发中心。同时，位于上海张江的汉高上海创新体验中心正在扩建中，总投资约 5 亿元，建成后将成为其全球第二大黏合剂技术创新中心，为中国和亚太地区的客户提供支持。该中心将于 2025 年竣工并投入使用。

汉高上海创新体验中心正在扩建中（效果图）。

当好"东道主"，营商环境更优化

进博会是中国构建新发展格局的窗口、推动高水平开放的平台和全球共享的国际公共产品。中国看世界，世界也在看中国，上海全力以赴当好东道主，始终保持第一次办展时的激情和干劲，让优化营商环境与高水平对外开放相向而行。

"本届进博会上海将继续在参展便利化上下功夫。在出入境方面，将聚焦外籍展客商和参展企业两大主体在出入境业务办理方面的实际需求，推进落实'为外籍展客商提供换发多次入境有效签证'等便利措施。海关已发布了第七届进博会通关须知和便利措施，进一步简化特许审批手续以及部分产品参展相关证书要求。"上海市政府副秘书长、城市服务保障领导小组办公室主任刘平介绍，在证件办理方面，本届进博会将进一步优化证件办理流程，压缩办证时间，逐步扩大电子证试用范围。

另据记者获悉，为向来自境外的进博会展客商提供全方位的支付便利，2024年上半年，上海实现超7万多台终端POS机支持受理外卡支付，较 2023 年年末增长 1.1 倍。

上海着力推动城市数字化转型，加快建设具有世界影响力的"国际数字之都"，以托举上海营商环境软实力的不断提升。

面向展客商，本届进博会将借助 AI 及数字化技术，升级数字化服务窗口，进一步优化找展商、看展馆、查活动等服务功能。同时，展馆内将增设智能会务服务点，优化展会现场 AI 智能应答功能。而服务保障部门在强化安保交通、展品通关、能源通信保障、气象监测预报、食品药品和特种设备安全监管等智能化应用的基础上，将进一步优化"进博一张图"功能，用各部门间数据融合应用的"一盘大棋"，确保进博会各项服务安全高效。

文 / 解放日报　吴卫群

（本文首次刊发时间为 2024 年 7 月 27 日）

搭上"进博快车"就是抓住中国机遇

　　6月，西门子医疗全球首款光子计数CT在上海交通大学医学院附属瑞金医院投入运行，它曾亮相第六届中国国际进口博览会，如今这束"光"照进生活，让更多患者受益；7月，科技护肤品牌

南京东路的进博集市城市会客厅已集中展销20多个国家和地区产品。【张伊辰　摄】

AP 媛彬在久光百货（静安店）开出首店，将在亮相第七届进博会后实施全国拓店计划；8 月，首批马来西亚猫山王鲜榴莲即将抵沪，品牌商摩拳擦掌，计划把限量版的鲜榴莲带到进博现场……

在第七届中国国际进口博览会迎来开幕倒计时 100 天之际，众多参展商已马不停蹄忙碌起来，大家都赶着搭上"进博快车"，抓住进一步全面深化改革、推进高水平对外开放的"中国机遇"。

从"准不准"到"快不快"

榴莲，是都乐近年来"死磕"的一件水果"宝贝"。"宝贝"有两层含义：其一，榴莲是近几年收获开放政策最密集的水果之一，2023 年中国榴莲进口量近 140 万吨，"准入"带来了巨大商机；其二，它的货值很高、利润丰厚，一如它金灿灿的外壳。"2024 年进博会上，榴莲仍将是'王炸'。"都乐中国市场部总监王娜表示，都乐已预定马来西亚猫山王鲜榴莲的进博首发"C 位"。

准入，是这家全球水果巨头决定"进博首发什么"的关键风向标。2023 年，菲律宾榴莲获准输华，都乐顺势在第六届进博会首发黄金普雅榴莲。2024 年 6 月 19 日，中国与马来西亚共同签署一系列协议，其中就包括《马来西亚新鲜榴莲对华出口植物检疫要求议定书》。王娜坦言，准备工作已经紧锣密鼓地展开，首批马来西亚猫山王鲜榴莲预计下个月以空运方式运抵中国市场。

鲜果市场的丰富度，是中国高水平开放的一道缩影。过去 7 年来，中国新开放的水果品类达到 98 个，而在之前的 6 届进博会上，都乐带来了其中 12 个品类的新品，并且全部变成了"爆品"。准入之后，考验的是速度，其中通关便利化是关键一环。王娜仍以鲜榴莲为例，从榴莲"树上熟"掉落，到在地检验检测，从包装、空

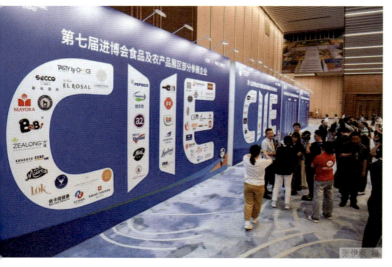

第七届进博会推介现场。【张伊辰 摄】

运到送达中国消费者手中，只要哪个环节稍慢一步，就会影响水果的品质和口感。如今，都乐可以做到在 2 天之内完成所有流程，这背后正是得益于进博会的一系列贸易便利化政策。

易腐坏的水果"宝贝"是贸易便利化的获益者，高精尖的新材料同样获益匪浅。2023 年进博会上，肖特首次展出的零度微晶玻璃成了技术装备展区的"网红"展品，并顺利"配对"成为青海墨子巡天望远镜的"视网膜"。由于这一高性能材料产自肖特德国美因茨工厂，而且体积大、价值高，在跨国长途运输和通关方面遇到了诸多挑战。肖特集团相关负责人透露，多亏了中国的通关便利化政策，这一材料顺利从德国运到国内加工装配后，最近已抵达青海冷湖天文观测基地。

从溢出效应到"首发经济"

首发首秀，永远是进博舞台上的关键词。在这辆"进博快车"上，从首发到爆发，从展品到商品，速度变得越来越快。

爱茉莉太平洋集团最近已确定了 2024 年进博新品名单，其中科技护肤品牌 AP 媛彬就是首次登陆进博会，并将借此契机布局中国市场。谈起这一 2024 年 2 月才焕新的品牌，爱茉莉太平洋集团上海研发中心负责人周淇很有信心，因为它开辟了一条崭新的护肤赛道——"医美后"护肤。"如今，热玛吉、光子嫩肤成为全球年轻消费者乐于尝试的非手术类抗衰项目，品牌独有的'绷带'专利配方及技术，可形成封闭式超导膜，为美容项目协同增效。"

有意思的是，让进博会溢出效应与上海"首发经济"形成市场联动，已成为参展商"朋友圈"公开的秘密。7月中旬，AP媛彬已在久光百货（静安店）开出内地首店，爱茉莉太平洋代表理事兼社长金昇焕这样形容上海的魅力——这里是助力品牌迅速向全球市场扩张的重要一步。在进博会亮相后，品牌还计划在全国范围内开设更多线下门店。

过去的6届进博会，上海累计引进首店5840家，其中亚洲级别以上首店逾80家，首发首展效应明显。在市商务委主任、进博会城市服务保障领导小组办公室常务副主任朱民看来，进博会在上海举办，是上海经济社会发展的重要动能引擎。上海正紧紧围绕"展品变商品、展商变投资商"功能定位，持续放大进博会溢出带动效应。

从进博会溢出效应到上海"首发经济"，

进博会吉祥物"进宝"。

双轮驱动为参展商带来更大机遇。就在几天前，美乐家（中国）日用品有限公司刚刚获颁成为外资研发中心，2024年企业还决定把进博会的展位从过去的108平方米拓展到153平方米。两者之间大有关联，美乐家（中国）市场副总裁吴殷揭秘：企业在进博会完成全球首发的美丽健康饮品、儿童营养食品，都大获成功，带动了产品销量，上海工厂还因此刷新生产纪录。基于此，美乐家作出了加码外资研发中心的决定，致力于用更多本土化配方的研发来拓展市场。

从本土化创新到全球价值链

多特瑞中国总裁麦欧文（Owen Messick）最近梳理精油原材料分布时惊讶地发现，中国已跃居成为企业精油植物原材料来源最多的国家。"我们发布的中国精油原材料已超过20种，包括枫香、草果、蓝莲花等，这一部分的业绩正以每年50%的速度提升。"他告诉记者，"我们在第七届进博会也加大了投入，展台面积从200平方米扩大至300平方米，展品数量、首发新品数都将创新高。"

随着"进博快车"提速，麦欧文对溢出效应有了更深的思考。他认为，进博会打通了一种双循环——将欧美萃取技术带来中国，将中国传统芳香植物带向世界："2024年，我们希望推动中国传统植物走上一条高附加值、高技术含量的发展道路，并将这种本土化创新融入全球产业链中，让香气传遍全球。"

从未来发展趋势看，越来越多的本土化创新将借助进博会走向全球。2024年，波士顿科学将带来一款兼具"中国智造"和"中国制造"元素的产品——AVVIGO+血管内超声系统。波士顿科学中国区副总裁达波（Da Bo）透露：这款产品由波士顿科学中国团队

进博集市"城市会客厅"。【中新社记者殷立勤　摄】

参与研发，2023 年 9 月已获得欧盟 CE 认证和美国食药监（FDA）批准，率先出口海外，而其核心主机全部由中国生产，进一步将本土化创新嫁接到全球产业价值链中。

七赴"进博之约"，西门子医疗大中华区总裁王皓坦言，西门子医疗始终将进博会视为全球医疗创新与技术交流的重要窗口，加速全球创新资源与本土市场的深度融合，共同催生新质生产力，让进博会成为"本土智慧、全球共创"的展示地。

距离第七届进博会开幕还有百日，新一批展品已经到来。位于静安区茂名北路丰盛里的"飞利浦健康生活 Lab"全球首家线下体验中心、4 月刚拿到牌照的新一代制氧机和 7 月刚获批的飞利浦移动超声系统先瞳 5500 已经入场，并将在 2024 年进博会首展首秀。

飞利浦（中国）集团传讯部高级经理陈玮说："进博会溢出效应进入了新的阶段，我们将更多地把在中国研发的技术和产品通过进博平台带向全球。"

文／文汇报　徐晶卉　张天弛　郭凡熙
（本文首次刊发时间为 2024 年 7 月 27 日）

"东方之约"再续前缘，中国机遇全球共享

自 2018 年以来，年年举办，从未爽约，"越办越好"的中国国际进口博览会，已经成为中国构建新发展格局的窗口、推动高水平开放的平台、全球共享的国际公共产品。

世界目光将再次聚焦黄浦江畔，见证"东方之约"再续前缘。7 年来，"进博磁力"不降反升，全球客商在此共绘蓝图、共享机遇、共创未来，书写更多的进博故事。7 年来，进博纽带紧密相连，为中国经济高质量发展提供动力，为全球经济复苏带来机遇。进博第七年，中国开放的大门越开越大。

进博效应持续释放

进博会是世界上首个以进口为主题的国家级博览会。从一个数字可直观感受它

在第七届进博会开幕倒计时 100 天之际，展前供需对接会在国家会展中心（上海）举办。
【陈梦泽 摄】

搭载零度微晶玻璃的墨子巡天望远镜。【采访对象供图】

乐高集团在进博会上首发的新品大多以中国文化为灵感来源。【张钰芸　摄】

的力量——784.1 亿美元，这是第六届进博会按一年计意向成交金额。这不仅彰显了中国高水平开放的魅力和与全球共享市场的诚意，也令上海的国际化成色更足，全球影响力更大。

7 年来，各国企业共享中国发展机遇，收获更多市场红利。"六届进博会，我们在展台上迎来了 20 万参观者，首发 24 款产品，绝大多数都以中国文化为灵感来源。"乐高集团高级副总裁、中国区总经理黄国强说，乐高集团已在中国 120 多个城市开设了超过 480 家品牌零售店，线上线下渠道合作也更加紧密，"如此高人气，要归功于进博会上的精彩亮相"。

在 2023 年进博会上，德国肖特集团首次展出的零度微晶玻璃成为技术装备馆的"网红"展品，它是天文望远镜的"视网膜"，能让天文望远镜比人眼接收多一亿倍的光，视野更广，看得更为清晰。借助进博会平台，这一材料将被用于坐落在我国青海冷湖的墨子巡天望远镜，是目前北半球光学波段时域巡天能力最强的望远镜。

美国科技创新企业 3M 是连续参展七届进博会的"全勤生"，

2024 年将在首次设立的新材料展区带来以可持续为主题的首发新品和解决方案。从首届进博会开始，环境声音耳罩、云纤保暖材料和应用于半导体制造领域的研磨垫等首发展品一一亮相，订单也接踵而至。

"进博会的集聚效应，让 3M 得以一站式把握中国这一重要风向标市场的前沿脉搏，不仅有效满足了本土客户的多元需求，也推动更多源于本土、产自本土、面向世界的产品'走出去'。" 3M 全球资深副总裁兼中国总裁丁泓禹说。

"参展六届进博会以来，我们已经累计达到了六亿元人民币的销售额，促成了与正大集团等行业龙头企业的大宗交易。"奈卡塔健康品牌总监吕玥蓉说，尽管蜂蜜市场竞争激烈，但进博会却给荷塔威品牌带来了更大的发展平台，得以与优质企业在产业升级、产品创新、可持续发展等诸多领域达成合作。

加速创新产品落地

从世界工厂走向全球超市，进博会让中国大市场成为世界大机遇的同时，也为国内消费市场带来更多新产品、新服务，足不出户"买全球"的同时，享受到了更加美好健康的生活。

2024 年 72 岁的陈阿姨是一名退休会计，本应颐养天年，却不幸承受了帕金森病的痛苦折磨。2024 年 5 月，她植入了美敦力 Percept™ PC 可感知脑起搏器，6 月底正式开机。陈阿姨告诉记者，尽管目前仍在术后恢复期，但她说已经感到震颤减轻了，浑身也不再僵硬，如今正在积极尝试康复锻炼，心情也越来越轻松。

在神经科学领域，Percept PC 被《自然》杂志评价为"第一次真正打开了大脑的一扇窗口"。以参展第四届进博会为契机，该创

都乐将在第七届进博会上首发马来西亚鲜食榴莲。【张钰芸　摄】

新产品进入大众视线，在中国获批后已于2023年7月完成首批植入，在国内超30家医院投入临床应用，造福上百位患者。

从全球走到中国、从展品走到临床，进博会连接起了患者与创新产品之间的桥梁。连续参展进博会五年以来，雅培也展示了数百款生命科技创新产品，得益于进博会强大的溢出效应，这些前沿科技和产品加速获批，陆续落地中国市场，从展品变为中国大众用得好的医疗健康产品。在第五届进博会上"首秀"的AVEIR VR单腔植入式无导线心脏起搏器在近期完成了首批手术，为心动过缓患者带来全新的治疗选择；瞬感葡萄糖监测系统则已服务超过50万中国用户，成为糖尿病患者管理血糖的新武器。

　　"伴随进博效应，都乐已经成为中国消费者广为认可的'进口果篮'。"都乐中国市场总监王娜告诉记者，从 2018 年首届进博会开始，我国新开放进口的水果品类达到了 98 个，而都乐将其中的 12 个带到了进博会上首发，包括比利时红啤梨、巴西甜瓜、菲律宾鲜榴莲等，如今都成为市民"果盘子"里的明星产品。

　　"2024 年 6 月 24 日，海关总署发布 2024 第 72 号《关于进口马来西亚鲜食榴莲植物检疫要求的公告》。我们力争成为第一个将马来西亚鲜食榴莲引入中国的企业，都乐马来西亚猫山王榴莲和黑刺榴莲将登上进博首发舞台，借助进博会强大的溢出效应，让中国榴莲爱好者一饱口福。"

从参展商变投资商

　　7 年来，进博会推动展品变商品、参展商变投资商，溢出效应不断放大。越来越多的企业以进博会为跳板进入中国，不断坚定对中国经济发展的信心和深耕中国市场的决心。

　　六天参会体验的获得感，升级为 365 天营商环境的满意度。7 年来，上海与进博展商"双向奔赴"。2024 年上半年，上海新设外资企业 3007 家，同比增长 18.3%。全市新认定跨国公司地区总部 29 家、外资研发中心 14 家，分别累计认定 985 家、575 家。

　　7 月 25 日，第 39 批跨国公司地区总部和研发中心颁证仪式在人民大厦举行，美乐家（中国）日用品有限公司获颁成为外资研发中心。公司副总裁吴殷说，作为一家外商独资企业，美乐家已在中国市场耕耘 20 年，此次升级为外资研发中心，将为中国市场带来更多健康产品，2024 年在第七届进博会食品及农产品展区的展位就将从 108 平方米拓展到 153 平方米。

"我们在进博会上全球首发的美丽健康饮品、儿童营养食品，都大获成功，带动了产品销量，上海工厂还因此刷新生产纪录，基于此，美乐家作出了加码外资研发中心的决定，致力于用更多本土化配方的研发来拓展市场。"

"中国是汉高全球第三大市场，在全球业务中发挥着重要作用，汉高正不断加大在华研发和高端产品生产方面的投资。"德国汉高大中华区总裁安娜表示，2024 年年初，汉高消费品亚洲研发中心在上海落成启用，该中心投资约 1 亿元人民币，是汉高消费品牌在亚洲最大的研发中心。此外，汉高投资约 5 亿元人民币，位于上海张江的汉高上海创新体验中心正在扩建中，建成后将成为其全球第二大粘合剂技术创新中心，为中国和亚太地区的客户提供支持。该中心将于 2025 年竣工并投入使用。

老友收获满满，新朋蜂拥而至。运动生活方式品牌 lululemon 近日宣布将首次参展进博会，lululemon 全球首席执行官卡尔文·麦克唐纳（Calvin MacDonald）说："进博会有着举世瞩目的影响力，我们很荣幸能与四海宾朋共赴这场'东方之约'。借此机会，也将传递我们进一步投资并深耕中国市场的坚定承诺。"

立邦也将在技术装备展区新材料专区打造 300 平方米的展台，携多款全球首发、进博首秀的产品亮相。立邦中国区首席执行官钟中林表示，从进博见证者到参与者的身份转变，彰显了立邦对中国市场的不变承诺。"通过进博会这一'共创共享'的世界级平台，立邦将与全球伙伴建立紧密合作，共享新时代中国发展机遇。"

文 / 新民晚报　张钰芸　杜萱

（本文首次刊发时间为 2024 年 7 月 27 日）

后 记

　　光阴似箭，日月如梭。这已是我们连续第 3 年编撰《进博故事》图书。来自全球各地的"进博伙伴"倾情分享其独特经历，带我们重回进博会的火热现场，一起感受那份沉甸甸的收获。

　　这些值得被记录和传播的"进博故事"，不仅是进博会巨大成效和影响的最好印证，而且成为中国坚定推进高水平开放，与世界共享机遇、共商合作和共促发展的真实写照。

　　我们认真记录下这些故事，并以中英文双语加以呈现，期待这本书像永不落幕的进博会一样，穿越时空距离，打破地域界限，成为不同国家、不同民族、不同文化的个体和群体相互连接的桥梁与纽带。

　　本书的编纂得到了各级领导、各界人士的关心与指导，得到了故事讲述者的支持和配合。在此，对各方的鼎力支持与付出致以最诚挚的敬意。衷心感谢中共中央宣传部，进博会秘书处（商务部服贸司）、商务部新闻办、中共上海市委宣传部、中共上海市委对外宣传办公室（上海市政府新闻办），以及人民日报、新华社、中央广播电视总台、经济日报、中国日报、中国新闻社、解放日报、文汇报、新民晚报、上海广播电视台、澎湃新闻、第一财经、国际商报、凤凰卫视等各单位和媒体机构的大力支持与付出，在此一并致谢！

　　进博会和虹桥论坛是推动建设开放型世界经济的年度盛会，更是构建人类命运共同体的伟大实践。在编写过程中，我们深刻体悟

到，进博会仿佛一座巨大的宝藏，还有无数的可能性，还有更多更精彩的故事等待你我去挖掘、去续写。

我们以高度的责任感编写本书，竭尽所能做好每一个环节，但因时间仓促、水平有限，难免存在疏漏和错误。不足之处，敬请理解包容。

分享你的
进博故事

CIIE NEW ERA SHARED FUTURE
新时代 共享未来

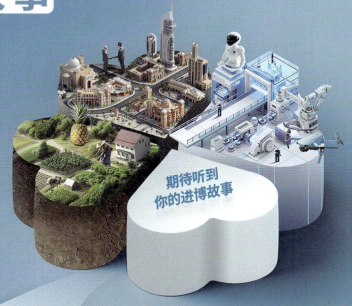

期待听到
你的进博故事

全球征集正式开启

投稿邮箱　ciiestories@ciie.org

征集时间　即日起至2025年7月26日

主办单位　中国国际进口博览局、
　　　　　　国家会展中心（上海）

支持媒体　人民日报数字传播、中国新闻社、
　　　　　　中国日报社新媒体中心、新民晚报、
　　　　　　看看新闻Knews、澎湃新闻、第一财经、
　　　　　　国际商报、凤凰卫视

支持平台　抖音、今日头条

扫码分享你的进博故事

衷心感谢交通银行对本书出版的大力支持！

中国的舞台
CHINESE STAGE   GLOBAL BRILLIANCE
世界的精彩

交通银行扎实做好金融"五篇大文章"

◎科技金融 ◎绿色金融 ◎普惠金融 ◎养老金融 ◎数字金融

交通银行
BANK OF COMMUNICATIONS
第七届中国国际进口博览会核心支持企业
CORE SUPPORT ENTERPRISE OF THE 7th CIIE

CIIE STORIES

China International Import Expo Bureau
National Exhibition and Convention Center (Shanghai) Co., Ltd.
China News Network

中国商务出版社
·北京·

CIIE STORIES

China International Import Expo Bureau
National Exhibition and Convention Center (Shanghai) Co., Ltd.
China News Network

ISBN 978-7-5103-5426-7
Published by China Commerce and Trade Press
No. 28, Donghou Lane, Anding Menwai Street, Dongcheng District, Beijing 100710
Printed in the People's Republic of China
http://www.cctpress.com
Email: bjys@cctpress.com
Tel: 8610-64269744 64266119
Price: CNY 189.00 USD48.00

Preface

As global partners continue to witness the growth and success of the China International Import Expo (CIIE), countless unforgettable moments have gradually accumulated, forming a series of captivating and memorable "CIIE Stories".

Each story shared by participants highlights vivid scenes of economic exchange, mutual trust, and mutual learning among civilizations, documenting the efforts, growth, and achievements of all "CIIE partners".

These "CIIE Stories" collectively written by people around the world, explore the path of innovation, telling tales of "Craftsmen strive for newness each day". They are stories of working together, sharing together, and winning together, akin to the adage "A myriad of flowers heralds the arrival of spring." They are stories of advancing civilization through cultural exchange and mutual learning, embodying the idea of "Though separated by a mountain, we'll share the same clouds and rain."

Since its inaugural event, the CIIE has acted as a colossal gravitational force, garnering a multitude of devoted followers. Since the launch of the latest global call for "CIIE Stories" a deluge of leads has poured in, solidifying its status as a vibrant testament to the CIIE's magnetic pull.

The narrators of "CIIE Stories" range from "first-time exhibitors" to

"returning guests" and "loyal attendees" who share a profound bond with the CIIE. This diverse group includes political dignitaries representing nations and international organizations, alongside experts and scholars engaging in the Hongqiao International Economic Forum. Each year, this event unites individuals who dedicate 365 days to meticulous preparation and spend 8,760 hours in anticipation. The "CIIE partners" not only secure valuable contracts and forge deep friendships but also collectively craft indelible memories.

Although their stories vary, gathering at the "Four-Leaf Clover" and attending the CIIE together has become their shared choice.

The CIIE appointment is an appointment with opportunities. Choosing the CIIE is choosing the great opportunities of the Chinese market, integrating into the embrace of the global market. Agricultural products from various countries board the "CIIE Express" and enter thousands of households.

Well-known pharmaceutical companies that participate in the exhibition give birth to "CIIE babies" year after year, while century-old stores use this opportunity to build a global cooperation chain. By proactively expanding imports, China has turned its market into a market for the world, a shared market, and a market for all. The CIIE opens the door of opportunity for all countries, injecting new impetus into the world economy.

The CIIE is a commitment to development. Choosing the CIIE means choosing to share the fruits of inclusive development in a closely interconnected global village. Specialty products from the least developed countries have become bestsellers thanks to the expo, artisans from distant lands have signed supply agreements at the event, and orders from China have helped improve livelihoods in faraway regions. As an international public good for all, the CIIE supports developing countries in benefiting from China's growth dividends, promoting cooperation and win-win outcomes worldwide.

The CIIE is a commitment to innovation. Choosing the CIIE means choosing a future driven by innovation. Multinational companies have promoted localized innovations under the theme "in China, for the World", startups have quickly integrated into innovation "ecosystems", and top experts have exchanged ideas at the forum. Inside and outside the CIIE, cutting-edge technologies and forward-thinking concepts converge, with global enterprises exploring new engines for future growth. As a window into China's new development paradigm, the CIIE serves as a platform for accelerating the growth of new productive forces and advancing high-quality development, becoming an "energy field" that helps companies win the future.

The CIIE is a commitment to openness. Choosing the CIIE means choosing to push economic globalization forward through openness and cooperation. China has announced substantial measures to expand openness at the CIIE, the Hongqiao International Economic Forum has released the *World Openness Report* and the latest World Openness Index for several consecutive years, and exhibitors and buyers from all nations have explored boundless opportunities in the open, cooperative atmosphere of the "Four-Leaf Clover" . Openness is the path to global

prosperity and development, and it is a hallmark of modern China. As a platform for promoting high-level openness, the CIIE raises the banner of openness, fosters a consensus on cooperation, and acts as a booster for trade liberalization and investment facilitation.

The "CIIE Stories" we share not only document the passionate dedication and beautiful visions behind the CIIE but also record the CIIE's efforts in building an open world economy and a community of shared future for mankind. The CIIE will continue to write more historic chapters on the path of promoting economic globalization that is more open, inclusive, beneficial to all, balanced, and win-win. The "CIIE Stories" will continue to be written by you, me, and more "CIIE partners".

Contents

Door of Opportunity

Door of Opportunity

Power of Innovation

Power of Innovation

Beauty of Development

Beauty of Development

Promise of Openness

Promise of Openness

Afterword

Door of Opportunity

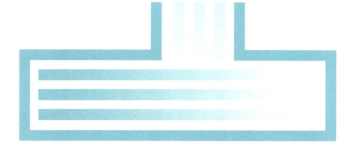

From French Farms to Chinese Dining Tables

People regard food as their primary need. Far away on the other end of the Eurasian continent, France, like China, enjoys a global reputation for its cuisine. Today, "Taste of France" travels across the seas, bringing "From French Farms to Chinese Dining Tables" into reality, enriching the taste buds of the Chinese people and meeting the increasing demand of more and more individuals in the country for a transition from "eating enough" to "eating well".

36-Hour Journey to China

There's a saying called "eating in Guangzhou". In this city famous for its cuisine, residents understand that the best dishes come from the freshest ingredients. Oysters, lobsters, mussels, and other seafood from France can be simply cooked or even eaten raw as if they were freshly plucked from the Atlantic Ocean.

Just two days ago, these sea delicacies were still being harvested; they were then inspected, packed, and flown directly to China. Thanks to a comprehensive rapid coordination mechanism established under the joint promotion of leaders from both countries, these fresh aquatic products can clear customs in-flight and upon landing are delivered via cold chain logistics straight to supermarkets, restaurants, and eateries.

Charente-Maritime is a major oyster-producing region in France. Jacques Kokolos, an oyster farmer from this province, says that their oysters can reach China in less than 36 hours.

For seafood producers like Kokolos, China is one of the world's largest consumers of aquatic products and presents a massive attraction. With the improvement of living standards, people have a growing demand for premium and distinctive goods, indicating an enormous market potential. "Lambert Oysters", an oyster exporter from Charente-Maritime, mentioned in an interview with French television that their exports to China increased more than fourfold between 2016 and 2023.

Authentic French Flavors

Maxim's, an authentic French restaurant in the Fifth Avenue, located in the center of

French wines exhibited at the French Pavilion during the 2nd CIIE [Photo / Zhang Yuwei, Xinhua News Agency]

Tianjin, China, is where French chef Alain Lemar serves as an executive chef. He says that many Chinese people have a yearning for French cuisine and come to taste it here.

What many regular customers often overlook is that the sauces used in preparing the dishes are the "soul" of the meal. With the smooth development of Sino-French trade and economic relations, French-origin condiments and ingredients is accessible to making these sauces. In fact, guests really enjoy this authentic French flavor.

In a supermarket in Nankai District, there is a wide variety of food items from France with diverse brands available. Liu Yang, a local resident, says, "My child really enjoys French cheese, and my parents have a preference for French wines. Nowadays, there are many import channels, and we can buy French wines at different prices according to our needs."

French meat products are also rapidly entering the Chinese market. Meng Fan, the chief representative for China of the INAPORC, states that China is currently the largest export market for French pork outside

A supermarket in Nankai District, Tianjin sells various types of imported cheeses from France and other places. [Photo / Wang Hui, Xinhua News Agency]

the EU. Maxence Bigar, Chair of the Foreign Trade Committee of INTERBEV, notes that French meat companies are actively engaged in the mechanism of "From French Farms to Chinese Dinner Tables", bringing a greater variety of high-quality French meat products to the Chinese market.

Mutual Benefits and Win-Win Cooperation

In recent years, there has been a continuous growth in Sino-French agricultural and food product trade. According to the General Administration of Customs of the People's Republic of China, France is China's top agricultural product import source within the EU and its second-largest agricultural trade partner. As of the first half of 2023, over 200 types of French agricultural and food products, including seafood, dairy products, meat products, breeding livestock, poultry, fruits, and others, had been approved for export to China, with nearly 7,000 French agricultural and food production enterprises registered in China.

In April 2023, under the joint promotion of the leaders of both countries, China and France established the mechanism of "From French Farms to Chinese Dinner Tables", accelerating the process of French agricultural and food products entering Chinese households. At the 6th CIIE held in Shanghai in November 2023, over 40 French agricultural and food companies made a collective appearance and engaged in face-to-face negotiations with Chinese buyers. Among them, Freshippo alone signed agreements with seven French companies on the spot to import French meat, cheese, and wine worth 3 billion yuan over the next three years.

Beyond agricultural and food trade, both sides have continuously expanded their cooperation. This includes strengthening agricultural technology collaboration, jointly training agricultural professionals, conducting exchanges on rural policies, enhancing people-to-people and institutional interactions, and promoting more fruitful partnerships in the agricultural sector.

The year 2024 marks the 60th anniversary of establishing diplomatic relations between China and France and China-France Year of Culture and Tourism. The Chinese Pavilion makes its debut at the historic Salon International de l'Agriculture. Additionally, France will be the guest country at the 2024 China International Fair for Trade in Services and the 7th CIIE in Shanghai. The two major agricultural countries are working together towards their shared goal.

Peng Mengyao, Yang Jun, Wang Hui

(Translated by Chen Xu)

CIIE Boosts Nicaragua's Food Access to Chinese Market

Nicaragua, known as the "Land of Lakes and Volcanoes," is located in the heart of Central America, bordered by Honduras to the north, Costa Rica to the south, the Caribbean Sea to the east, and the Pacific Ocean to the west. Thanks to its advantageous geographical location and climate, Nicaragua produces a wide range of high-quality agricultural products, earning it the title of the "Granary of Central America." Since the resumption of diplomatic relations between China and Nicaragua in December 2021, Nicaragua's top-quality products have rapidly entered the Chinese market, aided by the CIIE.

A Long-Awaited Opportunity

Following the reestablishment of diplomatic ties between the two countries, the word "China" has increasingly appeared in the daily lives of Nicaraguans. Many in the country have recognized that if their premium products could gain recognition in the Chinese market, it would present a significant economic opportunity for Nicaragua.

Less than a year after the resumption of relations, Nicaragua

Nicaragua makes its debut in offline participation in the 6th CIIE.

participated in the 5th CIIE's Country Exhibition virtually. In 2023, with the goal of expanding into the Chinese market, Nicaragua sent a high-level delegation to China to participate in the 6th CIIE, showcasing local products like coffee, seafood, beef, and rum to Chinese consumers. This marked the country's first in-person participation in the expo.

Ahead of the trip to China, several officials in the Nicaraguan delegation conveyed an optimistic outlook through media outlets. Laureano Ortega, the President's Advisor on Investment, Trade, and International Cooperation, expressed high expectations for the expo, saying, "We hope that Nicaragua's premium products will be well-received in the Chinese market. We also want to better understand the demand for our goods in China. Additionally, we hope this will attract more Chinese companies and entrepreneurs to invest in Nicaragua, particularly in industries like coffee cultivation and beef processing."

Iván Acosta Montalván, Minister of Finance and Public Credit, voiced the sentiment of Nicaragua's business community, stating: "This is their first exposure to such a massive market, and it's an opportunity the Nicaraguan economy has long been awaiting."

Michael Campbell, Nicaragua's Ambassador to China, on his first visit to the "Four-Leaf Clover" (the CIIE venue), also viewed the expo as a long-awaited opportunity for Nicaragua's business community. He expressed confidence in the Chinese market in a media interview, "We have many high-quality agricultural products, and I'm confident they will find their way into the Chinese market."

Opening the Chinese Market through the CIIE

"Chinese buyers lined up just to get a taste of Nicaragua's premium beef." More than a month after the 6th CIIE concluded, the scene was still vivid in the memory of José Bermúdez, Nicaragua's Minister of Development, Industry, and Trade. According to records, Nicaragua leads Central America in beef production. During the expo, Ambassador Campbell highlighted beef as one of Nicaragua's proudest products and expressed hope that more Chinese families could enjoy its delicious taste. In April 2024, during a meeting with a Chinese company, Ambassador Campbell revealed that Nicaragua has a cattle stock of six million, with over 80% exported to Europe and North America. The plan for the next five years is to double this stock, with China identified as the

most promising growth market.

In addition to beef, Nicaraguan lobster from the Caribbean coast became a "star product" at the 6th CIIE. The fresh, tender lobster meat drew long lines of visitors eager to taste this delicacy from a distant land. As the crowd gathered, Nicaraguan exhibitors enthusiastically promoted their offerings: "Our lobsters are sourced from the Caribbean Sea. Try some! And this crab meat, also from the Caribbean, is equally popular!"

Through the platform provided by the CIIE, Nicaragua's business community gained direct access to China's vast market of over 1.4 billion population and established connections with several Chinese companies. As a result, Nicaragua's products successfully made their way into the Chinese market, filling local businesses with great enthusiasm.

Sustained Benefits from Diplomatic Relations

In recent years, through active participation in the CIIE, Nicaragua's premium products have gradually gained recognition in China.

Nicaragua's Booth at the 6th CIIE National Exhibition.
[Photo / Xinhua News Agency]

This success is closely tied to the many benefits that have flowed from the resumption of diplomatic relations between the two countries.

In December 2021, China and Nicaragua resumed ambassadorial-level diplomatic relations, ushering in a new era of cooperation. The relationship has since developed rapidly, with practical cooperation in various fields advancing swiftly, injecting fresh momentum into Nicaragua's economic growth.

In July 2022, the two countries signed the Early Harvest Arrangement of the Free Trade Agreement Between the Government of People's Republic of China and the Government of the Republic of Nicaragua (herein after called "Early Harvest Arrangement") and jointly announced the commencement of negotiations for a comprehensive free trade agreement. Notably, Nicaraguan beef, which gained significant attention at the CIIE, was one of the agricultural products agreed upon for export to China under the Early Harvest Arrangement.

In December 2023, China and Nicaragua officially established a strategic partnership. The Joint Statement on the Establishment of a

On December 31, 2021, the reopening ceremony of the Chinese Embassy in Nicaragua was held in Managua, the capital of Nicaragua. [Photo / Xinhua News Agency]

Strategic Partnership noted Nicaragua's willingness to use platforms like the CIIE to expand exports to China.

Since the Free Trade Agreement between China and Nicaragua took effect on January 1, 2024, Nicaragua's exports to China have seen a notable increase. According to the latest customs data, from January to August 2024, the total value of Nicaraguan goods imported by China reached 47.508 million USD, marking a 156.7% year-on-year growth.

While Nicaragua's exports to China are experiencing rapid growth, new opportunities also bring new challenges. Ambassador Campbell pointed out that Nicaragua's current challenge is to quickly enhance the added value of its existing products and offer more goods and services that appeal to the Chinese market. To address this, the Nicaraguan Embassy in China plans to continue participating in investment and trade promotion activities, including the CIIE.

As the 7th CIIE approaches, Nicaragua is steadily advancing, from its online debut at the 5th CIIE, to its first in-person showcase at the 6th, and now as a guest country of honor at the 7th CIIE. With each step, Nicaragua is moving confidently towards the opportunities presented by the CIIE.

At the 7th CIIE Country Exhibition, Nicaragua will showcase its culture, tourism highlights, export products, and economic potential across several themed areas, presenting a comprehensive image of the country's strengths and unique charm. Under the continued benefits of resumed diplomatic relations, Nicaragua is poised for great success at the CIIE, and visitors are sure to be impressed by the country's offerings.

(Sources: People's Daily, Xinhua News Agency, CGTN, CCTV News App, Global Times, Beijing Daily App, Greater Bay Area Voice, Ministry of Foreign Affairs of the People's Republic of China, General Administration of Customs of China, Zhanjiang Cold Chain Logistics Association, etc.)

(Translated by Guo Yuhang)

Egypt Treasures Radiate Brilliance at CIIE

Bright's booth at the 6th CIIE.[Photo / cctv.com]

Egypt, an important African trading partner of China, has participated in the CIIE for six consecutive years, and also served as the guest of honor country at the first expo.

Through the CIIE, more and more Egyptian products are gaining recognition in the Chinese market, boosting confidence among Egyptian businesses.

Egypt's textile industry has long been a staple of the country's economy and is renowned worldwide, providing top-quality raw materials for the Chinese textile industry. Bright, an Egyptian dyeing and processing company offering a wide range of premium hand knitted yarns and threads, participated in the 6th CIIE in 2023. Within a few days, the company received numerous inquiries from businesses interested in becoming online and offline distributors of its products. The company's booth manager said, "We hope to use the CIIE to introduce our products to more Chinese consumers."

The spice industry is also a traditional industry in Egypt. In ancient times, a large number of spices were transported from countries like Egypt to China through the Maritime Silk Road. Today, by leveraging the CIIE, the Egyptian spice industry is encountering new opportunities in the Chinese market.

Last year, Hend Mahrous, export sales manager of Retaj, an Egyptian herbs exporter, participated in the CIIE for the first time, showcasing over 30 types of Egyptian specialty plant spices. "We came to China in search of business opportunities for our hometown's specialties. After participating in the CIIE, we have already received multiple orders, both from China and other countries," Mahrous said. Speaking about her achievements at the expo, she expressed great joy, stating, "The CIIE is truly a momentous event, not only bringing in orders but also offering hope for the future."

Egypt and China, both ancient civilizations, have utilized the CIIE to facilitate cultural exchange. Mahmoud Soliman, an Arabic language foreign teacher from Egypt's Cairo working at the School of Asian and African Studies of Shanghai International Studies University, became a volunteer at the 6th CIIE, participating in video broadcasts to share Chinese stories from an Egyptian perspective.

Expressing his happiness at being able to participate in the CIIE volunteer service as a foreign teacher, Soliman said, "Whether in terms

of economic cooperation or cultural exchange between China and Egypt, the CIIE serves as an excellent platform. As a teacher, I am eager to participate in and gain a deeper understanding of the CIIE." He also expressed his desire to act as a bridge by promoting economic and cultural exchanges between the two nations.

In April, a promotional event for the 7th CIIE was held in Cairo, with over 150 representatives from Egyptian government institutions, businesses, and trade associations in attendance. Sherif Al Mawardy, chairman of the Egypt Expo & Convention Authority, highlighted the outstanding results achieved by Egyptian companies participating in the 6th CIIE, providing them with a great opportunity to promote "Made in Egypt" globally. According to Mawardy, many Egyptian companies are preparing to attend this year's expo.

Mahmoud Soliman is involved in a livestream during the 6th CIIE.
[Photo / chinadaily.com.cn]

As 2024 marks the 10th anniversary of the establishment of the comprehensive strategic partnership between China and Egypt, Egyptian institutions and businesses are welcome to attend the 7th CIIE and introduce more high-quality and distinctive products to the Chinese and global markets.

A promotional event for the 7th CIIE is held in Cairo.

Sources: People's Daily, Xinhua News Agency, Guangming Daily, China Daily, China News Service, China Youth Daily, Hunan Ribao, Integrated media news center of Jiangsu Broadcasting Corporation, www.guancha. cn, Shanghai Education Television, WeChat account: sh_songjiang, International trade office of China National Textile and Apparel Council, WeChat account: SISUSAAS

(Translated by Zhao Guangmei)

Kazakh Businesses Flourish in Chinese Market

Kazakhstan businesses are gearing up to participate in the 7th CIIE on a larger scale than ever before to showcase a wider array of Kazakh products, said Arman Shakkaliyev, Kazakhstan's minister of Trade and Integration.

As one of China's neighbors, Kazakhstan has been an active participant of the CIIE since 2018. The nation's involvement in the expo gained further momentum after the launch of its export acceleration program in 2020.

The export acceleration program, designed to bolster Kazakh firms' international presence and enhance export capabilities, has been pivotal in motivating companies to explore global markers.

The QazTrade Policy Development Center, operator of the program, mobilized over 40 Kazakh organizations and enterprises to participate in the 6th CIIE, where they secured a large number of orders.

"Exporters from Kazakhstan show great interest in the CIIE," said Egemberdieva Asel Yerikovna, deputy chief executive officer of

QazTrade. She also recognized the CIIE as a valuable channel for showcasing Kazakh products to the vast Chinese market.

Kazakh enterprise Golden Camel, one of the beneficiaries of the CIIE, has established itself as a recognizable brand in the Chinese market. Over the course of six consecutive years participating in the expo, Golden Camel has witnessed a surge in orders from Chinese buyers, solidifying its position as a leading global producer with the ability to process 100 metric tons of fresh camel milk daily.

Botakoz Yelshibek, who served as a Kazakh volunteer at the CIIE since 2020, found her calling in Kazakh-China trade after being inspired by the expo's global reach and trade opportunities. Transitioning from a volunteer to an exhibitor in 2023, Yelshibek aims to introduce a wider variety of Kazakh cuisine to the Chinese market through the CIIE platform.

A few years back, Kazakh newspaper Kazakhstanskaya Pravda highlighted in a report that China's drive to increase the import

The Kazakh pavilion at the 6th CIIE attracts many buyers. [Photo / Xinhua News Agency]

Camel milk powder products from Golden Camel showcased at the 6th CIIE. [Photo / Xinhua News Agency]

Botakoz Yelshibek participates at the 3rd CIIE as a volunteer.
[Photo / courtesy of the interviewee]

of foreign goods not only contributes to its own economic growth but also benefits numerous other nations. The firsthand experiences and successes of Kazakh exhibitors in past editions of the expo serve as a vivid testament to the validity of this observation.

As the 7th CIIE approaches in the coming months, it will once again provide a gateway for the people of Kazakhstan into the vast Chinese market. Anticipation is high that Kazakhstan and China will strengthen their relations during this year's expo.

Sources: People's Daily, Xinhua News Agency, cctv.com, CCTV News app, China News Service, chinanews.com, Heilongjiang Daily,

JieFang Daily, Wenhui Daily, International Business Daily, WeChat account: DQRB6696060, WeChat account: kazembchina, Economic and Commercial Office of the Embassy of the People's Republic of China in Kazakhstan, official website of PwC.

(Translated By Zhao Guangmei)

CIIE Boosts Serbian Trade Ties with China

Serbia, China' first comprehensive strategic partner in Central and Eastern Europe, has an increasing number of businesses participating in the annual CIIE.

From 2018 to 2023, the number of Serbian exhibitors at the CIIE surged from 6 to 41, accompanied by a substantial increase in occupied exhibition space from approximately 100 square meters to nearly 700 square meters.

The products showcased by Serbian enterprises at the CIIE were mainly food and agricultural goods and consumer items. Through the expo, notable Serbian specialties such as wine, juice, cheeses, cereals, honey, jams, and meats have become popular among Chinese consumers.

The Serbian government has demonstrated its high regard for the CIIE, with the nation' President Aleksandar Vucic and Prime Minister Ana Brnabic addressing the expo' opening ceremonies through video messages and in-person appearances, respectively.

Serving as a bridge, the CIIE accelerates trade exchanges and fosters closer relations between China and Serbia. Brnabic, during her attendance at the 6th CIIE, highlighted the increasingly close cooperation between the two nations, noting a remarkable 185-fold increase in Serbian exports to China over the past decade.

The head of a Serbian company specializing in natural beverages and wines also highlighted the CIIE' significance in creating opportunities for Serbian exporters and strengthening global trade ties. He noted significant revenue growth and the formation of partnerships with numerous Chinese companies following his company' participation in the expo.

Jelena Grubor Stefanovic, director of the Chamber of Commerce and Industry of Serbia' representative office in China, has already begun preparations for the 7th CIIE following the conclusion of the 6th edition. She revealed that the rapid development of some Serbian businesses in China is attracting

The Serbian national pavilion at the 6th CIIE.

Serbian specialties showcased at the country' national pavilion during the 6th CIIE. [Photo / Chinese embassy in Serbia]

more participants to the CIIE, with a focus on showcasing products to Chinese consumers and understanding their preferences.

Stefanovic anticipates even greater opportunities for Serbian products in China following the signing of the China-Serbia Free Trade Agreement in October 2023, which will gradually eliminate tariffs on key Serbian exports to China.

"We plan to expand our exhibition space to accommodate more Serbian enterprises and provide them with opportunities at the CIIE," said Stefanovic.

Sources: Xinhua News Agency, China News Network, China Network, 21st Century Business Herald, China Business News, The Paper, Wenhui Daily, Southern Metropolis Daily, Shanghai Observer, Pudong Release.

(Translated by Zhao Guangmei)

Least Developed Countries Tap into Chinese Market Opportunities

The CIIE has provided a platform for the least developed African countries to showcase their unique agricultural products and access the Chinese market.

Sesame from Ethiopia showcased at the CIIE.

The African agricultural products pavilion at the 6th CIIE. [Photo / IC photo]

Since its first edition, the CIIE has actively invited the least developed countries (LDCs) to participate, offering each of them two free standard exhibition stands. Since the fifth edition, that number has increased to four.

In addition to the complimentary exhibition stands, the CIIE also identifies unique products with market potential from these countries and encourages them to be exhibited. Expo organizers assist exhibitors in connecting with buyers and partners, ensuring fruitful outcomes for them. Additionally, the CIIE creates opportunities for strong media coverage.

Since 2018, approximately 30 enterprises from LDCs have attended the CIIE each year in search of business opportunities. Many of these enterprises, with the support of international organizations, have made their presence felt at the expo. For instance, companies from Madagascar and Mozambique have participated through the International Trade Centre of the United Nations, while others from the Central African Republic, Niger, Angola, and Somalia have utilized the services of the European American Chamber of Commerce & Industry.

At the 6th CIIE, the China Chamber of Commerce of I/E of Foodstuffs, Native Produce and Animal By-products (CFNA) collaborated with entities such as ITC and Alibaba.com to establish an African agricultural products pavilion. The pavilion featured 20 agricultural exporters from nine of the least developed African countries, including Niger, Sudan, Ethiopia, and Benin, attracting considerable attention. Traditional African products like sesame, peanuts, and soybeans were the focus of Chinese buyers. The Benin booth was particularly popular, with a significant increase in online interest in Benin pineapples.

Data indicated that during the expo, the pavilion facilitated discussions between over 300 Chinese enterprises and African companies, with the intended purchase amounts exceeding expectations.

Sources: Xinhua, haiwainet.cn, www.un.org, CFNA

(Translated by Zhao Guangmei)

From "Sharing a Table" to "Owning 60 Square Meters"

In a modest corner of the 1st CIIE in 2018, Aker BioMarine, alongside other small and medium-sized enterprises, displayed its krill oil products on a shared table. At the time, the Norwegian biotechnology company could not have imagined that this small booth would open the door to major opportunities for its future growth.

Big Potential from a Small Booth

Aker BioMarine is dedicated to the sustainable development and utilization of marine biological resources. The company officially entered the Chinese market in 2015, gradually establishing a foothold by collaborating with Chinese clients and business partners, as well as participating in various industry expos.

To Aker BioMarine's surprise, their debut at the 2018 CIIE was an immediate success. Not only did their visibility increase, but partnerships with local companies also

Ren Yunli, director of the Gourmet Expo, live–streams at the Norwegian Seafood Pavilion during the 6th CIIE. [Photo / Norwegian Seafood Council]

accelerated, and their market share in China began to grow.

Aker BioMarine quickly realized that CIIE was more than just a large-scale exhibition—it was a dynamic platform. Here, they could not only showcase their products and technologies but also foster meaningful partnerships, promote idea exchange, and drive innovation. Additionally, the extensive exposure provided by CIIE proved invaluable for small and medium-sized enterprises (SMEs) looking to raise brand awareness and build trust with potential Chinese partners.

Since their first appearance at CIIE, Aker BioMarine has consistently attended the event, sending teams of marketing, sales, and technical experts every year. They carefully design their booth and meticulously

plan their participation, showcasing their innovative products and commitment to sustainability.

At the 5th CIIE, Aker BioMarine hosted a special seminar on "sustainable utilization of marine resources and a healthy future." By the 6th edition of the expo, the company had secured its own 60-square-meter booth, signed strategic cooperation agreements with nearly 30 clients, and supported seven live-streamed events, setting new sales records for krill oil products through these broadcasts.

The journey from "sharing a table" to "owning a 60-square-meter booth" has shown Aker BioMarine the immense potential of the Chinese market.

Mastering "Secret Code"

Unlike Aker BioMarine, which has been a "regular attendee" at the CIIE, the Norwegian Seafood Council made its debut at the 5th edition of the expo.

Though a novice, the Norwegian Seafood Council quickly found its footing, presenting under the theme "Norway, the Seafood Nation". By the 6th CIIE, they had already mastered the "traffic secret" for gaining attention. They invited Ren Yunli, a well-known food blogger, to live-stream directly from the "Norwegian Seafood Pavilion".

The live-streamed dishes included a Norwegian Arctic shrimp and mango Thai-style salad, a Norwegian salmon and avocado potato light salad, a Shanghai-style braised Norwegian Arctic cod, and an oil-free crispy Norwegian mackerel grilled Yunnan-style.

The food blogger's creative approach to cooking various types of fish showcased the delicious flavor of Norwegian seafood, while also revealing the many ways Norwegian seafood is making its way to Chinese dining tables.

A representative from the Norwegian Seafood Council stated, "CIIE is not only a platform for showcasing Norway's high-quality seafood, but also an important platform for enhancing international exchange and deepening Sino-Norwegian cooperation in seafood trade. We hope to leverage the CIIE's influence to further boost interest in seafood trade between Norway and China, strengthening cooperation and ties to meet the growing demand of Chinese consumers for premium seafood."

For the 7th CIIE in 2024, the Norwegian Seafood Council has refined its participation strategy. This time, it will be part of the Norwegian National Pavilion, aiming for a deeper understanding of the Chinese market.

With the spillover effects of the CIIE, the Norwegian Seafood Council quickly turned the "CIIE heat" into "trade heat".

Exhibits at the Norwegian Seafood Pavilion at the 6th CIIE. [Photo / Norwegian Seafood Council]

According to the latest data released by the Norwegian Seafood Council, as of July 2024, Norway exported approximately 89,856 tons of seafood to China, representing a 14% year-on-year increase, with a total export value of 4.87 billion Norwegian kroner (approximately 3.3 billion RMB). Among these exports, Norwegian salmon performed particularly well, with 26,876 tons shipped to China, generating 2.85 billion Norwegian kroner (approximately 1.9 billion RMB) in revenue.

Sigmund Bjørgo, director of the Norwegian Seafood Council, highlighted that in 2023, China was the fastest-growing market for Atlantic salmon consumption worldwide, with total consumption reaching 108,128 tons—an increase of 32,597 tons, or 43%, making China the 8th largest Atlantic salmon market globally. Moreover, China is currently the largest consumer of Atlantic salmon in Asia, consuming more than twice the amount compared to the second-largest market, Japan.

Becoming a "CIIE Recommender"

Norway's Prime Minister Jonas Gahr Støre had firsthand experience with the surging popularity of Norwegian seafood in the Chinese market. On the evening of September 10, 2024, during his visit to China, Støre made an appearance at the Shanghai East Hongqiao Center. After a brief tour, he donned a blue apron and personally promoted Norwegian seafood. Holding a tray, he invited guests to try Norwegian salmon and mackerel, enthusiastically saying, "Try it, it's very fresh."

Støre expressed his desire to export the freshest seafood to China and his hope to collaborate with relevant Chinese authorities to eliminate all barriers that make these products expensive for consumers.

By participating in the CIIE, Norwegian organizations such as Aker BioMarine and the Norwegian Seafood Council have reaped significant rewards, prompting Norway's official efforts to encourage more Norwegian companies and products to participate in future CIIEs.

On May 13, 2024, the 7th CIIE Norway Promotional Event was held in Oslo. It was the first time that a CIIE promotional event had been hosted in Norway, and it was warmly received by the local community.

During the event, data revealed that nearly 30 Norwegian companies participated in the 6th CIIE, marking a record high in both the number of participating companies and total exhibition space.

Wang Liming, a representative from Aker BioMarine, acted as a "CIIE Recommender" at the promotional event, strongly encouraging Norwegian companies to participate in future CIIEs.

Ole Henaes, at the Norwegian Promotional Event of the 7th CIIE. [Photo / Norwegian Seafood Council]

Exhibit booth of the Norwegian Seafood Pavilion at the 6th CIIE. [Photo / Norwegian Seafood Council]

Ole Henaes, Regional Director of Innovation Norway Asia and the Middle East, remarked that an increasing number of Norwegian businesses are engaging in trade and investment with China, with ongoing collaborations between companies from both nations in fields such as clean energy and seafood. He emphasized that the CIIE is an excellent platform for showcasing the latest products and technologies, fostering cooperation, and facilitating exchanges. Innovation Norway remains committed to promoting Norwegian products on the international stage, including in China, and will continue to organize businesses to participate in future CIIEs to help Norwegian companies expand their presence in the Chinese market.

Miao Lu

(Translated by Chen Xu)

Peruvian Alpaca Plush Toys Enter Chinese Market

The fluffy and vibrant alpaca plush toys showcased at the 6th CIIE captured the attention of many visitors.

These adorable handicrafts were crafted from alpaca wool by Peruvian artisans, including Oswaldo Mamani and his family.

Oswaldo Mamani showcases the giant panda plush toy made from alpaca wool. [Photo / Xinhua News Agency]

At 50 years old, Mamani has been creating and selling alpaca wool decorations since he was a teenager. In 2016, Chinese customer Ma Yuxia visited Mamani's small shop in Peru and purchased two alpaca plush toys, setting the stage for their eventual appearance at the CIIE.

At the inaugural CIIE in 2018, Ma brought Mamani's alpaca plush toys to the expo.

Despite being displayed in a modest nine-square-meter booth, this debut led to a surge in orders. Over 10 families from the Mamani clan are now engaged in the production of the toys, expanding their product range from alpacas to include pandas, penguins, rabbits, and dozens of other varieties.

Discussing their latest creation, the giant panda plush toy, Mamani explained, "We know that pandas are a symbol of China and are beloved in the country, so we got the idea to make panda plush toys from alpaca wool. We also noticed that the mascot at the CIIE was a giant panda."

From the 1st CIIE to the 6th, these Peruvian alpaca wool toys have been a part of every expo, showcasing their unique charm to the world.

"Taking our products to participate in the CIIE was our dream," Mamani said, adding that as traditional Peruvian artisans, "We are very grateful to China and Chinese consumers for appreciating and recognizing our work."

Peru, as the home to the largest population of alpacas globally, is a leading producer of alpaca wool textiles. Many families in the Peruvian Andes region raise alpacas and craft alpaca wool products for a living.

"China has opened up markets for our products," said Mamani. In his view, the continuous expansion of the Chinese market has contributed to the growth of the local handicraft industry in Peru.

"The Chinese market has potential, strong consumer power,

and rapid demand growth. We now deliver orders every two months, with each order ranging from 8,000 to 10,000 items," Mamani shared.

Thanks to Chinese market as well as their hard work, the Mamani family has reaped the tangible benefits of the "alpaca economy", expanding their single-floor workshop to three. "We love making handicrafts, and now we not only earn more money but also lead better lives," Mamani added.

Alejandra Bedregal, one of the Peruvian partners of the Mamani couple's collaboration with Chinese brands, said, "The CIIE, in particular, has broadened our horizons and given us a deeper understanding of the Chinese market, urging us to continue innovating and improving."

"I definitely want to go to China again to attend this year's CIIE," Bedregal expressed.

Xi Yue，Zhu Yubo, Li Muzi

(Translated by Zhao Guangmei)

A Peruvian artisan makes alpaca plush toys. [Photo / Xinhua News Agency]

Beauty of Development

Benin Pineapples Making Big Splash in China

The CIIE has emerged as a gateway for high-quality fruits from around the world to enter the Chinese market.

Last year, Benin's pineapples, one of the West African country's main export products, leveraged the 6th CIIE to accelerate the process of entering China. Benin pineapples were granted access to the Chinese market in September last year, with the first batch arriving in November.

Additionally, the CIIE provides multiple support policies, including free standard booths for least developed countries such as Benin, further facilitating the entry of their specialty agricultural products into the Chinese market.

Ahead of the opening of the 6th CIIE, Simon Pierre Adovelande, Beninese ambassador to China, welcomed the first batch of Benin pineapples at the Shanghai Pudong International Airport. In his view, participating in the 6th CIIE is an important move that benefits all of Benin. It signifies that China's vast market has opened its doors to Benin pineapples.

Due to the strong interest in food among Chinese consumers, Benin pineapples became the center of attention at last year's expo, leading to numerous orders being placed. An exhibitor from Benin expressed delight, highlighting the opportunity to sign major deals with Chinese companies.

The debut of Benin pineapples at the 6th CIIE also brought potential investment. "In addition to ordering Benin pineapples, we also plan to invest in building factories in Benin, using our planting technology and advanced management experience," said the head of Africa business at a Shanghai-based company.

To Adovelande, the debut of Benin pineapples at the 6th CIIE is a result of the collaborative efforts between China and Benin in developing the Belt and Road Initiative. Additionally, he harbors greater expectations for economic and trade exchanges between the two nations.

"The BRI has opened up the Chinese market to the world, and I

Visitors at the 6th CIIE sample Benin pineapples. [Ph1oto / Xinhua News Agency]

hope that Benin's cashews, cotton, and other specialty agricultural products can also enter China in the future," said Adovelande.

Sources: People's Daily, Xinhua News Agency, Guang-ming Daily, cctv.com, chinadaily.com.cn, chinanews.com, Global Times, Beijing Daily, Tide News, Yicai, cnxk.com, International Business Daily, xw.ejcccse.cn, Beijing Daily App.

(Translated by Zhao Guangmei)

Rwandan Delights Shine at the CIIE

Rwanda, a landlocked country in East-Central Africa, has actively participated in the CIIE for six consecutive years.

The driving force behind Rwanda's unwavering commitment to the CIIE lies in the concrete advantages the country has reaped from its

Rwanda's pavilion at the 2nd CIIE.

engagement with the Chinese market through the expo.

Rwanda is known for its abundant production of chili peppers, with its Habanero chili ranking among the spiciest globally. However, due to its intense heat and limited local consumption capacity, Rwandan chili peppers have often faced challenges in finding reliable markets.

The CIIE has opened up new avenues for Rwandan chili peppers. Following the inaugural CIIE, the Rwanda Development Board signed a memorandum of cooperation with a Chinese retail giant to promote Rwandan local products in China. This initiative led to a breakthrough for Rwandan chili peppers, which quickly gained popularity in the Chinese market, even becoming a popular item during the Chinese New Year.

Additionally, chili oil and dried chili peppers from the country also gained popularity at the expo, with orders for $2 million worth of chili oil at the 1st CIIE and 17 metric tons of dried chili peppers at the 4th CIIE.

Besides chili peppers, Rwandan coffee and tea have also emerged as standout products at various editions of the CIIE.

One of the country's coffee brands, Gorilla's Coffee, made its debut at the CIIE in 2018. "The CIIE is an open platform that promotes trade and opportunities for sharing,"said David Ngarambe, chief executive officer of Gorilla's Coffee.

Since participating in the CIIE, the company's sales in the Chinese market have continuously grown, leading to the development of several commercial partnerships and further integration into the international market.

Rwanda Mountain Tea Ltd made its debut at the 2nd CIIE, where it reached a partnership agreement with a Chinese import-export trader to introduce its full range of seven premium tea drinks to China, selling them on e-commerce platforms.

With the Rwandan government actively promoting high-quality products like avocados to enter the Chinese market, future CIIE editions are expected to showcase even more high-quality Rwandan products.

Sources: People's Daily, Xinhua News Agency, people.cn, CCTV News, Beijing Daily, Economic Herald, China Today, Cankao Xiaoxi, Shanghai Observer, The Paper, Knews, Chinafrica, China—Africa Economic and Trade Research Institute, China—Africa Trade Research Center, beijingreview.com.cn, hangzhou.com.cn, official websites of related companies.

(Translated by Zhao Guangmei)

Ethiopian Agricultural Products Soar in Chinese Market

Ethiopian coffee has been rapidly gaining traction in the Chinese market in recent years, with sales growing at a staggering rate of 27 percent annually.

This rapid growth has been significantly boosted by platforms such as the CIIE and cross-border e-commerce, which serve as effective gateways for overseas brands to enter China and present numerous opportunities for Ethiopian businesses.

One standout success story is the Ethiopian coffee brand Gera, which showcased roasted coffee beans at the 3rd CIIE. During the expo, the brand's Yirgacheffe and Sidamo coffees were signed up to a prominent cross-border e-commerce platform, immediately available for consumers.

During the 5th CIIE, Ethiopian highland coffee with vibrant orange packaging was drawing eyes. After being showcased in an e-commerce livestream during the expo, 17,000 boxes were sold in just one evening. Online sales of Ethiopian coffee surged 300 percent during the 6th CIIE.

Traditionally, Ethiopian coffee growers and processors only

accounted for less than 10 percent of profits in the export trade, with the majority of profits lying in distribution and sales. Leveraging the CIIE for cross-border e-commerce sales has effectively reduced trade costs, benefiting Ethiopian coffee farmers and allowing Chinese consumers to enjoy premium coffee beans at more affordable prices.

Witnessing the growing popularity of Ethiopian coffee among Chinese consumers, Tefera Derbew Yimam, Ethiopian ambassador to China, expressed great delight. He noted that China has become one of the primary importers of Ethiopian coffee. Ethiopian coffees have received rave reviews at the CIIE over the years, prompting many businesses to showcase their products at the event. "The embassy will continue to facilitate Ethiopian business participation in the expo," Yimam said.

Ethiopia's pavilion at the CIIE.

Ethiopian products at the 6th CIIE attract buyers.

Coffee trade is just one aspect of the trade relationship between China and Ethiopia. Products like sesame seeds and green beans from Ethiopia have also made their way to supermarkets, stores, and retail markets in China.

At the 6th edition of the expo, Ethiopian sesame trader Duka Engineering & Trading Plc reached a preliminary cooperation agreement with Shandong's Ruifu Sesame Oil Co Ltd, which would purchase 6,000 metric tons of sesame seeds.

In October 2023, Ethiopia and China upgraded their bilateral relationship to an all-weather strategic partnership. In a joint statement, China expressed its desire to continue encouraging and supporting Ethiopian exports to China, including agricultural and food products.

With the Chinese market serving as a key driver of Ethiopian exports, Ethiopia's distinctive offerings are expected to make a splash at this year's expo, presenting vast business opportunities for its enterprises.

Sources: People's Daily, Xinhua News Agency, CCTV financial channel, haiwainet.cn, gmw.cn, rmzxb.com.cn, International Financial News, International Business Daily, WeChat account: Enter_Ethiopia, Haibao News, Tianxia Quancheng app, Alibaba Design Innovation Center, Fana Broadcasting Corporate S.C.

(Translated by Zhao Guangmei)

Tanzanian Specialty Products Ride "CIIE Express"

In a testament to the burgeoning economic partnership between China and Tanzania, the CIIE has emerged as a pivotal platform for showcasing Tanzania's unique products to a global audience.

Over the past six years, Tanzania has consistently showcased its agricultural products at CIIE, with its renowned coffee taking center stage. Coffee, a staple among Tanzania's traditional export crops, thrives in the country's southern highlands, particularly around Mount Kilimanjaro. The volcanic soil of the Kilimanjaro region imbues the coffee with a luxurious texture and a delicate acidity, rendering it truly distinctive.

While exporting agricultural products to China typically entails more intricate procedures than regular goods, the CIIE has streamlined the process through a range of favorable policies, facilitating Tanzanian coffee companies like Afri Tea & Coffee Blenders (1963) Ltd in exporting their coffee products to the Chinese market.

At the 6th CIIE, Afri Tea & Coffee Blenders found a coffee distributor for its products. Beyond mere transactions, the company aimed to use CIIE as a gateway to the Chinese market, seeking to

The Tanzania's pavilion at the 6th CIIE.

establish enduring partnerships and construct a robust and dependable supply chain.

Cashews, another jewel in Tanzania's agricultural crown, also made a significant impact at the expo. In 2023, the 6th CIIE yielded promising results for Tanzania, with cashews being the top-selling Tanzanian product at the event. Tanzanian cashews have become one of the most popular Tanzanian specialties at the expo.

Moreover, seaweed sourced from Zanzibar, Tanzania, a distinctive product with versatile applications as a food ingredient or industrial resource, seized the opportunity to showcase itself to the Chinese audience at the CIIE.

With the backing of the economic and commercial office of the Chinese embassy in Tanzania, Tanzanian entrepreneurs showcased seaweed-based products like soaps, teas, and essential oils for the first time at the CIIE.

A Tanzanian businessman expressed optimism that if Zanzibar seaweed gains a foothold in the Chinese market through the CIIE, it could significantly contribute to local female employment, improving their economic status and living standards.

The CIIE has become an excellent platform for promoting trade

Abdulhakim Mulla (left), head of Afri Tea & Coffee Blenders, introduces the company's coffee offerings to Chen Mingjian, Chinese ambassador to Tanzania (middle).

[Photo / JieFang Daily]

between China and Tanzania, serving as an important window for enhancing economic and trade exchanges.

In 2023, the bilateral trade volume between China and Tanzania reached $8.78 billion, an 8.9 percent increase year-on-year. China has remained Tanzania's largest trading partner for eight consecutive years. To promote bilateral trade, China has granted zero-tariff treatment for 98 percent of Tanzanian products, including avocados, seafood, and cashews.

As China and Tanzania gear up to celebrate the 60th anniversary of their diplomatic relations this year, the enduring partnership stands as a beacon of China-Africa cooperation, setting an example of South-South Cooperation.

Looking forward, the 2024 Summit of the Forum on China-Africa Cooperation to be held in Beijing in September and the 7th CIIE set for November in Shanghai will continue to provide further avenues for dialogue and cooperation between the two nations. The 7th CIIE, in particular, will highlight the tangible outcomes of cooperation between China and

Seaweed–based products like soaps, teas, and essential oils on display at the CIIE.
[Photo / Xinhua News Agency]

Tanzania, advance the Belt and Road Initiative, taking Sino-Tanzanian trade to new heights of mutual benefit.

Sources: Xinhua News Agency, JieFang Daily, Xiaoxiangyan, the economic and commercial office of the Chinese embassy in Tanzania.

(Translated by Zhao Guangmei)

Laotian Agricultural Products Flourish in Chinese Market

Since the opening of the China-Laos Railway in December 2021, an increasing number of Laotian products have been transported to China by train.

While the China-Laos Railway serves as one of the links between Laotian products and the Chinese market, the CIIE, the world's first national-level import-themed trade fair, has played a crucial role in introducing Laotian products to Chinese consumers.

In 2018, Laotian tea company Three Six Manor showcased their tea products crafted from locally sourced ancient trees at the inaugural CIIE. The unique tropical flavors and rich tea brew made Laotian tea products a standout at the expo, attracting a flurry of orders. Following this success, Laotian tea companies, including Three Six Manor, began exporting their tea products to China.

In the subsequent years, in addition to Three Six Manor, companies like Gold Champa and San Wan Lao have also presented their ancient tree tea products at the CIIE, diversifying tea options for Chinese consumers. The increasing popularity benefited from the expo has positioned ancient tree tea as a new flagship product for Laotian agricultural exports.

Saysomphet Norasing, director of the trade promotion department at Laos' Ministry of Industry and Commerce, said that the country looks forward to leveraging favorable conditions such as China-Laos Railway and utilizing platforms like the CIIE as well as the vast Chinese market to promote Laotian ancient tree tea globally and benefit more Laotian people through the tea industry.

Laos' ancient tree tea products showcased at the 6th CIIE. [Photo / Xinhua News Agency]

Apart from tea products, the Department of Agriculture and Forestry in Laos' Luang Namtha province signed an international agricultural economic and technical cooperation agreement with Guizhou An Guang International Supply Chain Co at the 6th CIIE, focusing on high-quality chili cultivation and procurement supply chain cooperation projects.

Since the beginning of 2024, the cooperative project has been yielding results. As of May this year, An Guang International has selected and cultivated four high-quality chili varieties in Luang Namtha, and is currently applying for a certificate of origin for quality agricultural products.

Sample chili cultivation trial field in Luang Namtha province. [Photo / Eyes News]

Additionally, the high-quality chili cultivation area led by the demonstration base in Luang Namtha is in the process of applying for inclusion in the list of agricultural products eligible for export to China. The projected total yield of chili for 2024 is over 15,000 metric tons, with an expected export value of over 70 million yuan ($9.63 million).

Currently, preparations for the 7th CIIE are progressing smoothly, and more Laotian products are expected to dazzle Chinese consumers again at this year's expo.

Sources: People's Daily, Xinhua News Agency, cctv.com, chinanews.com, Farmers' Daily app, Wenhui Daily, Renmin Tiedao, Youth Daily, Guiyang Daily, jschina.com.cn, gog.cn, Eyes News, The Guizhou People's Association for Friendship with Foreign Countries, WeChat account: sitxyh1.

(Translated by Zhao Guangmei)

Cambodia Eyes CIIE to Explore Opportunities

Cambodia, a country renowned for its rich culture, tourism attractions, and diverse agricultural products, has been expanding its export markets and promoting tourism through its participation in the annual CIIE since 2018.

As a major global rice exporter, Cambodia has been actively seeking opportunities to expand into international markets. At the 6th CIIE, Cambodian jasmine rice featured at the Cambodian pavilion garnered interest from buyers, sparking inquiries about pricing and future collaborations.

Oknha Song Saran, chairman of the board of the Cambodia Rice Federation (CRF), said there had been an increase of Cambodian rice exports to China following its presence at the CIIE. "I believe Cambodian rice will become more and more popular in China," he said.

Lun Yeng, secretary general of CRF, also agreed that the CIIE has played a significant role in promoting the export of Cambodian rice to China. "We hope more Chinese consumers will enjoy pollution-free Cambodian rice through the CIIE."

According to data released by CRF in January, Cambodia exported a total of over 650,000 metric tons of rice in 2023, with 212,800 tons being shipped to China. China has become the largest market for Cambodian rice exports.

In addition to rice, Cambodia is also a significant mango production hub in Southeast Asia, blessed with ample sunshine and abundant rainfall that contribute to the fruit's delicate texture and rich aroma.

In May 2021, a refrigerated container cargo ship carrying fresh Keo Romeat mangoes from Cambodia docked at Qinzhou Port in South China's Guangxi Zhuang autonomous region, marking the first-ever export of Cambodian fresh mangoes to China. Mangoes, following bananas, became the second fresh fruit directly exported from Cambodia to China.

While the export of mangoes to China is a significant milestone, the true turning point came with the 4th CIIE held six months later, when Cambodian mangoes were promoted at the expo and drew much interest from buyers.

Cambodian rice products showcased at the 6th CIIE.

Keo Romeat mangoes from Cambodia at the CIIE. [Photo / Yunnan Daily]

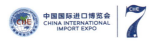

Cambodia's unique decorative items showcased at the booth of Cambodia Angkor Air during the 5th CIIE. [Photo / Cambodia Angkor Air]

Chea Munyrith, president of the Cambodian Chinese Evolution Researcher Association, said that Cambodian fresh mangoes will become widespread in the Chinese market and around the world through the CIIE.

The CIIE has not only stimulated exports of Cambodian agricultural products but has also showcased the country's abundant tourism attractions. Cambodia Angkor Air, for instance, made its debut at the 5th CIIE, highlighting iconic elements of Cambodian culture such as the intricate Apsara carvings from Angkor Wat.

"Chinese tourists enjoy traveling to Cambodia and visiting Angkor Wat, "said Yin Zheng, general manager of the Cambodia Angkor Air Shanghai representative office." We hope to build an air bridge connecting the two countries by leveraging the CIIE to facilitate cultural and tourism exchanges,"Yin added.

According to Cambodia's Ministry of Tourism, in the first quarter of this year, Cambodia attracted 190,000 visitor arrivals from China, up 43 percent compared to the same period in the previous year. Ticket revenue from Angkor Wat increased by 38.2 percent year-on-year.

Penn Sovicheat, the Cambodian Ministry of Commerce's secretary of state and spokesperson, appreciated that the CIIE demonstrates China's unwavering commitment to boosting global trade, promoting multilateralism, and opening up its market to the outside world.

Due to the huge potential of the Chinese market, Cambodia

The Cambodian Ministry of Commerce calls on businesses in the country to actively participate in the 7th CIIE. [Photo / khmertimeskh.com]

has confirmed its participation in the 7th CIIE, aiming to enhance partnerships and foster collaborations with China.

Sources: People's Daily, Xinhua News Agency, Economic Daily, chinanews.com, rmlt.com.cn, China Tourism News, Knews, Orient International, Yunnan Daily, WeChat account of related firms, Khmer Times.

(Translated by Zhao Guangmei)

Overseas Chinese Businesses and CIIE: A Tale of Mutual Growth

As both "guests" and "hosts," overseas Chinese businesses (enterprises founded by overseas Chinese) experience a unique sensation when participating in the CIIE. They support and engage in this global event in various ways, while the CIIE, in turn, opens doors of opportunity for their growth. Behind the continuous improvement of the CIIE lies the mutual achievements between overseas Chinese businesses and the expo.

Deep Emotional Connection as "Hosts"

"Participating in the CIIE every year is not only a smart business decision but also driven by a strong emotional resonance," said Zhai Jingli, vice-president of Sinar Mas Group APP (China). For seven consecutive years, Sinar Mas Group APP (Asia Pulp & Paper Co.,Ltd.) has been an active participant in the CIIE. "We see the CIIE as the most anticipated event each year. We are both 'guests' and 'hosts' here."

The CIIE provides a platform for overseas Chinese enterprises, including Sinar Mas Group APP, to showcase themselves and connect with global resources.

Sinar Mas Group APP's exhibit booth at the 3rd CIIE. [Photo / Sinar Mas Group]

Chia Tai Group (also called: Charoen Pokphand Group or CP Group), an iconic overseas Chinese business with over a century of history, was founded in Thailand in 1921 and entered China in 1979. It was the first foreign company to invest in mainland China after the country's Reform and Opening-up policy and has since established over 600 enterprises in China.

CP Group has participated in every CIIE to date. "The CIIE has created an important platform for CP to engage in exchanges and cooperation," said Xie Yi, senior vice chairman of CP Group and CEO of CP Investment Co., Ltd. On one hand, the CIIE has deepened CP's "Buy globally, sell globally" trade strategy. On the other hand, it attracts global buyers and partners, helping the company

explore new market channels and discover new business opportunities.

Yihai Kerry Arawana Holdings Co., Ltd. President Mu Yankui also expressed deep affection for the CIIE, stating, "This is a platform where China sets the stage for the world to participate and share. We've witnessed the continued success of the CIIE, and the expo has broadened our business development as well."

Oishi, a well-known brand among Chinese consumers, was founded by the Philippines-based Liwayway Holdings Co., Ltd.. Starting as a small family-run workshop in Manila in 1946, the company became a limited corporation in 1966, and by 1993, it had invested in manufacturing plants in China. Oishi's brand has steadily gained more

CP Group's booth at the CIIE. [Photo / CP Group]

recognition. Larry Chan, Chairman of Oishi China Co., Ltd., is a third-generation Chinese Filipino, born and raised in the Philippines. Under his leadership, elements of Philippine Chinatown and the "Three Treasures of the Chinese Filipino" were showcased at Oishi's CIIE booth. For Xu, participating in the CIIE has strengthened Oishi's confidence in establishing deeper roots in China.

A "Fast Track"

From a "global expo" to a "global platform," the CIIE has captivated Chinese-owned businesses worldwide. Their deep participation in the expo has also shortened the distance between their countries of residence and China. Leveraging the CIIE as an opportunity, these companies have accelerated their integration into the Chinese market and are sharing in the country's growth.

Founded in 1938 by renowned Indonesian-Chinese businessman Huang Yicong, Sinar Mas Group Asia Pulp & Paper Co.,Ltd. subsidiary entered China as early as 1992. Today, APP's products and business span the globe.

Oishi's booth at the 4th CIIE.
[Photo / Oishi]

Wilmar International's exhibit booth at previous CIIEs.
[Photo / Wilmar International]

"The CIIE not only helps Indonesian companies integrate into the Chinese market more smoothly, but it also serves as a crucial 'fast track' to access China," said Zhai Jingli. She emphasized that the CIIE is a stage for showcasing products and technology, as well as an essential window for understanding China's investment policies and identifying partnership opportunities. Over the past six years, APP has garnered over $700 million in intended orders at the CIIE, fully demonstrating the strong international procurement power of the expo.

"There is a Chinese saying, 'A rising tide lifts all boats.,'" noted Xie Yi. The spillover effect of the CIIE continue to unfold, and CP Group has achieved remarkable growth in China. Its agribusiness, food, retail, pharmaceuticals, real estate, and financial sectors have all seen significant progress, with investments covering every province in the country.

In addition to seizing CIIE opportunities for their own companies, overseas Chinese businesses have also actively served as bridges, helping companies from their countries of residence expand into the Chinese market. At the 5th CIIE, Larry Chan devoted extra time to promoting Philippine food products.

Known as the "Fruit Basket of the Pacific", the Philippines exports a wide variety of tropical fruits like bananas, mangoes, and papayas worldwide. Larry Chan noted that China's vast market and potential are incredibly attractive to Philippine businesses. "Resource sharing and market connectivity—China's market is the world's market, a shared market, and everyone's market. China's commitment to deepening

reforms and expanding openness will create endless opportunities for Philippine businesses," he added.

"Bridge Builders"

Over the past seven years, overseas Chinese enterprises and the CIIE have jointly written new chapters of openness, cooperation, and shared futures. Leveraging the expo's spillover effects, these businesses have quickly expanded to global markets, building bridges toward an open world economy.

One of the moments that left a lasting impression on Larry Chan was Oishi's unexpected encounter with a government delegation led by Uzbekistan's Deputy Prime Minister at the inaugural CIIE. Following that interaction, Oishi acquired land in Uzbekistan and established a factory there, formally launching the project. Xu remarked, "Opportunities like this are rare and invaluable, and this was one of the surprises CIIE brought us."

Growing from a snack food company into a diversified multinational food group, Oishi is now actively expanding into more overseas markets, setting up product lines in various countries, and offering new products and services to consumers worldwide. "As a Chinese businessman, like my father before me, I have full confidence in China, and I look forward to starting from Shanghai and discovering even more surprises," Larry Chan said.

CP Group not only organized 26 business units to participate in the 6th CIIE but also leveraged its position as a Chinese-owned enterprise to help high-quality Chinese specialty products reach global markets, creating the group's "dual strategy".

Xie Yi noted that CP Group's "buy globally, sell globally" approach allows them to assist more Chinese companies in exploring Southeast Asian markets. "We are eager to use our strengths in funding, technology, and cultural integration to establish more platforms for cooperation and exchanges, bridging China and other countries in various fields."

Zhai Jingli emphasized that the continuous participation in the CIIE also serves as a driving force for enterprises to elevate their own development, broaden their business horizons, and strengthen their influence. "A single flower does not make spring," Zhai said. "In the future, we hope to help more Chinese companies go global and tap into larger markets and opportunities."

While the experiences of overseas Chinese businesses at the CIIE vary, participating in the annual CIIE has become their shared commitment. The stories of mutual growth and achievements between these businesses and the CIIE are ongoing and yet to be continued.

Fan Yubin

(Translated by Chen Xu)

Power of Innovation

CIIE Accelerates Medical Innovation

Since its inaugural edition in 2018, the CIIE has emerged as a vital platform for showcasing innovative medical solutions, including treatments for rare diseases, and driving global medical enterprises to innovate and invest in China.

Leveraging the CIIE, numerous innovative drugs and medical devices have entered the Chinese market, providing Chinese doctors and patients with a plethora of new treatment options.

Siemens Healthineers' Naeotom Alpha, the world's first photon-counting CT scanner, has become commercially available in China just two years after its debut at the 4th CIIE.

Jerry Wang, head of China at Siemens Healthineers, said: "The CIIE has garnered attention from multiple parties, including medical products and healthcare security authorities, facilitating the expedited introduction of innovative medical devices."

Gilead Sciences' AmBisome, a drug for treating invasive fungal infections, was showcased at the 5th CIIE. It similarly received approval from China's National Medical Products Administration to enter the market just three months after the expo.

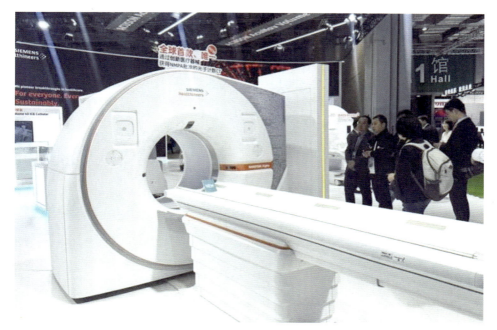

Siemens Healthineers' Naeotom Alpha showcased at the 6th CIIE.
[Photo / Xinhua News Agency]

The CIIE has also played a significant role in accelerating the approval process for new indications of existing drugs.

Japanese pharmaceutical company Takeda's Revestive®, which is used for treating short bowel syndrome, was also featured at the 5th CIIE. Within six months after the expo, it entered trial use in medical institutions in the Boao Lecheng International Medical Tourism Pilot Zone in Hainan and received official approval from the NMPA just 15 months after the expo.

In addition to facilitating the transition of exhibits into commercial products, the CIIE has also prompted exhibitors to boost investment in China and expedite their localization strategies.

Benlysta showcased at the 2nd CIIE. [Photo / The Paper]

For example, Boston Scientific's Polaris, a PCI (percutaneous coronary intervention) guiding device, caught the attention of Shanghai's drug regulatory authority at its CIIE debut in 2019. In July 2022, the company obtained a license to produce the device in China and the first Polaris then rolled off the line in a Shanghai factory in September of the same year.

Through the CIIE, certain exhibits have also earned inclusion in China's national medical insurance catalog, which benefits the Chinese people and contributes to the Healthy China 2030 Initiative.

At the 6th CIIE, biopharmaceutical company GSK showcased its Benlysta for the fifth consecutive year. During the five years, Benlysta has been included in China's medical insurance coverage list to treat systemic lupus erythematosus in adults and children.

Vocinti, another CIIE exhibit from Takeda, used in treatment for reflux esophagitis, was also included in China's medical insurance coverage list in 2020.

"We will accelerate the introduction of more flagship products in China and actively participate in building China's medical innovation ecosystem," said Sean Shan, senior vice-president of Takeda and president of Takeda China, adding that the company will also empower the high-quality development in Chinese healthcare and contribute to the realization of Healthy China 2030 Initiative.

Sources: Xinhua News Agency, China News Network, China Network, 21st Century Business Herald, China Business News, The Paper, Wenhui Daily, Southern Metropolis Daily, Shanghai Observer, Pudong Release.

(Translated by Zhao Guangmei)

Healthcare Companies Expand Their "Suitcases"

At every edition of the CIIE, the Medical Equipment and Healthcare Products Exhibition Area is always full of fresh innovations, featuring a large number of high-tech debut products. It consistently ranks as one of the most popular exhibition zones, attracting considerable attention with its many first launches, shows, and demonstrations.

In 2023, Gilead Sciences, a global leader in biopharmaceuticals, participated in the CIIE for the second time. Transitioning from a "first-time exhibitor" to a "returning participant", Gilead expanded the size of its booth fivefold, doubled the area for showcasing its innovative products, and set up a dedicated section for its research pipeline. This area focused on presenting Gilead's global R&D pipeline and its clinical research and product launch plans in China.

In 2024, Gilead Sciences will join the CIIE for the third time, further expanding its "suitcase". At its 500-square-meter booth, the company will again showcase its growing product portfolio and innovative achievements, fully demonstrating its strength in medical innovation and its exceptional collaborations with partners to benefit

Gilead Sciences exhibit booth at the 6th CIIE. [Photo / Gilead Sciences]

Chinese patients. The exhibits will cover key areas such as virology, oncology, and mycology, with several investigational drugs being unveiled for the first time. Gilead's vice-president and general manager of China, Jim Jin, expressed great anticipation for the company's third participation in the expo.

"CIIE Babies"

Headquartered in Foster City, California, Gilead operates in more than 35 countries and regions worldwide. In 2017, the company officially launched its commercial operations in China. Over the past seven years, 11 of Gilead's globally leading drugs have been approved in China, with

8 of them included in the national medical insurance catalog.

China is one of Gilead's three most important strategic markets globally. Having participated in the CIIE twice, Gilead has witnessed the expo's spillover effects and experienced the rapid launch of its exhibited medicines.

In the Medical Equipment and Healthcare Products Exhibition Area, exhibitors are accustomed to affectionately referring to innovative drugs and devices that have transitioned from exhibits to products through the CIIE and are being used in China as "CIIE babies".

Every year, following the CIIE, a batch of these "CIIE babies" is born. After Gilead's debut at the 2022 CIIE, it successfully gained

Visitors at the Gilead Sciences exhibit booth. [Photo / Gilead Sciences]

its own "CIIE babies", including two new drugs in the antifungal and oncology fields. One of them, Ambisome®, an antifungal medicine, was approved by China's National Medical Products Administration just three months after the expo, demonstrating the "Chinese speed" of making innovative drugs accessible faster.

At the 6th CIIE in 2023, Gilead's "star product" planned for the Chinese market, Lenacapavir, a long-acting HIV drug, made its debut and attracted significant attention.

Jim Jin believes that the CIIE plays a vital role in accelerating the overall process of bringing innovative drugs to market, becoming a true "accelerator" for pharmaceutical innovation.

Expanding "Ecosystem"

After participating twice, Gilead has found that the CIIE has subtly become an "accelerator" driving its growth in China. Through this open platform, Gilead continues to strengthen collaboration and exchange with various partners.

At the 5th CIIE, Gilead partnered with the Chinese Foundation for Prevention of STD and AIDS to launch a 3-year Hepatitis C case follow-up and management project, supporting the national effort to eliminate Hepatitis C as a public health threat.

At the 6th CIIE, Gilead signed a cooperation agreement with the Chinese Foundation for Prevention of STD and AIDS and Control to promote a rapid HIV treatment initiation project, encouraging early access to standardized care for those with HIV. Additionally, it partnered

Gilead's products showcased at the CIIE. [Photo / Gilead Sciences]

with the CSCO Foundation to establish the "CSCO-Gilead Oncology Research Fund", aimed at advancing research in the oncology field.

These projects are vivid examples of Gilead's deepening win-win collaboration with China's healthcare ecosystem through the CIIE. Jim Jin noted that Gilead looks forward to further expanding its "circle of friends" in the medical ecosystem via the CIIE platform.

Increasing R&D Investment

As an essential platform for foreign enterprises to seize opportunities in China, the CIIE has become a critical channel for leading global pharmaceutical companies to connect with the Chinese market. Through its participation in the CIIE, Gilead has experienced firsthand the "exhibit to product" effect of the platform and witnessed China's determination to share development opportunities with the world. This has further strengthened Gilead's confidence in deepening its roots in the Chinese market and advancing local pharmaceutical innovation.

Today, an international consensus has been reached that the Chinese market has become a market for the world. Since 2022, Gilead China has vigorously invested in local research and development, initiating multiple clinical research projects, including Phase III clinical trials in sync with global research, covering various diseases in the fields of oncology and virology. The aim is to promote more innovative therapies to be "synchronously" launched in the Chinese market, benefiting more patients in need.

Gilead is committed to breaking through the impossible. Jim Jin stated that Gilead will continue to focus on patients and explore

 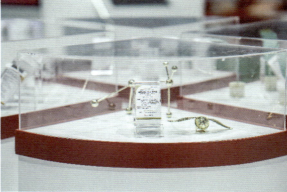

Gilead's "CIIE babies" . [Photo / Gilead Sciences]

Jim Jin, Gilead Sciences' Global vice–president and general manager of China, at the CIIE. [Photo / Gilead Sciences]

innovative cooperation with various partners, enhance multi-channel development, improve the accessibility of marketed drugs, and consistently build its local R&D capabilities, allowing more innovative medicines to benefit Chinese patients as early as possible.

Fan Yubin

(Translated by Chen Xu)

A Landmark Event in the Corporate Annals

"The Chinese market is open and attractive." The CIIE is continuing to send this strong signal to the world. Ichiro Yubaraki, who has just become general manager of Tokyo Marine Nichido Fire Insurance (China) Co.(hereinafter referred to as Tokyo Marine), has already felt the value of the signal. In his view, leading enterprises to participate in the 7th CIIE is his priority after taking office in 2024.

"By participating in the CIIE, we can learn the latest initiatives of various industries, understand the most cutting-edge technological trends, and build new business models in combination with our own business." Ichiro Yubaraki believes that in order to create a win-win situation, the expo is "an excellent platform to inspire thinking".

Cultivate deeply in China

Tokyo Marine was founded in 1879 as the first property insurance company in the history of Japan. As a Fortune 500 company, Tokyo Marine has been operating in China for more than 30 years.

Many multinational companies regard the CIIE as a "new channel" to understand and enter the Chinese market, and for "established" foreign

Ichiro Yubaraki, director and general manager of Tokyo Marine Nichido Fire Insurance (China) Co., LTD. [Photo / Kang Yuzhan]

companies that have been deeply engaged in China for many years, the CIIE has a deeper meaning.

"The CIIE opens the door for us to seize cooperation opportunities and access to the Chinese market, helping us to enhance social value while realizing economic value." Said Ichiro Yubaraki.

In 1992, Shanghai became the first pilot city in the Chinese mainland to open up to the outside world in the insurance industry, and many foreign-funded insurance companies successively settled in Shanghai. In 1994, Tokyo Marine opened a branch office in Shanghai, which was the first foreign property insurance company in China.

After 30 years in Shanghai, Tokyo Marine is not only a witness and beneficiary of the development of China's insurance industry, but also a participant and promoter.

The Priorities

Reviewing the development trajectory of the past 30 years, Tokyo Marine will take "three consecutive years of participation in the CIIE" as a landmark event and record the development of enterprises in China. There are countless exhibitions attended by established foreign enterprises. Why is participation in CIIE a priority?

"The CIIE provides a platform for Tokyo Marine to show its strength and achievements." In Ichiro Yubaraki's view, the CIIE is also a vindicator for enterprises to appreciate the global development trend and adjust their development strategy in China.

"China has a huge market size, rapid economic growth and a constantly improving business environment." Having worked in Guangzhou, Shenzhen and Shanghai, Ichiro Yubaraki has his own observation and understanding of the Chinese market. In his view, with the increase of Chinese residents' wealth and awareness of risk protection, China's insurance market demand shows a trend of diversification and personalization, coupled with the continuous improvement of the policy environment, "all of which provide a broad space for the development of foreign insurance companies".

Years of working experience in China have made Ichiro Yubaraki feel the rapid changes in the Chinese market and the continuous technological innovation, "in such an environment, enterprises need to participate in solving social issues to adapt to the growth of the Chinese market".

Energy conservation and low-carbon have become an important

direction of enterprise operation, health care industry and aging innovation have become a new incremental space for business, and a large number of enterprises are carrying out industrial upgrading...... The "frontier wind" at the CIIE is an excellent opportunity for foreign companies to grasp the pulse of the Chinese market.

In 2021, under the theme of "Providing Peace of mind, Security and Contributing to a Sustainable Future", Tokyo Marine made its debut at the CIIE. In 2022, Tokyo Marine Nippon Motor (China) incorporated the "sustainable development strategy" into the company's business strategy, and combined with China's national strategy and market trends, identified four priority areas: green transformation, health and elderly care, disaster prevention and mitigation, and industrial upgrading.

Cross-border cooperation

"At this time, we are facing more and more complex social issues, such as climate change, aging population and so on." Ichiro Yubaraki feels that these social problems cannot be solved by one company alone, but require broader cooperation among enterprises to discuss solutions.

"By continuing to participate in the CIIE, Tokyo Maritime Nippon Motor (China) has met new partners and "our 'circle of friends', as we say in Chinese, keeps expanding," Mr. Ichiro Yubaraki said.

On the big stage of CIIE, "co-creation" is not only taking place between enterprises, but also new sparks of cross-border cooperation are emerging between different industries.

At the 5th CIIE, Tokyo Marine Nippon (China), Panasonic

Electric Equipment (China) Co., LTD., and Omron (China) Co., LTD., which belong to three different industrial fields of insurance, electrical manufacturing and automation solutions, signed a contract to establish a health promotion industry alliance. The three Japanese enterprises in China have reached cross-border cooperation on the stage of Jinbo, giving full play to their respective product and service advantages, and jointly building a big health service ecosystem.

As an in-depth continuation of cross-border co-creation, at the 6th CIIE "China-Japan Health Promotion and Innovation Technology Development Forum", Tokyo Marine Nippon Motor (China) and China Association for Rehabilitation Technology Transformation and Development joined hands to launch a government-industry-university-research cross-border dialogue, and jointly explore a new path for the integrated development of smart health industry in multiple fields.

"By participating in the CIIE, we can not only conduct in-depth exchanges and

At the 5th CIIE, the Health Promotion Industry Alliance was established. [Photo / Tokyo Marine]

2024 marks the 30th anniv—ersary of Tokyo Marine's investment and business in China.
[Photo / Tokyo Marine]

learn from domestic and foreign counterparts, but also discover more cooperation opportunities and potential markets, so as to realize the simultaneous improvement of the company's economic value and social value." The enlightenment of the CIIE is that enterprises can achieve steady progress by working together, said Ichiro Yubaraki.

The 7th CIIE coincides with Tokyo Marine's 30 years of investment and business in China. Ichiro Yubaraki said that participating in the 7th CIIE is a milestone for the development of Tokyo Marine in China and a new starting point for win-win cooperation. "Please come to our booth and have a look."

Li Shuzhi

(Translated by Zhang Youchao)

Top-tier Projects for CIIE Regular Exhibitors

L'Oréal's connection with the CIIE dated back to a letter in 2018. The letter outlined China's preparations for the CIIE and its plan to invite foreign businesses to share in China's development opportunities.

Upon reading the letter, the immediate reaction of Jean-Paul Agon, the then Chairman and CEO of L'Oréal China, was "This idea is fantastic." L'Oréal quickly became one of the first enthusiastic supporters of the CIIE, taking the lead in participating in the exhibition.

As a regular exhibitor at the CIIE and the rotating chairman of the council of the CIIE Enterprise Alliance for five consecutive terms, L'Oréal will participate in the exhibition for the seventh consecutive year in 2024 and has once again served as the "dual chairman" of the Council of the CIIE Enterprise Alliance and the Daily Consumer Goods Professional Committee.

Exhibits, goods, best sellers

L'Oréal's firm choice to participate in the CIIE is because the company is full of confidence in China's future development. Every year, L'Oréal customizes themes for its exhibition, bringing the latest trends and the most appealing new brands, products, technologies, and concepts

that captivate Chinese consumers to the CIIE.

Today, the CIIE has become a top-tier project for L'Oréal globally, serving as the preferred platform for the global debut of L'Oréal's new products and technologies.

Over the past seven years, L'Oreal has launched nearly 20 new international brands and dozens of beauty and black technologies at the CIIE. Many new products have changed from "exhibits to commodities, and from commodities to popular products" on the CIIE platform.

L'Oréal is deeply integrating into the CIIE and continuously increasing its investment. In 2024, L'Oréal will set up the largest single booth in the daily consumer goods industry at the 7th CIIE, covering 672 square meters. On this stage, L'Oréal will create a main booth full of artistic charm, offering the audience a grand feast that combines technology, culture, and artistry.

At that time, L'Oréal will not only debut global new products, popular beauty technology, and cross-industry collaborations for sustainable consumption, but will also decode the scientific "artistry" behind the skincare, makeup, haircare, and perfume categories.

The CIIE is not only a stage for global new products and technological debuts but also a grand event that bridges different cultures and promotes international exchange and cooperation. In 2024, coinciding with the 60th anniversary of the establishment of diplomatic relations between China and France, France will be the guest country of honor at the CIIE, showcasing to the world the longstanding friendship between the two countries and highlighting the fruitful results of their practical cooperation.

As a witness and participant of the friendship between China and France, L'Oreal will enter the French Pavilion to pay tribute to the friendship between China and France, so that French elegance and Chinese charm can reflect each other, and jointly write a beautiful and shared movement of China-France cooperation.

Sharing, co-creation and win-win

The story of cooperation at the CIIE has continued. In 2019, L'Oreal met Oriental Beauty Valley at the 2nd CIIE and jointly created the "BIG BANG Beauty Technology Innovation Program" to create a win- win situation with start-ups with cutting-edge technologies and promote open innovation in beauty technology.

In April 2023, during French President Emmanuel Macron's visit to China, witnessed by ministers of the two countries, the French track in the "BIG BANG Beauty Technology Innovation Plan" was officially upgraded to a Sino-French strategic project. One year later, Meitgu Oriental signed a strategic cooperation memorandum with CTIBIOTECH, the winner of the 2023 BIG BANG China-France track, to help CTIBIOTECH enter the Chinese market. This cooperation further highlights the spillover effect of the CIIE.

The CIIE welcomes industry leaders to bring their own black technologies, and vigorously supports start-ups to bring their own skills to this world-class stage.

The CIIE's support for "openness, cooperation, innovation and win-win" coincides with L'Oreal's BIG BANG project. In 2023, L'Oreal

At the 6th CIIE, L'Oreal North Asia Beauty Technology Co–creation Incubation
Exhibition unveiled. [Photo / L'Oreal]

successfully expanded its BIG BANG project from China to Japan
and South Korea. Taking this opportunity, L'Oreal invited innovative
companies from Japan, South Korea and France to jointly participate in
the CIIE to explore the unlimited opportunities in the Chinese market.

The overseas start-ups said they were impressed by the CIIE.
Here, they not only felt the vitality and innovative atmosphere of the
Chinese market, met like-minded partners and potential partners, but
also received policy "service packages" from governments at all levels
in China. They are eager to have more "close contact" with China, which
supports open innovation. Like L'Oreal, they have changed from "first
return guest" to "repeat guest" and then to "resident guest" at CIIE!

The spillover effects of the CIIE have made L'Oreal feel the
vitality and potential of the Chinese market, and strengthened L'Oreal's

L'Oreal BIG BANG Beauty technology creation camp North Asia division winning enterprise award ceremony. [Photo / L'Oreal]

determination to deeply cultivate the Chinese market. In 2024, L'Oreal increased its investment in the Chinese market. The Smart Operation Center located in Suzhou, Jiangsu Province was officially launched in April 2024, hoping to further meet the increasingly personalized consumption upgrading needs of Chinese consumers.

As an old friend of the CIIE, L'Oréal will remain committed to supporting the expo. During the signing ceremony to attend the 7th CIIE, L'Oréal has already secured its participation for the 8th CIIE.

Fan Yubin

(Translated by Zhang Youchao)

From 46% to 71%: Envisioning a Sustainable Future

Michelin, which has been associated with racing since its birth, got a head start at the CIIE. In late September 2023, an innovative product of Michelin, tires with 63% use of sustainable materials, was cleared by Shanghai Customs in "seconds" after rapid review, and became the first entry exhibit of the 6th CIIE. The green tire quickly became a star exhibit after making its Asian debut at the CIIE.

Demand leads innovation

46% in 2021, 53% in 2022, 63% in 2023...... As the proportion of sustainable materials continues to increase in CIIE after CIIE, Michelin's "CIIE story" is also constantly "updated". At the 7th CIIE, Michelin will continue to demonstrate its

Michelin booth at the 6th CIIE. [Photo / Michelin]

commitment to sustainable materials and its ability to put breakthrough technologies into practice, once again showcasing its first product in Asia—a new tire with 71% sustainable materials.

Sustainable development is related to the long-term prosperity of human society and has become a global consensus and guide for action. Michelin has proposed that 100% of its tire products will be made from bio-based, renewable and recyclable materials by 2050.

Since the successful development of pneumatic tires by Michelin in 1895, tires have always been a crucial link in the automotive industry chain. In recent years, electrification and intelligence have become emerging growth points in the automobile market, and the global sales of

Michelin's Mission H24 hydrogen energy race car with 46% sustainable material ratio tires at the 4th CIIE. [Photo / Michelin]

supporting tires have gradually recovered, with significant growth in the Chinese market. Sales of tires for passenger vehicles in China reached 132 million units in 2023, ranking first among major regions in the world.

With the continuous improvement of global automobile production requirements for tires, it is the general trend for tires to move toward high-end and green. Michelin sees a huge demand for high-quality development in the automotive industry in China.

China became the world's largest new car market in 2009, and is now a well-deserved car production and consumption power. According to data released by the China Association of Automobile Manufacturers, China's automobile production and sales have ranked first in the world for 15 consecutive years, with the annual production and sales reaching 30.161 million and 30.094 million units respectively in 2023. In the first eight months of 2024, 18.674 million and 18.766 million vehicles were produced and sold in China, respectively.

The continuous release of demand in China's super-large market has enabled enterprises including Michelin to accelerate their innovation track, or adjust their strategies or upgrade their products to meet the new market demand and achieve their own development.

Ye Fei, president and CEO of Michelin China, said that the current take-up rate of Michelin brand tires in the high-end new energy vehicle market is more than 30%.

"We want to explore new prospects for green development in China. With the platform effect of CIIE, enterprises can not only better display cutting-edge innovation achievements, but also build more diversified connections. Although Michelin has a high market share in the middle and high-end new energy vehicle market, it still needs to flexibly adjust production according to market and customer demand in order to keep pace with the rapid development of the current Chinese auto industry." Ye Fei said the annual CIIE is an important opportunity for companies to quickly obtain demand and feedback.

Competition stimulates innovation

Headquartered in Clermont-Ferrand, France, Michelin is committed to improving the sustainable mobility of people and goods. Michelin (China) Investment Co., Ltd. was established in Shanghai in 2001 and now has nearly 7,000 employees and 3 factories in China.

For more than 100 years, Michelin has been adhering to the concept of "competition, in order to advance", and has never stopped chasing and innovating. In the "super show" of the CIIE, where leading enterprises in the industry compete together, 12 of the world's top 500 automobile companies, including Volkswagen, Toyota and Hyundai, and 3 leading automobile tire companies, including Michelin and Prometeon, compete for brilliance with new products. Michelin advocates the concept of "everything is sustainable", which is unique in these exhibits and leads the innovation frontier.

At the 6th CIIE, Michelin arranged its booth into a "Michelin Track Paradise" of more than 500 square meters to show its diversified achievements in the process of sustainable development. In Ye Fei's

view, sports events are more like real-world technology laboratories, playing a vital role in innovating sustainable solutions.

In 2024, Michelin will participate in the CIIE for the fourth time. Under the theme of "Michelin Adventure", it will display innovative technologies from road to sky and even space, so that the audience can see a Michelin that "innovation goes beyond the road". At the same time, Michelin will debut in Asia at the 7th CIIE "Lunar Rover without pneumatic tires", which can adapt to the extreme conditions on the moon. In China, Michelin wants to lead industry changes and reshape people's lives with locally tailored innovation, Ye Fei said.

Thanks to the CIIE, new products, technologies and services of many enterprises, including Michelin, have made their debut at the Four-leaf Clover and entered the Chinese market, driving China's industrial upgrading and consumption upgrading, contributing to high-quality development and providing more new opportunities for the world.

Michelin exhibited 63% sus–tainable material ratio tires at the 6th CIIE. [Photo / Michelin]

Collaboration for Innovation

At the CIIE, scenes of exhibitors collaborating and negotiating with business partners, shaking hands, and signing contracts are frequent, with each mutually beneficial agreement serving as a vivid testament to the concept of "win-win cooperation".

"Cooperation" is also the key word for Michelin to participate in the CIIE. Through the CIIE platform, Michelin gets closer to consumers and partners, and has the opportunity to obtain cooperation intentions from more surrounding enterprises in the industrial chain and ecosystem, thus reserving more resources for innovation.

"Participating in the CIIE will give us more opportunities to strengthen cooperation and exchanges with companies upstream and downstream of the industrial chain, explore sustainable development experience and technology with other companies, and jointly promote the industry to move towards a greener and more sustainable direction," Ye Fei said.

In previous CIIE, Michelin has reached a series of cooperation, including purchase orders, tire business, race business and other cooperation, so as to better understand the Chinese market and consumers.

The CIIE is a platform to promote dialogue and cooperation. Michelin, who is well aware that "communication brings cooperation", held seven dialogues on different topics at the 6th CIIE, inviting professionals from different fields to participate in discussions. In Ye Fei's view, "this kind of direct dialogue with global peers, government

Michelin booth at the 3rd CIIE. [Photo / Michelin]

figures, experts, scholars and industry leaders is very rare".

An exhibition brings together the world and benefits the world. Looking ahead, CIIE will work with Michelin and other "old friends of CIIE" and more new partners to drive development through innovation, bring better life experience to people and contribute to sustainable development.

Fan Yubin

(Translated by Zhang Youchao)

"Triple Jump" Achieved at the CIIE

Black lines stretch far and wide on the silver ground running through the coordinates of the LeBron James Innovation Center and the Xinjiangwan Neighborhood in Shanghai...

High-tech research equipment of the Nike sport research lab showcased at the 6th CIIE.
(Photo / Nike)

At the well-designed stage of the 6th CIIE, Nike announced that it would establish a Nike Sport Research Lab in Shanghai, which has become another vivid example of the CIIE to "shift exhibitors to investors" and intensify efforts to attract and utilize foreign capital.

For this hundred-year-old sports brand, such a brand-new sport research lab is of great significance as it can be called its "innovative brain". After its establishment, the lab will become Nike's first sport research lab in Asia.

Why did Nike announce such an important decision at the CIIE? Ma Zheng, vice-president of the government and public affairs of Nike greater China said, "In the context of globalization, the CIIE serves as a wonderful platform to enhance economic opening of various countries as well as global dialogue and exchanges, providing an opportunity for Nike to participate in China's economic development and work together to create a better future. We are eager to join it. At the CIIE every year, Nike shows the global innovation results and announces important investment programs in China. This has become our custom."

in China, for the world

At the 6th CIIE, Nike displayed a part of the "neuron" of its "innovative brain", drawing flocks of visitors to watch. Foot scanner can record the data of one's foot size so as to make fitter shoe tree. Pressure mapping and force measuring plates can identify one's stride and judge which parts of the shoe sole need to be shock absorbed according to one's point of strength when one walks or jumps in order to reduce pressure…

Nike China sports research lab release site. [Photo / Nike]

A former basketball player of the Chinese national team who has also been to the CIIE, also thinks that the Nike sport research lab is the "most attractive site" in Nike's booth, because athletes can acquire the sports equipment that better fit them with the help of the lab.

According to Ma Zheng, the launching of its "innovative brain" in China will help Nike better understand Chinese athletes and consumers, and design and produce innovative goods that cater more closely to the needs of the local market. "In a sense, it will spearhead Nike's innovation around the world."

A few years ago, the team of Nike Greater China found what Chinese women needed were a pair of light, comfortable and uniquely stylish sneakers, and transformed this observation into an innovative product successfully. As soon as the debut of the brand Nike Motiva of sneakers at the CIIE, it won immediate recognition of the global audience.

"This is a typical case, in which we back-feed the global innovation based on the demand of the Chinese consumers," said Ma Zheng. From "in China, for China" to "in China, for the world", the CIIE has become the "catalyst" of such a change.

Getting Higher and Higher

Nike is regarded as an "early bird" of the Global Fortune 500 companies to seize opportunities in China. As early as the beginning of China's reform and opening-up in the 1980s, it had signed production contracts with the shoe factories in Tianjin and Shanghai. In 1981, Nike set up its China headquarters in Shanghai.

In 2021, the 4th CIIE coincided with the 40th anniversary of Nike's entry into Chinese market. At its CIIE booth, Nike showcased 40 special moments and took the important products made during its development in China as its exhibits in order to tell the vivid stories of the growth of Nike together with Chinese sports.

Over more than 40 years of development, China has achieved "triple jump" in the position of Nike's global market. From a key

The exhibition marking the 40th anniversary of years of Nike's entry in Chinese market debuts at the 4th CIIE. [Photo / Nike]

manufacturing and export base in the world, it has risen to the second global single market apart from the United States, and then leapt to the leading innovative center across the world based on its original foundation.

The CIIE has played an essential role in assisting the "triple jump". "The CIIE is not only a six-day expo, but also part of the activities throughout the enterprises' annual development plans and goals. Either from the perspective of investment, or the perspective of technological

and brand development, all enterprises involved will benefit from its spill-over effect," said Ma Zheng.

"Upgrading"

In 2020, at the 3rd CIIE, a special zone for sports goods and events was established for the first time, with Nike being among the first exhibitors. "Four-leaf clover" has frequently been the stage for Nike to announce important investment projects.

"China is gradually becoming the center of innovation in the world, so it is to Nike. We shared the valuable experience and knowledge as well as the innovative spirit obtained in China with the world through the CIIE," said Ma Zheng.

Nike's first automated detaching technological process for disused sneakers on display at the CIIE. [Photo / Nike]

Nike has attended the CIIE for four consecutive times, becoming the "CIIE's old friend". Moreover, representative programs implemented are presented at every CIIE.

At the 4th CIIE, Nike announced to build its China Technological Center in Shenzhen to accelerate its digital transformation and firmly grab the online opportunities. At the 5th CIIE, it announced that it would establish the "Automatic Running Warehouse" in Nike China Logistics Center so as to achieve highly intelligent automation and lights-out operation, and great boost the efficiency of its supply chain and resilience.

In addition to these programs, the CIIE has also offered a platform for Nike to promote collaborative development among enterprises, universities, and research institutions. At the 6th CIIE, Nike declared its plan to conduct deep cooperation with Tsinghua University in sustainable development. The two sides would work together to carry out the "special plan for deep integration in carbon neutrality among enterprises, universities, and research institutions". Nike also cooperated with the Institute of Ecological Civilization and Circular Economy at Tongji University to develop the first automated detaching technological process for disused sneakers, by which it built up an environment-friendly sports field through recycling used sneakers.

In the eyes of Ma Zheng, "With the continuous upgrading of the CIIE in recent years, the exhibitors have been acquiring a stronger sense of gain." At the upcoming 7th CIIE, Nike will be "upgraded" together

with the CIIE. According to Ma, Nike will take "running" as its "secret weapon" to further demonstrate its future development space and long-term commitment to the Chinese market.

Miao Lu

(Translated by Liu Yanling)

All-time Exhibitor in Sync with China's Development

The "six-constant climate station" integrating air conditioning and fresh air functions, the "BetteRRRy" cloud analysis service for battery asset management and life extension, and the combined cooling, heating and power (CCHP) project using 5kW pure hydrogen fuel cells... Panasonic, a "perfect attendance exhibitor" at the CIIE, debuts quite a few futuristic technologies every year.

Panasonic's new products and technologies enjoy great opportunities for exposure at the CIIE. Tetsuro Homma, global vice-president of Panasonic Holdings Corporation and group regional head for China & Northeast Asia, said that Panasonic defines the CIIE as a "global strategic exhibition", where it showcases many innovative products and technological

Panasonic's booth at previous CIIE. [Photo / Panasonic]

achievements every year and releases the Group's strategy in China.

Showcase latest products and accelerate the delivery of benefits

Starting from the 2nd CIIE in 2019, attending the CIIE has become a fixed schedule that Tetsuro Homma has never missed. Each time, he will come to the Panasonic booth, interact with the audience on-site, and demonstrate its products and services.

"For foreign businesses, the CIIE acts as an excellent stage for us to showcase latest products and solutions to China," said Tetsuro Homma. "We can accelerate the delivery of benefits and get timely market feedback by presenting the latest high-tech products and concepts to Chinese consumers through the Expo."

The Expo gives more than just an opportunity for Panasonic's business exposure. Over the past 7 years, Panasonic has been expanding its circle of friends. It has inked a number of memorandums of cooperation with many partners during the CIIE, including up to 15 cooperation agreements signed at the 6th CIIE alone.

Panasonic, a time-honored Japanese company, is known far and wide in the Chinese market. Since its entry into the Chinese market in 1978, Panasonic has extended

Panasonic's booth at previous CIIE. [Photo / Panasonic]

its business from the cathode ray tube (CRT) and home appliances to the current three key businesses, namely healthy and intelligent living space, new energy auto parts, and intelligent manufacturing, all of which are closely associated with China's economy and society.

In 2019, Panasonic Group established China and Northeast Asia Company, a regional company that combines business and regional omnibus functions. That year, Panasonic advanced for the first time at the CIIE the strategy of building the "No. 1 Healthy Eldercare" brand business, and promoted the establishment of the first eldercare community in China, Yada Panasonic Community.

At that time, Panasonic's hope to promote healthy eldercare in

China was just a concept. As the CIIE progresses, Panasonic's age-appropriate products and solutions rooted in its 20 plus years' eldercare expertise in Japan have been well received by Chinese government, enterprises and consumers. The Yada Panasonic Community was officially completed in 2022. Today, there are 35 such home appliance and housing integration projects in China.

Gain insight into market changes and keep abreast of the pace of China

Tetsuro Homma said that China is a manufacturing powerhouse, as well as a major country in consumption, engineering and innovation. With a huge domestic market demand and a complete industrial and supply chain, China is always ready to accept new technologies and shows great potential for economic development, which provides broad opportunities for the development of foreign-funded enterprises in China. For Panasonic, China is an important market for it to boost its performance across the board.

In his view, the Chinese market is undoubtedly distinctive in the world. "For foreign businesses, the Chinese market is appealing for both its huge size and the consumers' readiness to embrace new concepts and technologies."

For foreign-funded companies like Panasonic, the CIIE is an excellent platform to keep abreast of the latest developments and changes in the Chinese market. "Through participating in the CIIE, we have enhanced our ability to quickly adapt to new technologies and market changes, and keep up with the pace of the Chinese market and China's development," said Tetsuro Homma.

From the inaugural CIIE's emphasis on the theme of "Century- old Enterprise's Full Range of Home Appliances" to subsequent focuses on "Health, Elderly Care," "Cleanliness," and "Life and Environment," and culminating in the theme of "Smart Life, Smart Society" at the 7th CIIE, it's evident that Panasonic's exhibition themes have consistently mirrored the shifting market dynamics and consumer trends in China.

Tetsuro Homma said that the CIIE brings together the products and technologies presented by outstanding enterprises from all over the world, and acts as an important platform and window for the world and China to learn about each other. "Through the CIIE, we feel that China

Panasonic's booth at previous CIIE. [Photo / Guo Zhihua]

is opening up wider to the world, and the Chinese market is playing an increasingly important role in the world."

Seeing is believing and embrace a better future with openness

Yuki Kusumi, CEO of Panasonic Group, visited the new product release platform of the CIIE for the first time at the 6th CIIE. "China speed is global speed, and China cost is global cost", he said and requested that Panasonic must advance its global business with "China speed" and "China cost".

A new product showcased by Panasonic at previous CIIE. [Photo / Panasonic]

"China is opening up wider to the world, giving a great fillip to Panasonic, a company that has been operating in China for more than 40 years." As Tetsuro Homma disclosed, executives of almost all of Panasonic's business units visited China in the past years to learn about market trends and seek cooperation opportunities. Panasonic will as always showcase new products and unveil new investment plans at the 7th CIIE to seek a better future with China's economy.

"Seeing is believing. I also hope that more foreign executives will come to China to see this ever-changing and innovating market and deepen their understanding of the Chinese market," said Tetsuro Homma.

Fan Yubin

(Translated by Ni Weisi)

Bocom: Contributing Financial Power to High-Level Global Opening-Up

Swipe left, swipe right, make a fist…In front of an air holographic screen, visitors can easily access detailed global case studies of financial services promoting high-quality development with a simple finger swipe. At the CIIE, Bank of Communications uses such interactive displays to

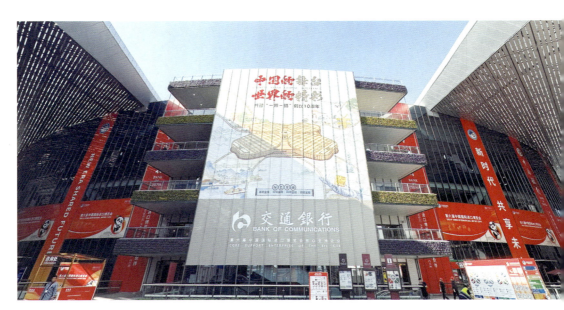

Bocom showcases at the 6th CIIE. [Photo / Bocom]

make its intangible financial products and services more tangible and accessible.

CIIE is the world's first national-level exhibition focused on imports, where the demand for international procurement and investment promotion continues to grow. Bocom remains committed to serving the physical economy as its core mission, emphasizing its role as the "lifeblood" of finance. By focusing on cross-border financial services and innovating comprehensive financial solutions, it builds a "financial bridge" for greater global openness.

Digitization Empowering Cross-Border Trade

At the 6th CIIE, Bocom showcased several major initiatives, including the launch of its "Digital Trade Service" cross-border financial solutions, the "Silk Road E-commerce" comprehensive financial service platform for cross-border e-commerce, and new corporate channels along with a digital ecosystem service plan. These efforts highlighted Bocom's innovations in digital financial services to the world.

Leveraging financial technologies such as AI algorithms and big data analysis, Bocom continues to optimize its products, with a strong focus on providing enhanced financial support for micro and small foreign trade businesses. It aims to expand its financial services for new foreign trade business models like cross-border e-commerce.

Digitalization has become a major trend in the transformation of financial institutions. Bocom has fully embraced this wave of digital development, using its fintech advantages to provide efficient, high-

quality, one-stop financial services for CIIE. This ongoing effort also supports the broader spillover effects of the expo.

Before the 7th CIIE, Bocom successfully facilitated cross-border RMB settlements for core CIIE support enterprises and designated insurance service providers using the central bank's Multilateral Digital Currency Bridge.

This was the first reinsurance payment transaction in the shipping trade scenario. By utilizing the "point-to-point" technology of the Digital Currency Bridge, Bocom achieved fast clearing, significantly reducing the delays and high fees often associated with traditional cross-border payments.

Bocom has also intensified its research into market and client needs, steadily advancing new offshore international trade financial services. It has integrated itself into cross-border transactions involving bulk commodities like food, energy, and minerals, continuously improving its scenario-based financial services and making cross-border trade payments under intellectual property rights more convenient for tech companies.

Bank of Communications Showcasing at the 6th CIIE.

[Photo / Bocom]

At the innovation incubation area of the 6th CIIE, Bocom presented its latest digital achievements, including corporate online banking, a new version of corporate mobile banking, open banking, and mini-programs. Bocom's open banking services focus on the needs of import-export enterprises and platform institutions, providing tailored foreign remittance services. It also offers a full-process, online, scenario-based cross-border payment solution for new types of foreign trade.

According to statistics, Bocom leveraged its advantages as a digital capital project pilot to attract and utilize foreign investment. In the first half of 2024, the business volume increased by more than 130% year-over-year.

Green Finance, Empowering Low-Carbon Transformation

A digital RMB recycling bin for discarded bottles at Bocom booth has drawn many visitors' attention. By depositing a used water bottle, visitors can receive a digital RMB "red envelope". Through this interactive display, Bocom hopes to raise public awareness about green development.

Beyond the booth design, Bocom has been actively involved in the Hongqiao International Economic Forum and other events at CIIE. The bank has shared insights on themes such as "Developing Green Investment and Trade, Building a Global Ecological Civilization" and "High-Quality Development of Foreign Trade in the New Era and Trade Facilitation," sharing its expertise and collaborating to build an open ecosystem.

To integrate service for Shanghai International Shipping Center development with green and low-carbon initiatives, Bocom hosted the 6th Hongqiao International Economic Forum Shipping Finance Member Forum . Under the theme "Concentrating High-Energy Shipping, Serving a New Development Pattern," government agencies, industry experts, scholars, and others were invited to explore cutting-edge trends in shipping finance related to low-carbon and digitalization, aiming to create a "Chinese solution" for shipping industry collaboration.

During the forum, Bocom's subsidiary led the initiation of the "China Shipping Leasing Innovation Alliance", aimed at boosting high-level shipping industry clusters and paving the way for new development patterns in the shipping industry.

Technology Inject Momentum to Innovation

On the path to supporting the development of sci-tech enterprises, Bocom has employed a multi-pronged approach—equity, debt, loans, leasing, and trusts—injecting financial momentum to promote high-level scientific and technological self-reliance.

At the "Focusing on New Technology, Collaborating for a Future of Innovation" Technology Finance Forum for HQF Members, organized by Bocom, representatives from the government, banking, and business sectors gathered to discuss the future integration of technology and finance.

During the event, Bocom launched its "Bocom Sci-Tech" brand for the first time, providing full lifecycle service solutions for tech-driven companies, supporting the growth of industry clusters.

Shanghai is a key hub for technological innovation in China. In this fertile ground, the Bocom leverages its local advantages and global network to build communication platforms for local innovation parks, enhancing the "soft environment" for technological innovation. Through the platform provided by the CIIE, Bocom launched its "Global Innovation Hub" service plan under the "Bocom Sci-Tech" brand for the first time, showing the bank's efforts to improve the local innovation ecosystem.

As a comprehensive financial holding group, Bocom's subsidiaries also actively support the global business operations of high-quality sci-tech enterprises by providing "hard support." During the 6th CIIE, Bocom Investment, Bocom International Trust, and Bocom MSIG Life jointly launched a fund of funds (FOF) dedicated to investing in sci-tech enterprises in Shanghai. In collaboration with leading hard-tech investment institutions, Bocom established four industry-themed sub-funds focused on foundational software, integrated circuits, advanced manufacturing, and optoelectronic chips and commercial aerospace. Bocom Financial Leasing also introduced a specialized product system, "FastTech Lease (Kuaiyizu)," "TrustTech Lease (Xinyizu)," offering efficient financial leasing services to more tech-focused small and medium enterprises (SMEs). It has further accelerated the integration of production and finance in partnership with industrial partners, driving equipment procurement through innovative SPV mechanisms in free trade zones.

Bocom's "Freighter"

A cargo ship named "Bocom" loaded with containers sails toward distant destinations, with the words "Cross-Border

Financial Services, Integration of Onshore/Offshore, Domestic/Foreign currencies" written above it. This is the scene depicted in Bocom's CIIE-themed poster.

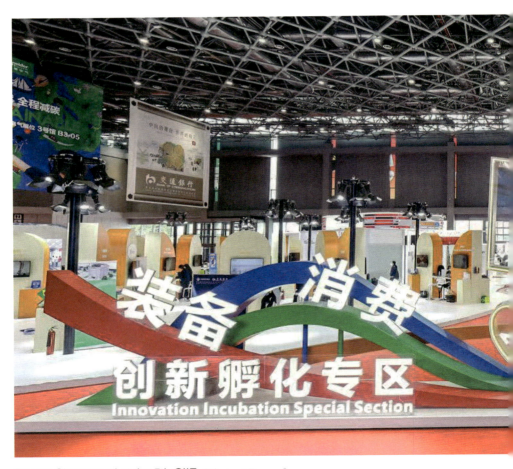

Bocom Showcased at the 5th CIIE. [Photo / Bocom]

Bocom actively supports landmark projects under the Belt and Road Initiative (BRI) and smaller livelihood initiatives with a strong focus on green, digital, and technology cooperation in BRI-related projects.

Data indicates that Bocom provides credit enhancement support for projects under the Belt and Road Initiative using guarantee products, with a 92% year-on-year increase in guarantee amounts to Belt and

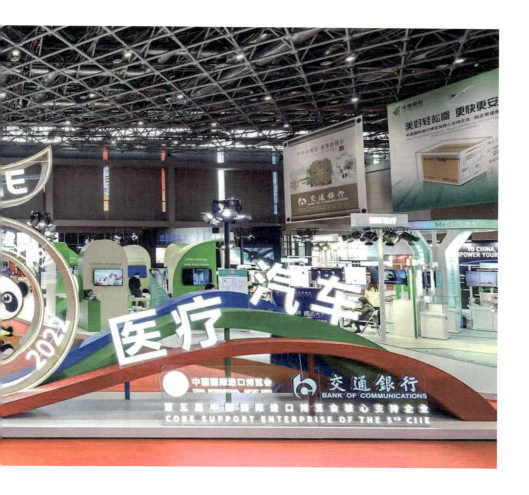

Road partner countries in the first half of 2024. Bocom also continuously enriches the range of convertible currencies for Belt and Road partner countries, having launched nine small currencies along the Belt and Road such as the UAE Dirham, Hungarian Forint, and Polish Zloty in recent years for business of Forward Settlement and Sale of Foreign Exchange and Foreign Exchange (Forex) Trading Products, making 27 currencies available for clients to exchange, reducing exchange costs for businesses and promoting bilateral trade and investment.

In the process of serving CIIE exhibitors, Bocom fosters mutual trust with enterprises, continuously expanding the depth of business cooperation. For example, a subsidiary of an exhibitor at CIIE, Company A urgently needed to register in the "List of Foreign Exchange Receipts and Payments for Trade Companies" to meet its first import payment demands. As the legal representative of the company was a foreign individual, according to the policy at the time, the registration required the company to send someone to the foreign exchange bureau counter for processing, which was time-consuming and challenging. Bocom thoroughly understood the company's needs, recommended the optimal business processing solution, and ultimately met its trade payment requirements accurately within the timeframe.

In 2024, Bocom will participate in CIIE for the seventh time, and for the third time as a "core supporting enterprise" . Bocom remains committed to providing efficient, high-quality, one-stop financial services for CIIE, amplifying the event's spillover effects, injecting vitality into

China's economic development, and contributing to the growth of the global economy.

Miao Lu

(Translated by Chen Xu)

Promise of Openness

7 Years on - Charm of the CIIE Remains

The 7th CIIE will be held in Shanghai from November 5 to 10, 2024. On the occasion of the 100-day countdown to its opening ceremony, Sun Chenghai, deputy director-general of the CIIE Bureau, introduced the latest progress. As of then, over 50 countries and international organizations have confirmed their participation in the Country Exhibition, with the contracted exhibition area for corporate exhibits exceeding 360,000 square meters. The progress in organizing trade delegations and professional audience attendance is ahead of the same period in 2023. It is expected that more professional audiences will attend the 7th CIIE.

Seven years on, what contributes to the enduring charm of the CIIE?

Allows outstanding products from the National Exhibition and Convention Center (Shanghai) to broader markets

"Theland, as an imported brand that has grown through the empowerment of the CIIE, is not only a witness to the openness of the expo but also a beneficiary," stated Sheng Wenhao, CEO of Theland Asia Pacific Region.

Since the inception of the CIIE, Theland has never been absent and has unveiled new products each year. In 2024, it will launch a "full-chain low-carbon milk", showcasing its exploration and development of green new quality productivity, from enclosure-free farming in pastures to hydrogen fuel transport, and the use of renewable geothermal energy in factories. Sheng noted, "As global economic growth enters a slow lane, multinational enterprises are seeking new engines for growth and reshaping global supply chains. China's continuous nurturing and development of new quality productive forces provides vast opportunities

Össur's exhibits at the CIIE help more individuals with disabilities.
[Photo / Tian Hong]

for innovation and transformation for multinational corporations. We believe that 'next China will still be China'."

How significant is the spillover effects of the CIIE? Zhu Min, director of the Shanghai Municipal Commission of Commerce, elaborated that Shanghai is closely aligning with the functional positioning of "transforming exhibits into commodities and exhibitors into investors" and continuously amplifying the spillover effects of the CIIE. The remarkable products showcased at the expo are moving from the National Exhibition and Convention Center (Shanghai) to the more tremendous domestic market, which is reflected in three evident trends.

The progress of Silk Road e-commerce cooperation is evident. The construction of the Shanghai pilot zone for Silk Road e-commerce cooperation is fully underway. Such consumption-promoting events as the Shanghai Online Lunar New Year's Shopping Festival and the Shanghai Silk Road E-commerce Carnival have been organized, facilitating the transformation of expo products into e-commerce commodities.

The effects of a year-round display and trading platform is evident. The trading volume at Hongqiao Import Commodity Exhibition and Trade Center reached RMB 17 billion in 2023, with a cumulative establishment of 23 sub-centers in cities such as Suzhou and Shaoxing. 63 national pavilions and 13 branches have been established for the Greenland Global Commodity Trade Hub, promoting over 5,000 products identical to those showcased at the CIIE to enter the domestic market. The CIIE Bazaar on Nanjing East Road has gathered products from over

20 countries and regions, becoming a go-to destination for global visitors to discover new products and experience international goods.

The effect of first launches and exhibitions is evident. Since the inception of the CIIE, Shanghai has introduced a total of 5,840 first stores, among which over 80 are first store in Asia or above.

Transforms participants' sense of gain into satisfaction with the business environment

The CIIE not only facilitates "buying global, selling global" but also showcases China's firm determination to expand high-level openness and create a platform for Chinese and foreign enterprises to collaborate.

LEGO, which has participated in the CIIE for six consecutive years, has made significant progress in the construction of its theme park resort project's first phase. Exhibitor Straumann at the 4th CIIE has initiated the industrialization of its high-end implant project, which is expected to reach production by 2025. A "all-time" participant of all seven

LEGO's Monkie Kid caravan activity. [Photo / the interviewed company]

sessions of the CIIE, Lesaffre, has partnered with Shanghai Qingmei Group to develop Chinese-style pastries tailored to foreign consumers' tastes, aiding Qingmei in expanding its international market.

The experience gained from six days at the expo has been upgraded to a year-round satisfaction with the business environment as Shanghai continues to optimize its business environment to attract foreign investment. By aligning comprehensively with international high-standard economic and trade rules, Shanghai is advancing its high-level and multi-dimensional institutional openness, implementing initiatives to promote global partnerships for foreign investment, and enhancing the brand of "Invest in Shanghai" series activities. The city has held multi-level government-business communication roundtables and policy dissemination activities for foreign enterprises to facilitate "mutual engagement" with the CIIE exhibitors. In the first half of 2024, 3,007 new foreign-funded enterprises were founded in Shanghai, reflecting an 18.3% year-on-year growth. The city has recognized 29 new regional headquarters of multinational companies and 14 foreign research and development centers, bringing the total to 985 and 575, respectively.

Zhang Kailan, senior manager of Public Affairs at L'Oréal North Asia, noted that L'Oréal is a "all-time" participant at the CIIE. The expo has become a "flagship" project for L'Oréal globally, serving as the preferred platform for the launch of new products and technological innovations. Over the past six years, L'Oréal has debuted nearly 20 international new brands and dozens of cutting-edge beauty technologies at the CIIE. Many products were transitioned "from exhibits to commodities and then best-sellers".

The genuine spillover effect of the CIIE has allowed L'Oréal to fully experience the immense vitality and potential of the vast Chinese market, reinforcing its commitment to further investment in China. At the 2nd CIIE, L'Oréal, in collaboration with the Oriental Beauty Valley, launched the "BIG BANG Beauty Tech Innovation Program". In 2022, it established its first investment company, Meicifang, outside of its headquarters in Shanghai. In April 2024, its smart operations center in Suzhou officially commenced operations.

Enables global enterprises to discover new projects, partners, and opportunities

From 73 to 150, and then to 300, an increasing number of technology-driven startups and small and micro enterprises have boarded the fast track of Chinese innovation since the innovative incubation special area was first established at the 4th CIIE in 2021.

Sun Chenghai noted that, as of now, the scale of the innovation incubation special area for the 7th CIIE has exceeded the overall level of 2023. This year, the exhibition planning will focus on four major areas, namely digital economy, green and low-carbon technologies, life sciences, and manufacturing technologies. It will continue to host awards and create an innovative incubation ecosystem that integrates projects, policies, investments, finance, and promotion, so as to provide technological resources and collaboration opportunities for global startups and small- and micro enterprises exploring the Chinese market.

The Korea Innovation Center (KIC China) will participate in the 7th CIIE for the first time as a recommending agency in 2024. It will bring six South Korean tech startups in fields such as artificial intelligence, biopharmaceutical, and new materials to the innovation incubation special area of the exhibition. "The CIIE is one of the most influential exhibitions globally. We hope to connect with Chinese investors and partners through this platform and enhance the competitiveness of the South Korean startup and high-tech industry," said Kim Jong-moon, a representative from KIC China, expressing high expectations and confidence for the inaugural CIIE journey, "China has the most complete industrial supply chain in the world. It is necessary to cooperate with Chinese industries to enhance technology. We hope to promote cooperation in the technology field between our two countries through the CIIE."

In 2024, Spain's National Innovation Center will bring 20 Spanish startups to the innovation incubation special zone of the CIIE, covering fields such as digital economy, aerospace, and manufacturing technologies. A representative from the center stated, "the Spanish startups participating in 2024 not only possess high-tech capabilities but also demonstrate significant confidence and enthusiasm for the Chinese market, with a strong desire to

3M will be present in the newly established new materials special section in the Intelligent Industry and Information Technology Exhibition Area. [Photo / organizer]

enter it. We hope to find Chinese partners and discover new opportunities for development through the CIIE platform. We believe this participation will lay a solid foundation for deeper cooperation in the future."

"The CIIE platform has been continuously upgraded to meet the new demands of the Chinese market." 3M, a global leader in technology innovation and another "all-time" participant at the CIIE, has showcased its offerings in various zones over the past six sessions, including consumer electronics and home appliances, technology lifestyle, medical devices and healthcare products, equipment technology, as well as energy-efficient, low-carbon and environmental technologies. At the 7th CIIE, 3M will be present in the newly established new materials special section in the Intelligent Industry and Information Technology Exhibition

Area. Focusing on low-carbon and sustainability themes, it will present a series of globally leading climate technologies and solutions. Ding Hongyu, senior vice-president of 3M Co and president of 3M China, remarked, "the aggregation effect of the CIIE allows companies to grasp the forefront of the Chinese market in a one-stop manner. Over the past six years, 3M has met new demands with new products, sparked new inspiration with new trends, and promoted more locally sourced and produced products to the world."

Tian Hong, People's Daily

This article was first published on July 30, 2024.

(Translated by Li Donglin)

A Powerful Resonance of Openness Gathering New Quality

As the world's first national exhibition themed exclusively on imports, the CIIE has expanded its "circle of friends" over the past seven years, bringing together new faces, new technologies, and new perspectives. Through the CIIE, an increasing number of foreign-invested enterprises continue to view China positively and remain committed to investing in the country.

Sun Chenghai, deputy director-general of the CIIE Bureau, announced that the 7th CIIE will be held from November 5 to 10, 2024, in Shanghai. To date, the contracted exhibition area has exceeded 360,000 square meters, with over 150 companies signing contracts for seven consecutive years, thus writing a new chapter of mutually beneficial cooperation.

In addition to the arrival of familiar friends, the 7th CIIE will also welcome new participants.

The New Zealand brand, Tracel, will participate in the expo for the first time in 2024. Having officially entered the Chinese market in June 2024, its oral beauty products coincided with the June 18 shopping

festival, achieving sales of over RMB 10 million in the first month, prompting the brand to exclaim that their performance "far exceeded expectations".

The sports lifestyle brand Lululemon also recently announced its first participation in the CIIE. According to Calvin McDonald, chief executive officer of Lululemon, the CIIE holds significant global influence and Lululemon is honored to join friends from around the world for this "oriental appointment".

It is reported that more than 50 countries and international organizations have confirmed their participation in the 2024 CIIE Country Exhibition. Notably, countries such as Norway, Benin, and Burundi, as well as international organizations like UNICEF, will be making their debut at the expo. In the Business Exhibition, Global Fortune 500 companies like Mitsubishi Corporation will also make their first appearance. Industry leaders in the new materials sector, including Nippon Paint and Invista, as well as in the transportation sector, such as Aptiv and Alstom, have also signed contracts for the first time, further expanding the CIIE's "circle of friends".

At the Pre-Expo Supply-demand Matchmaking Meeting for the 7th CIIE, exhibitors and purchasers engaged closely, with "new quality productive forces" becoming a high-frequency buzzword at the event.

"Currently, multinational enterprises are searching for new growth engines. China's new quality productive forces, driven by innovation and centered on enhancing full-element productivity, are generating new appeal in the global economic landscape," Sheng Wenhao, CEO of

The Pre−Expo Supply−demand Matchmaking Meeting for Food and Agricultural Products, Medical Devices and Healthcare Exhibition Area of the 7th CIIE.
[Photo / Fang Zhe,Xinhua News Agency]

Theland Asia Pacific Region. He added that in 2024, Theland will focus on "CIIE New Quality" as a key theme, leveraging the dual tracks of "green and digital" to implement outcomes in China.

In terms of exhibition setup, the 7th CIIE will deeply explore the exhibition potential of cutting-edge technology fields, contributing "CIIE strength" to the acceleration of new quality productive forces. Notably, a special demonstration area for new materials will be established for the first time. Confirmed to debut in this area are Global Fortune 500 companies and industry-leading enterprises from countries including the United States, Japan, Germany, Singapore, Brazil, and Italy, along with some "hidden champion" enterprises in niche sectors.

"China remains our strategic focus for global business growth and investment. Our choice to debut in the special demonstration area for new materials aligns perfectly with our business development direction," said Kyle Redinger, vice-president of Upstream Nylon Asia-Pacific, Invista.

Held concurrently with the CIIE, the 7th Hongqiao International Economic Forum will be held under theme "High-Standard Opening up for Universally Beneficial and Inclusive Economic Globalization". During the main forum and related sub-forums, the World Openness Report 2024 and the new World Openness Index will be released to contribute wisdom to promote global openness.

Gathering global wisdom with an open stance, the innovation incubation special section aims to provide opportunities for display and communication of small and micro enterprises and technology startups worldwide. Since its establishment at the 4th CIIE, over 500 overseas innovative achievements have been showcased on this platform.

A foreign exhibitor (left) introduces the company's products.
[Photo / Chen Haoming]

The number of exhibitors in the first year was 73, which increased to 150 in the second year, and then to 300 in the third year. Currently, for the 2024 CIIE, the number of participating enterprises in this area has surpassed that of the previous year, with expectations to reach a new high of 350 exhibitors. The figures presented during the Publicity Roadshow for the Innovation Incubation Special Section of the 7th CIIE & the CIIC Signing Ceremony are very impressive.

According to Angel Prieto, vice-president of External Affairs at the Spanish Innovation Center, in 2024, a total of 20 Spanish startups will debut in the innovation incubation special section, covering fields such as digital economy, aerospace, and manufacturing technology. These participating Spanish startups not only possess high technological content but also demonstrate a strong desire to enter the Chinese market. They are now actively engaging with governments and industrial parks across China to facilitate the implementation of more projects.

"Hosting CIIE demonstrates China's commitment to collaborate with more countries in a way that is inclusive and beneficial, releasing new development momentum," said Wang Wen, executive dean of Chongyang Institute for Financial Studies at Renmin University of China (RDCY).

Zhou Lei, Wang Moling, Xinhua News Agency

This article was first published on July 26, 2024.

(Translated by Li Donglin)

The CIIE Promotes Mutual Benefits and Win-Win Cooperation

Since 2018, the CIIE has consis-tently graced the shores of the East China Sea and the banks of the Huangpu River in every golden autumn. Friends from across the globe gather for this "Oriental Appointment" to strive for greater progress in cooperation.

"The CIIE, an event to be held on an annual basis, will feature good performance, good results and continued success in the years to come," declared Chinese President Xi Jinping at the inaugural ceremony of the 1st CIIE, a promise that still resonates profoundly.

Following this commitment, the CIIE has successfully hosted six sessions. The stories of the CIIE continues to unfold and its effects are ever-increasing, painting a beautiful tapestry of deep integration and win-win development between China and the world. Exhibits are transformed into commodities to enter households far and wide from here. Through tangible and practical actions, China has opened its doors ever wider, offering nations the opportunity to share in its development dividends and providing businesses with the chance to thrive in the Chinese market, thus crafting a new grand chapter of shared opportunities and mutual growth.

Embracing the world with open arms

On May 14, 2017, Chinese President Xi Jinping announced at the Belt and Road Forum for International Cooperation in Beijing that China would host the CIIE starting in 2018. In the following spring, he once again earnestly promoted the CIIE to the world at the Boao Forum for Asia. He said, "it is not just another expo in an ordinary sense, but a major policy initiative and commitment taken of our own accord to open up the Chinese market. Friends from around the world are welcome to participate in the Expo."

Since then, China has repeatedly extended "CIIE invitations" to the world, from the Shanghai Cooperation Organization (SCO) Qingdao Summit to the Ministerial Meeting of the China-Arab States Cooperation Forum, from the BRICS Business Forum to the Summit of the Forum on China-Africa Cooperation (FOCAC).

The international community is filled with anticipation: what vitality will this first national-level expo centered on imports bring to the world economy?

On November 5, 2018, the inaugural CIIE opened, illuminating the world with an "Oriental Appointment" that left a brilliant mark in human history. Heads of state from 16 countries, royal representatives, deputy or vice heads of state, or heads of government from 11 countries, and leaders from 13 international organizations gathered in Shanghai, along with over 400 foreign guests at the ministerial level or above. More than 3,600 enterprises participated in the event and over 400,000 domestic and international buyers attended for negotiations. The total exhibition

area reached 300,000 square meters. It has resulted in a cumulative intended turnover of USD 57.83 billion for the year.

Reflecting on the 1st CIIE, Leon Wang,executive vice-president, International and China President at AstraZeneca, expressed his amazement, "I did not expect such high standards for the expo, nor such significant support from the Chinese government, and I certainly did not anticipate the global participation to be so vast. The platform effect of the CIIE is unmatched by other exhibitions. It is truly a pioneering initiative."

Since then, regardless of the ever-changing global landscape, the CIIE has consistently occurred as scheduled. Its prominence has increased, with more exhibitors and a continuous rise in transaction volumes.

The 6th CIIE recorded an intended transaction amount of USD 78.41 billion, a 6.7% increase from the previous year. 72 countries and international organizations participated in the Country Exhibition and 3,486 enterprises from 128 countries and regions attended the Business Exhibition, displaying 442 representative new products, technologies, and services. The number of participating Fortune Global 500 companies, industry leaders, and innovative SMEs reached an all-time high. All 15 major global vehicle brands, 10 major industrial electrical enterprises, 10 major medical device companies, three major mining giants, and four major grain traders participated in the expo.

The CIIE is thriving and its spillover effects continue to amplify. Domestic and international dignitaries, prominent business leaders, and experts from various fields gather at the CIIE to discuss innovation and openness and promote cooperation, sparking ideas and mutual inspiration. The African media outlet "Invest in Africa" commented that the CIIE provides an international platform for countries to showcase their products and serves as a venue for discussing significant issues such as foreign trade, the global economy, and global governance.

Countries are increasingly viewing the CIIE as a premier venue for launching global new products, selecting cutting-edge technologies, and promoting innovative services, and actively joining the big CIIE family. New friends become old friends, and "first-time visitors" turn into "repeat attendees". With more stories about the CIIE have been recorded, the consensus in the international community is that China's market has become a market for the world, a market shared by all, and a market accessible to all.

Yin Zheng, executive vice-president of China & East Asia Operations, Schneider Electric, noted that the CIIE fully demonstrates the achievements of China's high-level opening-up, providing significant opportunities for global enterprises to deepen their engagement in China and pursue mutually beneficial cooperation. Participation in the CIIE has become Schneider Electric's most valued "Chinese Appointment". In the six consecutive sessions of the CIIE, Schneider Electric has expanded its booth size each year, increasingly showcased green and advanced products and solutions, and broadened its industry coverage and "circle of friends".

The CIIE effect unleashes vast opportunities

Exhibitions are a gathering place for the achievements of human civilization and reflect the trajectory of prosperity and growth of the host country. In 1851, the United Kingdom successfully held the first Great Exhibition of the Works of Industry of all Nations, showcasing its dominant position as the world's factory. The 1933 Chicago World's Fair heralded the dawn of industrial technology, with Ford's automobile assembly line presenting a new mode of production and lifestyle. Today, the CIIE, in a historic manner, illuminates the path for the world economy shrouded in uncertainty and injects confidence into it.

The boundless potential of China's vast market is widely regarded by the international community as a crucial support for the stable and enduring development of the Chinese economy, as well as a focal point for businesses from various countries to continue investing in China. Aiming at the inherent demands of high-quality economic development in China and aligning with the common expectations for win-win cooperation from the international community, China positions its own advancement within the framework of human progress. Through open initiatives such as the CIIE, it actively opens its market to the world, allowing nations to hitch a ride on the fast track of China's development.

From century-old and time-honored brands to cutting-edge startups, from powerful Fortune Global 500 companies to nimble SMEs, from longstanding participants to newcomers attending for the first time... exhibitors are eager to showcase their competitive advantages at the CIIE, explore new possibilities for cooperation, and express their unwavering confidence in the Chinese market as well as their high expectations for the CIIE spillover effects.

Products such as coffee from East Timor, chocolate from Switzerland, and milk from New Zealand… are increasingly entering the Chinese market through the CIIE, allowing consumers to "buy global" without leaving the country. It not only helps them to fully enjoy the dividends of economic globalization but also creates greater space for the optimization and upgrade of China's consumer market.

A series of signings and collaborations further invigorate the spirit of innovation among Chinese enterprises and increase development opportunities. Domestic and foreign companies join hands to enlarge the market pie, bringing a significant surge of momentum to the recovery and development of the world economy.

Medtronic, a medical technology company, has participated in the CIIE for six consecutive years. Geoff Martha, chairman and CEO of Medtronic, stated that the CIIE serves as an important platform for multinational medical companies to share opportunities in the Chinese market and showcase cutting-edge medical technologies. Thanks to the powerful market influence of the CIIE, Medtronic's products and services can benefit Chinese patients more quickly.

Tobias Wahl, board chairman of the Hawk brand at Kärcher Group, noted that by riding the "CIIE Express", multiple Kärcher cleaning products have swiftly occupied the market, opening the door to opportunities in the Chinese market. The significant outcomes from participating in the CIIE have strengthened the company's confidence to

continue deepening its engagement and investing in China, facilitating its transformation "from an exhibitor to an investor".

At the CIIE, not only do the developed economies showcase impressive exhibitor numbers, but the developing countries are also writing their own remarkable stories.

During the 1st CIIE, Bangladesh's Dada Group Ltd. exhibited jute handicrafts made by impoverished women, garnering interest from purchasing groups. With the assistance of Chinese partners, the company's products entered Shanghai's department stores and launched online shops to explore the e-commerce mode.

An exhibitor from Mali learned that the CIIE organizers were inviting Malian entrepreneurs to participate in without any barriers and providing free booths. She signed up without hesitation and was then delighted to find that Malian products were well received at the CIIE. Substantial sales of decorations and handicrafts were realized within just a few days.

Firmly advancing economic globalization

In recent years, the global economic recovery has been sluggish and economic globalization has faced headwinds, with protectionism and unilateralism becoming increasingly rampant. At the same time, a new round of technological and industrial revolutions is emerging, leading to an accelerated evolution of the international division of labor and a profound reshaping of global value chains. All these imbue economic globalization with new connotations and give rise to new momentum for growth.

The international community fully recognizes that economic globalization is an objective requirement for the development of social productivity and an inevitable result of technological progress. Building barriers with closed doors and shifting blame onto others is not the correct solution to the issues at hand, while reverting the vast ocean of the global economy to isolated lakes and streams is contrary to historical trends. The intermingling of national interests and the shared destinies of countries are inevitable trends. The continuous creation of better lives is a common expectation of the people worldwide. It is the shared responsibility of governments of various countries to ensure that economic globalization benefits all people globally.

The original intention and pursuit of hosting the CIIE reflect China's clear understanding and scientific judgment of the prevailing global development trends. For this reason, China is resolutely leading economic globalization towards a more open, inclusive, equitable, balanced, and win-win direction.

Multinational corporations are both the promoters and beneficiaries of economic globalization. Rising anti-globalization sentiments and trade protectionism as well as uncertainty in the global economic and trade landscape present numerous challenges for the production and operation of multinational corporations. Through hosting the CIIE, China demonstrates to the world its sincere commitment to opening its market and warmly invites exhibitors from all countries to deepen mutual understanding, exchange, and collaboration with the Chinese market for making greater progress.

International experts believe that hosting the CIIE, like "holding the key to tomorrow," is a powerful measure to support the continued development of economic globalization.

Kristalina Georgieva, managing director of the International Monetary Fund (IMF), stated that over the past few decades, the world has benefited immensely from economic globalization. Economic globalization has been the driving force behind everyone's pursuit of a more prosperous future, which underscores the great significance of the CIIE and the necessity of this platform for the international community.

As a Chinese saying goes, "A single flower does not make spring, while one hundred flowers in full blossom bring spring to the garden." Alongside hosting the CIIE, China has successively implemented a series of significant measures to promote higher level opening-up, lower tariff levels, shorter negative lists, more convenient market access, and more transparent market rules... The institutional environment for foreign enterprises to enter the Chinese market is continuously being optimized, making the channels for sharing opportunities in China more accessible.

The international community clearly sees that China's CIIE is not a choice of expediency. It is a future-oriented pragmatic action taken to embrace the world and promote common development. China will continue to reform and open up and is committed to promoting the development of economic globalization and building an open economy, is embracing the world with a more open and inclusive attitude to work together with countries around the world for common development and the construction of a community with a shared future for mankind.

Even before the opening of the 7th CIIE, many exhibitors have already reserved tickets for the 8th CIIE. On July 3, 2024, the launch ceremony for the 8th CIIE's exhibition recruitment was held, with 26 companies signing contracts on-site, becoming the first batch of exhibitors for the 8th CIIE. The exhibition area booked reaches 15,000 square meters. Through their actions, enterprises from various countries clearly express their consensus that economic globalization is the unstoppable tide of the times and China is a central force propelling this tide forward.

The CIIE serves as a bridge for global cooperation. This groundbreaking initiative in international trade history is driving a new future of shared prosperity between China and the world!

Yuan Yong / Economic Daily News

This article was first published on July 12, 2024.

(Translated by Li Donglin)

7th CIIE Likely to Prove Solid Growth Platform for Many Companies

July 24, 2024，a view of a matchmaking event for the 7th CIIE. [Photo / Chen Mengze]

The robust demand of the Chinese market and the improving business environment in the country make China a big growth opportunity for companies wishing to further expand their operations, said corporates that have registered to participate in this year's CIIE.

The seventh edition of the annual CIIE, to be held in Shanghai from Nov 5 to 10, will start its 100-day countdown on Saturday (July 27).

With more than 360,000 square meters of exhibition area already signed up, this year's CIIE will see some new participants, said Sun Chenghai, deputy director-general of the CIIE Bureau, the expo's organizer, during a news conference on Wednesday (July 24).

Japanese trading company Mitsubishi

Corp, US material provider Invista, French transportation company Alstom, Ireland-based auto technology supplier Aptiv and New Zealand's beauty nutritional drink brand Tracel Health will all make their CIIE debut this year.

Special demonstration areas will be set up for the first time to showcase the progress made by companies specializing in new materials, autopilot technology, low-altitude economy and energy storage for cars, said Sun.

Charlie Wang, chief marketing officer of Tracel Health, said: "In recent years, we saw demand in the Chinese market for healthcare products. Female consumers' demand for oral products is continuously growing. Sales of our products exceeded 5 million yuan ($687,132) in the first month after their debut on Tmall Global (the cross-border e-commerce site of Alibaba Group) in late May, topping its category. Through the CIIE, we hope more consumers will get to know the brand."

Shanghai-based discount grocery retailer HotMaxx will also exhibit at the CIIE for the first time this year as a buyer. According to the company's co-founder Nick Zhang, the CIIE serves as an important platform via which Chinese companies and consumers can understand "the progress being made elsewhere in the world".

Zhang said: "A large number of the products sold in our stores have just entered the Chinese markets, receiving recognition among Chinese consumers unexpectedly. We look forward to partnering with the CIIE exhibitors to see more innovative products and hope to come back in every edition."

French beauty giant L'Oreal has attended all the past six editions of the CIIE. It has introduced more than 20 new brands into the Chinese market via the expo, making up the majority of the 31 brands that the company has launched in China so far. A new air dryer featuring the application of infrared rays and higher efficiency will debut at this year's show.

More importantly, L'Oreal has expanded its footprint in China by announcing increased investments at the CIIE.

In May 2022, L'Oreal set up Shanghai Meicifang Investment, its first investment company in China. Four months later, Meicifang made its first investment move by picking up minority stakes in Chinese fragrance brand Documents and biotech company Shenzhen Shinehigh. In February, L'Oreal acquired a minority stake in To Summer, a local premium fragrance brand.

"It is all because of the huge market demand and growth potential of the Chinese market", said Lan Zhenzhen, president of public affairs at L'Oreal North Asia and China.

According to Sun of the CIIE Bureau, over 150 companies will participate for the seventh consecutive year at the upcoming CIIE. New Zealand dairy giant Fonterra is one of them.

Fonterra's Shanghai innovation center started operations in 2020. Its Wuhan application center, the 6th of its kind in China, broke ground in May and is scheduled to start operations in September, according to Justin Dai, vice-president of Fonterra Greater China.

Zhu Min, director of the Shanghai Municipal Commission of Commerce, said CIIE exhibitors have expanded their operations in China. Danish building-block toy company Lego, which has attended all the previous six editions, has seen the first phase of its Legoland theme park in Shanghai taking shape. Swiss dental implant company Straumann Group, which attended the fourth edition, is expected to see the first phase of its implant project in central Shanghai go operational in 2025.

Shi Jing, Wang Xin / China Daily

This article was first published on July 26, 2024.

Guests from All over the World Gather at the CIIE

In 100 days, the 7th CIIE will begin. People from all over the world will gather for the expo as appointed. As Shanghai redoubles its efforts to establish itself as an international center for economy, finance, trade, shipping and scientific and technological innovation it will undergo

another refinement through the CIIE and showcase an extraordinary chapter to the world.

Transforming exhibits into commodities, the "debut economy" shines brighter

The successful hosting of six sessions of the CIIE has promoted Shanghai's development as an international consumption center.

The Hongqiao Import Commodity Exhibition and Trade Center (Hongqiao Pinhui) serves as the main platform for the expo's "6 days + 365 days" exhibitions, achieving a trading volume of RMB 17 billion in 2023. It has established 23 sub-centers in cities like Suzhou and Shaoxing. Another year-round exhibition platform, the Greenland Global Commodity Trade Hub, has opened 63 national pavilions and 13 branches in China in total, facilitating the entry of over 5,000 products identical to those showcased at the CIIE into the domestic market.

On the eve of the 100-day countdown to the opening ceremony of the 7th CIIE, a new product launch for the Serbian Wine Festival was held at the Greenland Global Commodity Trade Hub, the expo's year-round trading service platform.

The successful hosting of the CIIE has significantly contributed to Shanghai's "debut economy". Since the

The launch ceremony of the new products of the Serbian Wine Festival held at the Green Global Commodity Trading Port, the perennial trading service platform of the CIIE.

inception of the expo six years ago, Shanghai has introduced a total of 5,840 first stores, including over 80 in Asian or above. In June 2024, the world's first photon-counting CT, which debuted at the 6th CIIE, will officially commence operations at Shanghai Ruijin Hospital. The device of lower radiation and higher resolution will benefit more patients.

As the 100-day countdown to the 7th CIIE begins, Abbott has announced its return to the expo with a series of new products. Throughout past sessions, Abbott has showcased hundreds of innovative life sciences technologies. Among them, the AVEIR VR single-chamber leadless cardiac pacemaker, which debuted at the 5th CIIE, has officially received approval in China and has recently completed its first surgeries, providing a new treatment option for patients with bradycardia. Following its debut at the expo, the MitraClip transcatheter mitral valve clip for minimally invasive treatment of mitral regurgitation has also successfully entered China, filling a domestic treatment gap with its innovative technology.

In recent days, exhibitors of the 7th CIIE have been eager to "tease" their new product launches that will shine in 100 days. Össur will present several bionic prosthetic products, including the global premiere of "Storm Runner Earth Sports Foot" designed for highly active users. Theland will debut its 4.0 A2 full-chain low-carbon milk. The term "full-chain" here indicates that after implementing low-carbon practices at the farm and factory, the company will launch New Zealand's first fleet of new energy milk transport vehicles in 2024, using cleaner hydrogen energy to approach "zero emissions" in dairy transportation. Fonterra anticipates bringing nearly 20 innovative products, including new offerings with nutrition that support healthy aging.

On the eve of the 6th CIIE, the State Council of China approved *The Plan for Establishing a Pilot Zone for Silk Road E-commerce Cooperation in Shanghai*. Since then, Shanghai has successfully hosted consumption-promoting events such as the Shanghai Online Lunar New Year's Shopping Festival and the Shanghai Silk Road E-commerce Carnival, facilitating the transformation of expo exhibits into e-commerce commodities. Shanghai has also promoted online-offline synergies,

creating national pavilions for "Silk Road E-commerce".

In April 2024, the Pakistan National Pavilion was open in Waigaoqiao, becoming the primary platform for Pakistani products showcased at the 6th CIIE to enter the Chinese market. Since the beginning of 2024, Shanghai has added three new "Silk Road E-commerce" national pavilions, bringing the total to 26. Reports indicate that staff at these national pavilions have been working diligently to prepare stock, planning to initiate multiple live broadcasts on-site as the grand event approaches, linking online and offline efforts to "provide support and generate excitement" for the 7th CIIE.

Exhibitors become investors, strengthening Shanghai's position as a foreign investment high ground

In addition to showcasing the latest and trendiest products, global enterprises are proactively seizing the opportunity presented by the CIIE platform to express their commitment to sustained investment in China. The successful hosting of six sessions of the CIIE has further solidified Shanghai's status as a premier destination for foreign investment.

In 2023, despite a sluggish global economic recovery, 6,017 new foreign-funded enterprises were established in Shanghai, reflecting a year-on-year increase of 38.3%. In the first half of 2024, the city registered 3,007 new foreign-funded enterprises, representing a growth of 18.3%. Additionally, 29 new regional headquarters of multinational companies and 14 foreign R&D centers have been recognized, bringing the totals to 985 and 575, respectively.

At the 6th CIIE, 3M's innovative products attracted visitors.
[Photo / Tang Yanjun, China News Service]

As a "all-time" participant at the CIIE, 3M will once again take the stage at the 7th CIIE, this time in the newly established new materials zone within the technology equipment exhibition area. Ding Hongyu, senior vice-president of 3M Co and president of 3M China, noted that since the inception of the CIIE, many of 3M's innovative achievements have transitioned from "exhibits to commodities." During the 5th CIIE in 2022, 3M announced plans for capital expansion at its Jinshan factory in Shanghai. "With robust support from the global board, the project commenced substantial operations within a year, with production expected to begin by the end of 2024." The expansion will involve an investment of RMB 400 million to RMB 500 million, marking one of

the largest capital increases in the past decade. "3M will continue to invest in its R&D center in Shanghai, focusing on new energy, consumer electronics, and sustainability," he added.

As reported, 3M has announced a commitment to invest USD 1 billion in sustainable development globally over the next 20 years to fulfill its environmental commitments. According to Ding, "A significant portion of this investment will undoubtedly be allocated to sustainable development in China."

"Exhibitors turn into investors." Henkel has also progressed together with the CIIE. "The CIIE platform has allowed Henkel to witness and participate in the development of China's industries and economy, strengthening its commitment to supporting local industry and talent development through sustainable local innovation services and continuous investment," stated Anna An, president of Henkel Greater China.At the beginning of 2024, Henkel Consumer Brands Asia R&D Center was inaugurated in Shanghai, with an investment of approximately RMB 100 million, making it the largest R&D center for Henkel's consumer brands in Asia. Meanwhile, Henkel's Adhesive Technologies Innovation Center in Zhangjiang, Shanghai is undergoing expansion with a total investment of about RMB 500 million. Once completed, it will become the second-largest adhesive technology innovation center globally, providing support for clients in China and the Asia-Pacific region. It is expected to be completed and operational by 2025.

Rendering of the expanded Henkel Shanghai Adhesive Technologies Innovation Center (design sketch).

Shanghai is fully committed to being a gracious host and optimizing its business environment

The CIIE serves as a showcase of China's new development paradigm, a platform for promoting high-level opening-up, and a public good for the whole world. As China looks to the world, the world is also watching China. Shanghai is wholeheartedly committed to being an exceptional host, maintaining the passion and drive evident during its inaugural edition, while aligning efforts to optimize the business environment with high-level opening-up.

"In this session of the CIIE, Shanghai will continue to focus on facilitating participation. In terms of entry and exit, we will focus on the actual needs of foreign exhibitors and enterprises in handling entry and exit procedures, and promote the implementation of convenient measures such as 'providing multiple-entry visas for foreign exhibitors'.

The customs have issued the entry and exit guidelines and convenient measures for the 7th CIIE, further simplifying the special approval procedures and requirements for certain product exhibition-related certificates," explained Liu Ping, deputy secretary-general of the Shanghai Municipal Government and director of the Urban Service Guarantee Leadership Group Office. He noted that this year's expo will further optimize the document processing workflow, reduce processing times, and gradually expand the trial scope of electronic certificates.

It is also reported that comprehensive payment convenience will be provided for foreign exhibitors and merchants participating in the CIIE. Shanghai has achieved the capability to accept foreign card payments at over 70,000 POS terminals in the first half of 2024, a 1.1-fold increase compared to the end of 2023.

Shanghai is actively promoting urban digital transformation and accelerating the establishment of a globally influential "Digital Capital" to continuously enhance its soft power of business environment.

For exhibitors and merchants, this year's CIIE will leverage AI and digital technologies to upgrade digital service windows, further optimizing functionalities such as finding exhibitors, exploring venues, and checking event schedules. Additionally, smart conference service spots will be established within the exhibition halls to enhance AI smart response capabilities. Building upon intelligent applications that strengthen security, transportation, customs clearance of exhibits, energy communication support, meteorological monitoring and forecasting, as well as the safety regulation of food, pharmaceuticals, and special devices, service assurance departments, will further optimize the "One Map for the CIIE" functionality. A coordinated effort of digital integration and application across departments will be utilized to ensure that all services for the CIIE are safe and efficient.

Wu Weiqun / JieFang Daily

This article was first published on July 27, 2024.

(Translated by Li Donglin)

Boarding the "CIIE Express" Means Seizing Opportunities

In June, the world's first photon counting CT designed by Siemens Healthineers was put into operation at the Ruijin Hospital of Shanghai Jiaotong University School of Medicine. It was first showcased at the 6th CIIE. Today it brings benefits to more patients like a light shining into their lives. In July, the tech brand Apex of Skincare (AP) opened its first store at the Jiuguang Department Store (Jing'an branch), and will conduct its plan of opening more stores across the country after the 7th CIIE. In August, the first batch of Malaysian Musang King fresh durians will arrive in Shanghai. The brand owner is eager to bring the limited version of fresh durian to the CIIE site.

As the 7th CIIE marks the 100-day countdown to its opening ceremony, many exhibitors are busy catching the "CIIE Express" to seize the "China opportunities" as the country strives to comprehensively deepen reform and promote higher-level opening-up.

The CIIE Bazaar City Arena located in Nanjing East Rd. is showcasing products from more than 20 countries and regions. [Photo / Zhang Yichen]

Witnessing Higher–Standard Opening up

Durian, a fruit "treasure" that has been keenly promoted in recent years. The term "treasure" has two meanings. First, Durian is one of the fruits that has benefitted most from the opening-up policies in recent years. In 2023, China's durian import reached nearly 1.4 million tons as the "access" has brought about huge business opportunity. Second, it is lucrative and profitable just as its golden shell. "In the 2024 CIIE, durian must still be the 'king'," said Wang Na, marketing director of Dole China. Dole has reserved the "central position" for the Malaysian

Musang King fresh durian in the debut of CIIE products.

Access is the main bellwether of the global fruit giant in deciding "what to launch first in the CIIE". In 2023, the Philippine durian obtained its access to the Chinese market. Dole took this opportunity to first launch the Dole Golden Puyat durian at the 6th CIIE. On June 19, 2024, China signed a series of contracts with Malaysia, including the *Protocol on Phytosanitary Requirements for the Export of Fresh Durian from Malaysia to China*. Wang said that the preparations are underway, and the first batch of Malaysian Musang King fresh durian is expected to reach the Chinese market next month by air.

The richness of the fresh fruit market epitomizes China's higher-standard opening up. Over the past seven years, 98 new varieties of fruit obtained access to China. At the previous six CIIEs, Dole introduced 12 of them, all of which have become best-sellers. A major test is about speed after the fruit got access. And the Customs clearance facilitation is a key link. Wang Na still uses fresh durian as an example. From the moment the durian gets ripe and falls from the tree, to on-site inspection and testing, from packaging and air transport to delivery into the hands of Chinese consumers, any slight delay in any step can affect the quality and taste of the fruit. Today, thanks to CIIE's series of trade facilitation policies, Dole is able to finish all the procedures within two days.

The perishable fruit "treasure" is the beneficiary of trade facilitation, so are the advanced and sophisticated new materials. At 6th CIIE, the zero-degree microcrystalline glass exhibited for the first time by Schott AG became a star in the technical equipment section and became the "retina" of the Qinghai Wide Field Survey Telescope (WFST) through successful "pairing". As this high-performance material is produced in Schott's factory in Mainz, Germany and is large in volume and high in value, it has faced many challenges in long-distance

The 7th CIIE promotion site. [Photo / Zhang Yichen]

transnational transportation and customs clearance. The head of Schott said that thanks to China's customs facilitation policy, this material has been smoothly transported from Germany to China for processing and assembly, and has recently arrived at the astronomical observation base in Lenghu, Qinghai Province.

Witnessing a Bigger Market

Debut is always a key word for the CIIE. On this "CIIE Express", the speed from the first launch to the explosion of popularity and from exhibits to commodities is getting faster and faster.

AmorePacific Group has recently set the list of new products for CIIE 2024, including the tech skincare brand AP, which will make its debut in the CIIE and be promoted in the Chinese market through this opportunity. Speaking of this new product just launched in February 2024, Zhou Qi, head of the Shanghai R&D Center of AmorePacific

169

Group, showed his confidence as the product has opened up a brand new skincare channel – the "post-cosmetic medicine" skincare. "Today, Thermage and photorejuvenation have become the non-surgical anti-aging program that the world's young consumers like to try. And our exclusive 'bandage' patented formula and technology can form a closed superconducting film, boosting the effect of the cosmetic program."

What's interesting is that leveraging the spillover effects of the CIIE in conjunction with Shanghai's "debut economy" to create a market synergy has become an open secret among the exhibitors. In mid-July, AP Apex opened its first mainland store at the Jiuguang Department Store (Jing'an branch). Kim Seung-hwan, CEO of AmorePacific described Shanghai as a charming city and an important step in helping the brand rapidly go global. After its debut in the CIIE, this brand also plans to open more physical stores across China.

In the past six CIIE events, Shanghai has introduced a total of 5,840 "first stores" of

different brands, including more than 80 first stores at the Asian level and above, demonstrating prominent effects of premier releases and exhibitions. According to Zhu Min, director of Shanghai Municipal Commission of Commerce and executive vice director of the Leading Group Office for the Guarantee of the CIIE City Service, the CIIE held in Shanghai serves as an important engine for Shanghai's economic and social development. Centering around the CIIE's functional positioning of "transforming exhibits into products and exhibitors into investors", Shanghai will continue to amplify the spillover and driving effects of the CIIE.

The dual drivers of the CIIE's spillover effect and Shanghai's "debut economy" have provided more opportunities for exhibitors. Just a few days ago, the Melaleuca Wellness Company has been approved as a foreign-funded R&D center. In 2024, it also decided to expand its CIIE booth from 108 square meters to 153 square meters. There is a strong connection here. Wu Yin, vice-president of marketing, Melaleuca (China), disclosed the story behind: the company's global debut of beauty and health drinks, and children's nutritional food at the CIIE were highly successful, driving products sales, and the Shanghai factory even set a new production record as a result. It was based on these achievements that Melaleuca decided to increase its investment in the foreign-fund R&D center, with a view to expanding the market through the R&D of more localized formula.

Witnessing Global Influence

In a recent review of the distribution of the raw materials of essential oil, Owen Messick, president of doTERRA China, was surprised to find that China has become the country with the most sources of raw materials of essential oil plants for the company. "We have released more than 20 types of essential oil raw materials from China, including sweetgum, black cardamom and blue lotus, among others. And the performance of this part is improving at a rate of 50% annually." "We are also increasing our investment in the 7th CIIE. Our booth will be expanded from 200 square meters to 300 square meters, and the number of our exhibits and premiere products will reach a record high," he said.

As the "CIIE Express" accelerates, Owen Messick has deeper reflections on its spillover effects. He thinks that the CIIE has opened up a kind of dual circulation-bringing the extraction technology from Europe and the United States to China, and taking the traditional essential plants from China to the rest of the world. "In 2024, we hope to promote the development of China's traditional plants along a high value-added and high-tech path, and integrate such localized innovation into the global industrial chain so that our aroma can be shared worldwide."

In terms of the future development trend, more and more localized innovations will go global with the help of the CIIE. In 2024, Boston Scientific will introduce the AVVIGO + intravascular ultrasound system, a product that combines the elements of both "Made in China" and "Intelligently Manufactured in China". Da Bo, vice-president of

Boston Scientific China, said that this product was developed with the participation of Boston Scientific's Chinese team. It obtained the CE certification of the EU and the approval of the U.S. Food and Drug Administration (FDA) in September 2023, and has been a leading export ever since. With its core mainframe completely manufactured in China, this product is another step to integrate localized innovation into the global value chain.

As a seven-time participant of the CIIE, Wang Hao, president of Simens Healthineers Greater China, said that the company has always regarded the CIIE as an important window for global healthcare innovation and technological exchange, aims to expedite the deep integration of global innovation resources with localized markets, and

CIIE Bazaar City Arena. [Yin Liqin，China News Service]

joins hands with partners to boost new quality productive forces, so as to make the CIIE a showcase featuring "local wisdom and global innovation".

With only 100 days to go before the opening of the 7th CIIE, a new batch of exhibits has arrived. The world's first offline experience center of the Philips Healthy Living Lab in Fengshengli of Maoming North Road in the Jing'an District of Shanghai, a new generation of Oxygen generator that just got license in April, and the Philips Portable Ultrasound System 5500 that was just approved in July are all ready for the exhibition. They will make their debut in CIIE 2024. "The spillover effects of the CIIE have come to another level. We will take more technologies and products developed in China to the rest of the world through the CIIE platform." said Chen Wei, senior manager of Philips (China) Group Communications Department.

Xu Jinghui, Zhang Tianchi, Guo Fanxi / Wenhui Daily

This article was first published on July 27, 2024.

(Translated by Liu Yanling)

Keeping "Oriental Appointment" for Globally Shared Opportunities

Since 2018, the CIIE, which has continuously held and improved annually, has become a showcase of China's new development paradigm, a platform for high-standard opening up, and a public good for the whole world.

In 100 days, the whole world will once again focus on Shanghai to witness the continuing of the "Oriental appointment". Over the past seven years, the "CIIE's magnetic force" has increased instead of decreasing. Global traders have drawn blueprints, shared opportunities and created future together here, charting more CIIE stories. The closely linked CIIE tie has provided momentum for the high-standard development of China's economy and

A Pre–Expo Supply–demand Matchmaking Meeting held at the National Conference and Exhibition Center (Shanghai) at the 100–day countdown to the opening of the 7th CIIE.

[Photo / Chen Mengze]

opportunities for global economic recovery. At the 7th CIIE, China will open its door even wider to the world.

Continuing to Release CIIE effects

The CIIE is the first national-level exposition themed on import in the world. One figure can directly show its force—USD 78.41 billion, which is the annually intended transaction amount of the 6th CIIE. It has not only demonstrates the charm of China's higher-standard opening up and the sincerity of China to share market with the rest of the world, but also makes Shanghai a more international and influential city.

Over the past seven years, enterprises from various countries have shared the opportunities of China's development and obtained many market dividends. "During the previous six sessions of the CIIE, we received 200,000 visitors at our booth and premiered 24 types of

The Wide Field Survey Telescope (WFST) carrying the ZERODUR® glass–ceramic. [Photo / courtesy of the interviewee]

LEGO products that draw Chinese culture debuted at the CIIE. [Photo / Zhang Yuyun]

products, most of which were inspired by the Chinese culture," said Paul Huang, senior vice-president of the LEGO Group and general manager of LEGO China. The LEGO Group has opened more than 480 brand retail stores in over 120 Chinese cities and its online and offline cooperation is getting closer. "Such a high popularity should be attributed to LEGO's remarkable demonstration at the CIIE."

At the 6th CIIE, the ZERODUR® glass-ceramic exhibited by Germany's Schott for the first time became the "celebrity" exhibit in the section of Intelligent Industry & Information Technology as it is regarded as the "retina" of astronomical telescope that can receive more than 100 million times light than human eyes with wider and clearer perspective. By means of the CIIE platform, this material will be used in the WFST located in China's Qinghai Province, which is the strongest telescope for exploring the universe in the optical band time domain of the north hemisphere at present.

The US technological innovation enterprise 3M has participated in the CIIE for consecutive seven years. In 2024, it will debut its latest products and solutions themed on sustainability at the newly set section of New Materials. Starting from the 1st CIIE, the premiere exhibits such as the ambient sound earmuffs, the cloud fiber thermal materials and polishing pads applied in the semiconductor manufacturing field have been put on display and followed by successive orders.

"Thanks to the CIIE's agglomeration effect, 3M could grasp one-step the earliest information of China – an important bellwether market. It has not only effectively satisfied multiple demands of domestic

customers, but also helped more products that originated from China, made in China, and oriented toward the world market to go global," said Ding Hongyu, senior vice-president of 3M Co. and president of 3M China.

"After participating in the previous six sessions of the CIIE, our sales volume accumulated has amounted to RMB 600 million, facilitating block transactions with leading enterprises in the industry such as Charoen Pokphand Group (CP Group)," said Hakatere Naturals Health Brand Director Lu Yuerong. Although the honeybee market is very competitive, the CIIE has provided a larger platform for the Hakatere Naturals brand to conduct more cooperation with quality enterprises in such fields as industrial upgrading, product innovation and sustainable development.

Accelerating the Application of Innovative Products

From the world factory to the global supermarket, the CIIE has turned China's super-sized market into abundant opportunities for the world. Meanwhile, it has also introduced more novel products and services for the domestic market, enabling Chinese consumers to "buy products made all over the world"in their country while enjoying better and healthier lives.

In 2024, 72-year-old lady Chen, a retired accountant, suffered from the Parkinson's disease at the age when she could live a happy later life. In May, she was implanted with the Percept™ PC sensible cerebral pacemaker of Medtronic, which will start working at the end of June.

Chen said that she was still in the postoperative convalescence, but she had felt the tremor subsiding and her body was no longer as stiff as before. Now she is trying rehabilitation exercises and getting more and more light-hearted.

In the area of neuroscience, Percept PC was appraised by *Nature* magazine as "a window that has truly opened the brain for the first time". Taking the 4th CIIE as an opportunity, this innovative product has entered the view of the public. After being approved in China, it finished its first batch of implantations in July 2023. Now more than 30 hospitals in China have put it into clinical application, which has benefitted hundreds of patients.

From the world to China and from exhibitors to clinical application, the CIIE serves as a bridge between patients and innovative products. Over the five consecutive participation of the CIIE, Abbott has also showed its hundreds of innovative life technologies. Thanks to the CIIE's strong spillover effect, these cutting-edge technologies and products have been approved faster and applied in the Chinese market, turning into well-received medical and health care products from exhibits. The Implantable AVEIR™ VR Leadless Pacemaker debuted at the 5th CIIE has completed its first batch of operations recently, bringing about brand new choice of treatment for patients with bradycardia. Moreover, the flash glucose monitoring (FGM) has served more than 500,000 Chinese users, becoming the new weapon for diabetes patients to control their blood sugar.

"With the CIIE's effect, Dole has been widely regarded as the

Dole will debut the Malaysian fresh durian at the 7th CIIE.[Photo / Zhang Yuyun]

'imported fruit basket' for Chinese consumers." Wang Na, marketing director of Dole China, said that since the 1st CIIE in 2018, the species of fruit newly opened for import to China has reached 98, of which 12 have been premiered by Dole at the CIIE, including Belgian red conference pear, Brazilian melon, and Philippine fresh durian. Today they have all been the star products in the "fruit plates" of urban residents.

"On June 24, 2024, the General Administration of Customs of China (GACC) issued its No. 72 Announcement of 2024, *Announcement on Phytosanitary Requirements for Importation of Malaysian Fresh Durian*. We are trying our best to become the first enterprise to introduce

Malaysian durian to China. Dole's Malaysian Musang King durian and black thorn durian will debut at the CIIE. And by means of its strong spillover effect, we would like to give the Chinese durian lovers a real treat."

"Two-way Efforts"

Over the past seven years, the CIIE has helped turn exhibits to commodities and exhibitors to investors. The spillover effect keeps expanding. An increasing number of enterprises have taken the CIIE as a "springboard" to enter the Chinese market with stronger confidence in China's economic development and firmer determination to cultivate the Chinese market.

The sense of gain during the six-day participation in the CIIE can be upgraded into satisfaction with the business environment for the whole year. Over the past seven years, Shanghai and the CIIE participants have reached out to each other. In the first half of 2024, 3,007 foreign-funded enterprises have been established in Shanghai, registering an increase of 18.3 year on year. In addition, 29 regional headquarters of transnational corporations, 14 foreign-funded R&D centers have been recognized with a total of 985 and 275 respectively.

On July 25, the certification ceremony for 39th transnational corporations' regional headquarters and R&D centers was held at the People's Tower in Shanghai. The Melaleuca Wellness Company was recognized as a foreign-funded R&D center. Wu Yin, vice-president of marketing, Melaleuca (China) said that as an exclusively foreign-owned

enterprise, Melaleuca has operated in the Chinese market for 20 years. The upgrading as a foreign-funded R&D center this time will help the company provide more healthcare products for the Chinese market. At the 7th CIIE in 2024, its booth at the section of Food and Agricultural Products will be expanded from 108 square meters to 153 square meters.

"We have achieved great success in the global debut of all the beauty and health drinks as well as the nutritious food for children. It has boosted the sales of these products, by which our factory in Shanghai has broken its production record. Based on these results, Melaleuca decided to enhance the foreign-funded R&D center with a view to engage in the R&D of more localized recipes to expand the market."

"As Henkel's third largest market in the world, China plays an important role in our global business. Henkel has been increasing its investment in the R&D and the production of high-end products in China,"said Anna An, president for China unit at Henkel AG & Co. In early 2024, the Henkel Consumer Goods Asian R&D Center was launched in Shanghai. With the investment of about RMB 100 million, it became the biggest R&D center of Henkel consumer goods in Asia. In addition, Henkel has invested RMB 500 million in the Henkel Shanghai Innovation Experience Center in Zhangjiang, Shanghai, which is under expansion. Once it is completed, it will become the second largest adhesive technology innovation center in the world and will provide customer support for China and the Asia-Pacific region at large. This center will be built up and put into operation in 2025.

While old friends have gained a lot, we have new friends coming in. The sports lifestyle brand Lululemon announced recently that it will attend the CIIE for the first time. Calvin MacDonald, CEO of Lululemon said, "The CIIE has a world-renowned influence. We are very honored to keep this 'Oriental appointment' with friends from all over the world. I would like to take this opportunity to extend our firm commitment to further investment and deeper cultivation in the Chinese market."

Nippon has also created a 300-square-meter booth at the section of New Materials in the section of Intelligent Industry & Information Technology to exhibit many products that will be debuted globally at the CIIE. Zhong Zhonglin, CEO of Nippon China said that the shift from the CIIE's witness to a participant has shown Nippon's unchanged commitment to the Chinese market. "Through the 'jointly built and shared' world-class platform of the CIIE, Nippon will conduct close cooperation with global partners and share China's development opportunities in the new era."

Zhang Yuyun, Du Xuan / Xinmin Evening News

This article was first published on July 27, 2024

(Translated by Liu Yanling)

Afterword

Time flies. This marks the third consecutive year we have compiled the book *CIIE Stories*. "CIIE partners" from all over the world have graciously shared their unique experiences, transporting us back to the bustling scenes of the expo and allowing us to relive the profound achievements it brings.

These "CIIE Stories" —worthy of being recorded and shared—are not only the best testament to the CIIE's significant results and influence but also a vivid reflection of China's steadfast commitment to high-level openness, sharing opportunities, and fostering global cooperation and development.

We have carefully recorded these stories and presented them in both Chinese and English, hoping that this book, much like the CIIE itself, transcends the boundaries of time and space, breaks geographical barriers, and becomes a bridge connecting individuals and groups from different countries, ethnicities, and cultures.

The compilation of this book has received care and guidance from leaders at all levels and people from various sectors, as well as support and cooperation from the storytellers. Here, we wish to express our most sincere respect and gratitude to everyone for their strong support and contributions. We would like to extend our heartfelt thanks to the Publicity Department of the Central Committee of the Communist Party of China, the Secretariat of the China International Import Expo (Trade in Service Department of the Ministry of Commerce), the Information Office of the Ministry of Commerce, the Publicity Department of the Communist Party of China Shanghai Municipal Committee, the Information Office of Shanghai Municipality, and media outlets such as People's Daily, Xinhua News Agency, China Media Group, Economic Daily, China Daily, China News Service, JieFang DAILY, Wenhui Daily, Xinmin Evening News, Shanghai Media Group, The Paper, Yicai, International Business Daily, and Phoenix Satellite Television. We really appreciate the tremendous support and contributions from all organizations and media outlets!

The CIIE and the Hongqiao International Economic Forum are not just annual events promoting the construction of an open global economy, but also important initiatives toward building a shared future for mankind. Throughout the creation of this book, we realized that the CIIE is like a vast treasure trove, filled with countless possibilities and even more inspiring stories waiting to be discovered and continued.

We approached the writing of this book with a strong sense of responsibility, striving to perfect every step of the process. However, due to time constraints and our own limitations, some oversights or errors may have occurred. We kindly ask for your understanding and patience with any shortcomings.

图书在版编目（CIP）数据

进博故事 =CIIE STORIES：英文 / 中国国际进口
博览局，国家会展中心（上海），中国新闻网编 .
北京：中国商务出版社，2024.10. -- ISBN 978-7
-5103-5426-7

Ⅰ . F752.61-282

中国国家版本馆 CIP 数据核字第 20243CH315 号

进博故事

JIN-BO GUSHI

中国国际进口博览局

国家会展中心（上海） 编

中国新闻网

出版发行：中国商务出版社有限公司
地　　址：北京市东城区安定门外大街东后巷 28 号　　邮　编：100710
网　　址：http://www.cctpress.com
联系电话：010-64515150（发行部）　　　　010-64212247（总编室）
　　　　　010-64269744（商务事业部）　　010-64248236（印制部）
责任编辑：张高平
责任校对：孙柳明　郭舒怡　周水琴
排　　版：廊坊展博印刷设计有限公司
印　　刷：北京华联印刷有限公司
开　　本：787 毫米 ×1092 毫米　1/16
印　　张：24.5　　　　　　　　　　字　　数：352 千字
版　　次：2024 年 10 月第 1 版　　　　印　　次：2024 年 10 月第 1 次印刷
书　　号：ISBN 978-7-5103-5426-7
定　　价：189.00 元（全二册）

INSPIRE THE WORLD
WITH CIIE STORIES

Tell Us Your Story

THE GLOBAL COLLECTION BEGINS

SUBMIT YOUR STORIES:
ciiestories@ciie.org

SUBMISSION TIME:
From now until 26th July 2025

ORGANIZER:
CIIE Bureau, National Exhibition and Convention Center (Shanghai)

SUPPORTING MEDIA:
People's Daily Digital Communication, China News Service,
China Daily New Media, Xinmin Evening News, Knews, The Paper,
Yicai, International Business Daily, Phoenix TV

SUPPORTING PLATFORMS:
Douyin, Toutiao APP

Scan the QR code and
submit your stories

Sincere thanks to Bank of Communications
for the publication of this book!

中国的舞台
CHINESE STAGE　GLOBAL BRILLIANCE
世界的精彩

交通银行扎实做好金融"五篇大文章"

◎科技金融 ⑤绿色金融 ◎普惠金融 ⑥养老金融 ◎数字金融

交通银行
BANK OF COMMUNICATIONS

第七届中国国际进口博览会核心支持企业
CORE SUPPORT ENTERPRISE OF THE 7th CIIE